A Lawyer Looks at the
CONSTITUTION

A Lawyer Looks at the
CONSTITUTION

Rex E. Lee

Brigham Young University Press

Library of Congress Cataloging in Publication Data

Lee, Rex E., 1935–
    A lawyer looks at the constitution.

    Includes bibliographical references and index.
    1. United States–Constitutional law.
2. United States–Constitutional history.   I. Title
KF4550.L37   342.75   81–1571
ISBN 0–8425–1904–1   347.302   AACR2

International Standard Book Number: 0-8425-1904-1
Brigham Young University Press, Provo, Utah 84602
© 1981 by Charles E. Jones, Trustee. All rights reserved
Printed in the United States of America
10 9 8 7 6 5 4 3 2

To Tom and Michael

CONTENTS

FOREWORD

This book was written by a distinguished lawyer to provide laymen with an understandable, professional description of the modern meaning of the United States Constitution. That could be a prescription for windy overgeneralizations and breezy superficiality. Not here. Although written with a light style and a brisk pace that is readable, interesting and informative, this book has the substance that will reward careful study and thoughtful consideration. It gives a brilliant perspective of the Constitution, providing overall illumination and sharp focus for the lay reader and a valuable road map for the lawyer or scholar who needs to locate his area of inquiry in preparation for research in greater depth.

This kind of writing is needed. Like most other professionals, lawyers generally do not deign to speak to laymen in any depth about their specialty. As a result, the people of the United States—even the most thoughtful and best educated—are generally at the mercy of journalists and pamphleteers of various persuasions to explain the content, workings, and complications of public laws and legal institutions of great interest to all.

Popular efforts to understand law and legal institutions have been distorted by superficiality and victimized by labeling and sloganeering. The principal loser is probably the judicial branch. Its public standing has probably suffered most from the current public disenchantment with law and legal institutions. Called "the least dangerous branch," the judiciary is also the most vulnerable. It has no formal representative to speak for it in the court of public opinion. A better understanding of the Constitution and the current problems and complexities of its interpretation is likely to help the standing of courts, especially the United States Supreme Court. For that reason, this is a book *amicus curiae*; that is, a friend of the court.

Rex E. Lee is uniquely qualified as the author of such a book. His legal experience of more than two decades has made him a top-ranked law graduate, a law clerk in the United States Supreme Court, a partner

xi

in a distinguished law firm, an experienced advocate in state and federal courts, the popular Dean of Brigham Young University's J. Reuben Clark Law School, an author and scholar of the law, and an Assistant Attorney General of the United States. As practitioner, teacher, scholar and administrator he is admirably qualified to teach the United States Constitution to his fellow lawyers and to interested laymen.

Dallin H. Oaks
Justice, Utah Supreme Court

January 1981

INTRODUCTION

In 1976 our nation celebrated a bicentennial anniversary. It was marked by nationwide celebration and public reaffirmation of time-honored values. In 1987 our nation will reach another bicentennial. The celebration of this second bicentennial will probably not be as enthusiastic as that of 1976; indeed, many people may not be aware of the significance of this occasion. But the event to be commemorated in 1987 is even more important than the event commemorated in 1976.

July 4, 1976, marked the two hundredth anniversary of the signing of the Declaration of Independence. The summer of 1987 marks the two hundredth anniversary of the drafting and signing of the United States Constitution, which was ratified by the required number of states two years later. If not for the Constitution, the Declaration of Independence would probably be remembered only as an interesting historical document. Its powerful words would be mere sentiment. The Constitution of the United States made this country a nation. By protecting individual freedoms, guarding against arbitrary government, and securing individual opportunity, it made the American political creed unique.

Most Americans know something about the Constitution. They have a general impression that it is important and that it provides for certain individual rights. Nevertheless, knowledge of the Constitution seldom goes beyond that general impression and a vague notion of law and liberty. Most of us know far too little about the Constitution – its origins, its adoption, and its subsequent role in defining the limits of government and the rights of the individual in society. Part of the reason for this is that most of the available materials on the Constitution have been written for lawyers, historians, and political scientists, not for the interested layman. While this book should be useful to lawyers and law students, I have written it primarily for the reader who has had no legal education but who has an interest in the Constitution and a desire to learn more about it.

What is the American Constitution? Obviously, it has something to do with law. But there are other sources of law that are not constitutional law. How does constitutional law differ from other laws? What are the relationships between the Constitution and other sources of law?

Why is the Constitution important, and why should we study it? How does it operate? What does it do? How does it limit the things that government can do? What kinds of effect does it have on Congress, on the president, and on the courts? How does it divide powers between the national government on the one hand and state and local governments on the other? How do these divisions of governmental power affect the individual American?

The study of constitutional law is aided by considering the entire field under two large subject headings. The first subject concerns the powers of government, both state and federal. The second deals with the protection of individual interests against the exercise of those governmental powers.

Most of the provisions of the seven articles of the original Constitution, adopted in Philadelphia during the summer of 1787, deal with the first subject, the powers of government. The first three articles distribute power among the three branches of government, and the entire body of the original Constitution, plus the Tenth Amendment, divides it between the national government and the various state governments. These matters of governmental power deal with structure: which governmental unit is constitutionally authorized to perform which governmental function—which can build dams, which can run a postal service, which can operate fire departments and schools, which can pass laws dealing with marriage, divorce, and adoption.

The Constitution spreads these powers among the three branches of the federal government. This is commonly called "separation of powers." The constitution also divides governmental powers between the federal government and the state governments. This is called "federalism." Both separation of powers and federalism have a common objective: each attempts to allocate governmental power and to prevent the accumulation of excessive power in any one unit of government.

The second great subject heading of constitutional law—protection of individual rights against the exercise of governmental powers—is rooted principally in the amendments. The Bill of Rights and the Fourteenth Amendment, for example, are not concerned with which government—federal or state—or which branch of the federal government has the authority to engage in a particular activity. Rather, the purpose of these parts of the Constitution is to prohibit or limit the exercise of any governmental activity that unduly infringes on individual interests.

In considering this second subject of constitutional law—protection of individual interests—it is helpful to bear in mind that anything government does will have an adverse effect on the interests of some individuals, even as it protects the interests of others. This is true of literally every governmental activity, including fighting wars, running postal services, building highways, cleaning up air and water, or providing police and fire services. In the great majority of instances, we simply accept this intrusion on individual interests as one of the costs of living in a civilized society, free from anarchy. In some cases, however, the interests of the individual prevail over those of the government.

The accommodation of these two conflicting sets of interests—those of the individual on the one hand and those of society as determined by society's elected representatives on the other—is the function of the Constitution. In this respect, the Constitution contains a series of governmental "thou shalt nots." The Constitution in effect says to government, "Yes, I have given to the federal branch the authority to impose an income tax and to wage war; I have given even broader authority to state governments, including authority to provide for schools, hospitals, and police and fire protection. But both the states and the federal government are prohibited from exercising those powers in certain ways. Government may build highways, for example, but may not take private property for that purpose without paying for it."

This book surveys the most important principles that make up the body of American constitutional law, dividing those principles into the two great subject headings, the powers of government, and the protection of individual rights against the exercise of those powers. The basic approach and purpose is to summarize and inform. Three caveats, however, are in order.

First, while I have attempted a survey of the entire constitutional law field and have included a discussion of at least most of the problems and the rules that the majority of people would agree are important ones, the treatment is not exhaustive. For reasons that will become more apparent in the book, constitutional law is such a dynamic and open-ended field, any attempt at an exhaustive treatment would probably be impossible even as a theoretical matter.

Second, while in each instance I attempt to state the law as it is, I do not always refrain from expressing my own views concerning what the law should be.

Finally, in addition to summarizing constitutional problems and principles, the book gives greater attention than might be expected in a general survey of constitutional law to the role of the courts in constitutional lawmaking. It has been said, and many people believe, that constitutional law has nothing to do with the Constitution, that constitutional law is only what the United States Supreme Court says it is.

While that statement represents a dangerous and largely inaccurate overgeneralization, the concern that it expresses lies at the foundation of all constitutional issues. One of the major focuses of the book, therefore, is an examination into what the role of the courts has been, and what it should be, in making constitutional law.

Many people have contributed to this book. The two most prominent have been my wife, Janet, who is also my ablest critic, and my research assistant Scott Isaacson, who toward the end of the process became almost as much a collaborator as research assistant. I am also grateful to my colleagues, Dallin Oaks, Carl Hawkins, Robert Riggs, Grant Nelson, Bruce Hafen, Reese Hansen, Neil York, Ed Kimball, and Martin Hickman, who read the manuscript at various stages and made valuable comments.

PART ONE
The Powers of
Government

Introduction to Part One

Part I of this book reviews the powers of government as they are allocated and defined by the Constitution. It is helpful to consider the constitutional issues of state and federal governmental power against two backgrounds. The first is the historical background, particularly the Constitutional Convention of 1787 and the Founding Fathers' view of how governmental power came from the people. The second is the distinction and the close relationship between the two roles of the Constitution: as an allocator of governmental power on the one hand and as a protector against governmental power on the other. In theory these two roles of the Constitution are distinct; for this reason Part I surveys constitutional grants of power, while Part II surveys constitutional limitations on governmental powers. In practice, there is a significant overlap between the two. There is no more effective guarantor of individual rights against the abuses of government than to spread power among the separate branches of the national government and to separate state and federal governments. Throughout the analysis, therefore, the reader should bear in mind that the separation of powers among the three branches of the federal government and the division of powers between the federal government and the fifty state governments also have another effect: the securing of individual rights. It is against government that the Constitution secures individual rights. The Constitution accomplishes this not only by express individual guarantees, but also by preventing concentrations of governmental power.

Part I consists of six chapters. Chapter 1 reviews briefly the history of the Constitutional Convention. Chapter 2 recounts the birth of the Bill of Rights and the struggle for ratification of the Constitution. Chapter 3 contains a general survey of the constitutional provisions. Chapters 4 and 5 discuss separation of powers, and Chapter 6 focuses on federalism.

CHAPTER ONE

The Philadelphia Convention of 1787

The Philadelphia summer of 1787 was unusually hot and humid. For the fifty-five delegates gathered in Philadelphia to deliberate as a Constitutional Convention, however, there were problems more serious than the unpleasant weather.

Scarcely a decade before the Philadelphia convention the colonies had gained freedom from British rule. During the War of Independence they had been governed under the Articles of Confederation, which had been drawn up in 1777 and ratified in 1781 and which were still in effect when the Constitutional Convention met in 1787. A century of experience with British imperial authority had taught the colonists to fear centralized authority. Often ignored in textbooks or dismissed as a prelude to the Philadelphia convention, the Articles are important in their own right and were the natural outgrowth of the revolutionary experience. The Articles created a "free league of friendship," under which the former colonies banded together as "The United States of America" but nonetheless retained their individual "sovereignty, freedom, and independence." As a result, when the war ended and the overriding necessity of unity passed, the Thirteen Colonies had little more in common than historical background, common borders, and mutual efforts to take advantage of each other.

The Articles of Confederation established the Continental Congress, where each state delegation had a single vote. The Articles did not establish a separate national executive or a federal court system. The unicameral Congress was given certain powers, including the authority to carry on diplomatic relations, requisition the states for men and money, coin and borrow money, regulate Indian affairs, and settle disputes between the states. More significant, however, were the powers that were withheld from Congress. The authority to regulate commerce and to tax were retained by the states. Most crucial legislation could only pass with a two-thirds majority; amendments to the Articles of Confederation required the unanimous assent of the states. Indeed, all ultimate ordinary lawmaking authority remained with the states. Congressional resolutions were merely recommendations. It was assumed that the states would enforce them, but there was no obligation to do so.

Some influential colonial leaders had perceived the Articles of Confederation as necessary only to pursue the Revolutionary War. The first draft was considered by the Continental Congress in July 1776, about the time of the Declaration of Independence, and the document was not legally established until March 1781, just seven months prior to the allied victory at Yorktown. No less a figure than Thomas Jefferson expressed the view that the delegates to the Congress established by the Articles should "destroy the strange idea of their being a permanent body, which has unaccountably taken possession of the heads of their constituents, and occasions jealousies injurious to the public good."[1]

Several occurrences during the decade of the 1780s contributed to the sentiment that substantial change had to be effected. Because of the splintered quality of their alliance, the states were unable to negotiate any effective trade agreements with European countries. Attempts to conduct foreign relations and even to provide basic protection resulted in frustration and embarrassment. The Barbary pirates seized American ships and sold their crews as slaves. Lacking any strong central authority, the states were unable to take effective preventive measures such as those enjoyed when their ships and crews operated under the protection of the British flag. Another development was the emergence of a new generation of leaders. After the war there emerged a growing number of nationalists, many of whom, like George Washington and Henry Knox, had served in the army and seen up close (too close, they would have said) the deficiencies of a government relying on essentially voluntary efforts on the parts of the several states to field an army and win campaigns. They were joined by politicians like Robert Morris and Benjamin Franklin, who had sat in Congress and experienced the same frustrations. Joining the generals and the old-hand politicians was a new generation of leaders, men like James Madison and Alexander Hamilton. They were younger men who had entered public life for the first time during the war and were imbued with a different vision of national purpose than some of their older colleagues who clung to more provincial ways. They did not share the fear of some, notably Richard Henry Lee and Samuel Adams, that a more vigorous national government would be dangerous. While Lee and Adams could admit that the war may not have been fought all that efficiently and that postwar problems were vexing, they warned that the cost of a more powerful national government would be diminished state power and fewer individual liberties. The nationalists retorted that government under the Articles had been safeguarded into impotency, making the Confederation a thirteen-headed hydra. As a matter of political survival, they concluded, the government had to be changed.

The division between nationalists (like Hamilton) and their opponents (like Lee) became more pronounced with each passing year after the 1783 Peace of Paris. Nationalists pointed to the uprising of debtor farmers in western Massachusetts in 1786 (now known as Shays's Rebellion) as convincing proof that the arm of the central government had to be strengthened. Capitalizing on the mild recession between 1783 and 1786, they also claimed that the American economy would collapse unless the national government were empowered to lay tariffs and regulate trade.

Virginians took the lead by calling for an interstate convention in September 1786 to discuss commerce in the new nation. Five states responded by sending delegates to Annapolis, Maryland, to deal with trade problems. Some, like James Madison of Virginia, hoped that the Annapolis meeting would lead to something much bigger. Members of the Annapolis Convention reached no satisfactory solution concerning trade because they quickly determined that commercial problems could not be separated from the larger problems of politics and government. Accordingly, they called for a general convention to meet in Philadelphia the next year "to render" the Articles of Confederation "adequate to the exigencies of the Union." The proposed convention was approved by the Continental Congress, which authorized the new convention to revise and amend the Articles.

Twelve states sent delegates to the Philadelphia convention. Rhode Island, the smallest and most faction ridden, refused to have anything to do with the convention and boycotted the proceedings. Twenty-nine delegates were on hand when the convention opened on May 25, 1787. A total of fifty-five attended at one time or another before the convention concluded its business on September 17. A few of the more prominent leaders of the Revolutionary Era were absent. John Adams and Thomas Jefferson were overseas, serving as foreign ministers in England and France, respectively. Fiery Samuel Adams was ill and stayed away from Philadelphia. Two great Virginia patriots, Patrick Henry and Richard Henry Lee, though elected as delegates, refused to attend—Henry complaining that he "smelled a rat." Both Henry and Lee were opposed to attempts to bolster the central government at the expense of the states, and they suspected that the convention would end up doing just that. During the Virginia ratification debates they objected vociferously to the work done in Philadelphia.

These notable absences notwithstanding, the delegates represented the best of American leadership at a time when leadership was this nation's greatest asset. It is safe to say that such a meeting of minds has never been duplicated. Though the Founding Fathers have been accused of being less than selfless and as concerned with protecting their elite status as they were in securing the liberties of their fellow citizens, few would deny that they brought a rare political genius into the Constitutional Convention.

George Washington, one of the representatives from Virginia, was elected to preside over the convention. Benjamin Franklin, now eighty-one and fast approaching the end of his brilliant career, was there as well. He did not play as active a role as some of his younger colleagues but he was, like Washington, an important calming influence. The most impressive state delegations were from Virginia—which, in addition to Washington, sent James Madison, George Mason, and Edmund Randolph—and Pennsylvania—which sent Gouverneur Morris and James Wilson. Alexander Hamilton of New York and Roger Sherman of Connecticut also figured in the political give-and-take that followed.

The work of all of the delegates was, of course, important. One man, however, clearly deserves the title of Father of the Constitution. This man was James Madison, then thirty-six years of age. He was not the official recordkeeper for the convention, but his notes of the debates and other convention proceedings have provided for succeeding generations the best understanding of what occurred during that historic summer. Far more important than his record-keeping, however, were his substantive contributions. He was not trained in any particular profession, but he was widely read and capable of clear and independent thought, remarkably unburdened by prevailing assumptions. Among the delegates, his was the clearest and the strongest voice for the proposition that the strong central government he deemed essential should derive its powers not from the states, in which the Articles of Confederation had vested virtually all sovereignty, but from the people. The concept was not the democratic notion that the total populace could be trusted to make sound decisions; it was rather that the powers of the new government should be powers of the nation as a whole—of all the people—rather than deriving from the individual states.

Almost all of the delegates could agree that their government was out of balance, though they could not always agree on how to set it right. Most could see that they had overreacted to their experience in the British empire when creating their new state governments and when drawing up the Articles of Confederation during the war. In the search for the "permanent foundation of freedom," state constitutions written between 1776 and 1780 had led to legislative supremacy and the emasculation of the executive and judiciary. Since so much of the conflict between colonists and imperial officials in London had been expressed as a contest between royal governors and administrators on the one hand and popularly elected assemblies on the other, Americans of the Revolutionary Era had developed a stilted view of politics. Building on Whig political theories that enjoyed a large following in the colonies, they came to see popularly elected legislatures as almost synonymous with the people. Thus it followed that, in their eyes, the best way to protect the interest of the people and control the passions of the rulers was to increase the power of the legislature and decrease that of the executive and judiciary.

In their reactions to what they interpreted as abuse of power by the executive and judiciary during the years preceding the Revolution, however, they had set the stage for abuse of power by the legislatures. Legislative supremacy, without effective checks, could prove as tyrannical as that of the other branches of government. Separation of powers did not work smoothly if, in separating those powers between executive, legislative, and judicial branches, one branch could rule unchecked. Though all the states except Pennsylvania had bicameral legislatures, the lower houses effectively ran the state governments. The legislature dominated the governor and the courts, and the legislature was in turn dominated by one of its parts.

Some of those gathered in Philadelphia shared the sentiments of John Adams, who took a dim view of this governmental dominance by one legislative chamber. Adams had been disheartened by the state governments established in 1776, feeling that the popular sovereignty institutionalized in the lower houses should be tempered by a natural aristocracy of "merit" in the upper houses and an executive role in government. The Massachusetts Constitution of 1780 codified Adams's ideas by providing a governor with real powers, an independent judiciary, and a congress composed of a house and a more aristocratic senate.

Though they might concur with Adams that balance needed to be restored, the delegates in Philadelphia were hardly of one mind. Much more was at stake than had been the case in Massachusetts. There were more diverse interests to be satisfied, more compromises that had to be made. Of most pressing importance was the division between representatives of the large and small states at the convention. Representatives from the large states believed that the small states enjoyed undue influence in the national government, far out of proportion to their population and size. Representatives from the small states feared that replacing voting by state with voting by individual representatives, with the number of representatives to be determined by population, would place them at a fatal disadvantage.

The small-state delegates had been thrown into a panic the very first week of the convention when Edmund Randolph submitted the "Virginia Plan." The Virginia Plan proposed to abandon the Articles of Confederation and draw up a new scheme of government which provided for an elected president, a federal court system, and a bicameral legislature with representation in both houses based on population. This plan, authored primarily by Madison though introduced by Randolph, favored the large states and, by implication, envisioned states as administrative agencies rather than sovereign political societies.

Delegates from the small states proposed their rival "New Jersey Plan" the next month. They wanted to keep the Articles intact and beef them up. They desired only to augment some of the powers of Congress and keep the state sovereignty written into the Articles. They contended that a national legislature based on popular representation would allow large states to bully their smaller neighbors. This could not be condoned, they argued, because the states are "so many political societies," each of them equal in importance.

The New Jersey Plan was voted down, but one part of it was kept after delegates from the smaller states threatened to walk out. To pacify them the convention agreed that the upper house of Congress, the Senate, would have its representation based on the states, while the lower house, the House of Representatives, would have its representation apportioned according to population. This concession, sometimes called "the Great Compromise," saved the convention from dissolution and also guaranteed that the Virginia Plan, altered only in this one area, would be passed. In so doing the delegates overstepped the original charge given them by the Continental Congress to amend the Articles; what they now proposed was a new form of government.

The delegates managed to head off a break between northern and southern states almost as serious as that between the large and small states by another compromise before the convention adjourned. Those states having substantial slave populations naturally wanted their slaves counted for the purposes of congressional apportionment. Northerners, incensed by the South's "peculiar institution," and fearful of the increased power this would give, consented to count slaves at a three-fifths ratio—and for taxation as well as representation. They also got the Southerners to agree that the overseas slave trade could be prohibited after twenty years.

The convention ended soon after, having drafted a new frame of government titled "The Constitution of the United States." Those who had remained in Philadelphia to sign it were, for the most part, pleased with their work. Madison, Washington, Franklin, and the other thirty-six signatories believed that they had salvaged the Revolution while restraining its excesses—that they had restored balance in government.

The convention adjourned September 17, 1787. The drafting was finished, the words were in place. The struggle over the new Constitution had not concluded, however; in many ways it had just begun. Before the government outlined in the Constitution could be organized the Constitution itself had to be ratified by the people. Ratification took longer than the drafting and was just as difficult. The principal issue was the absence of a bill of rights.

CHAPTER TWO

Ratification of the Constitution and the Bill of Rights

The Bill of Rights, with its assurances of freedom of religion, press, and speech and its promise of fair trials and security from unwarranted intrusion, is so familiar, and so important that we often forget that it was not part of the Constitution as adopted by the Constitutional Convention. The words "Bill of Rights" do not appear anywhere in the Constitution. What we call the Bill of Rights is contained in the first eight amendments, which, along with two other amendments, were added to the Constitution after it was ratified. The story behind the first ten amendments—why they were not included in the original work and how they later became part of the Constitution—is not only interesting and informative; it is also helpful in understanding constitutional law today.

The tradition of a written catalog of rights can be traced back in English history to Magna Charta and subsequent similar documents containing grants of power from the king to his subjects. The significance of Magna Charta is that, as early as 1215, English barons at Runnymede had extracted from their sovereign the promise that certain individual liberties would be guaranteed, including fair jury trials. Later the people of England won the guarantees of the writ of habeas corpus and a degree of freedom of religion and expression.

The Bill of Rights Issue at the Constitutional Convention

After the Declaration of Independence, eight of the Thirteen Colonies, beginning with Virginia in 1776, included in their state constitutions explicit statements regarding individual rights. Even those states lacking a separate enumeration of rights included in the body of their constitutions limitations on government that protected individual liberty. These state bills of rights, though drawing on English tradition, differed significantly in basic theory. Americans during the Revolutionary Era had become convinced that the people were sovereign, not the king, the governors, or even the legislatures. Thus, the bills of rights adopted by early American states were not "grants" of rights from political leaders. Rather, they were designed as limitations imposed on the government to protect the peoples' rights.

Many of the delegates to the Constitutional Convention had helped to write their own states' bills of rights, and nearly all had taken part in the ongoing debate over the nature of human rights and government. George Mason, delegate from Virginia and author of the bill of rights for that state, logically assumed that his motion to add a similar bill to the Constitution would pass. Why, then, was Mason's motion to append a bill of rights to the Constitution defeated unanimously by the convention?

There are several probable reasons why the convention chose not to include a written bill of rights. First, the framers were, above all else, struggling to organize a workable government with proper balance and clearly defined powers. They were pragmatic, politically astute, and experienced in the operations of government. They saw their problem as a practical one: designing a system that would work. All through the convention they had avoided any extravagant statements about human rights.

Second, nearly all of the state constitutions protected individual liberty. The framers thought that these rights were adequately preserved by the states. Also, the delegates looked on the Constitution as it stood as a kind of bill of rights. All of its provisions and the ideas behind it were aimed at forming a limited, carefully checked government, which the founders considered to be the surest protection of individual rights. The safest way to protect those rights, they believed, was to give government no power at all to deal with them. In other areas government intervention was necessary, but the Constitution provided checks and balances on that power. With this in mind, many of the delegates decided that a separate enumeration of rights was unnecessary. As Hamilton pointed out, "[W]hy declare that things shall not be done which there is no power [in Congress] to do?"[1]

Although the original Constitution lacked a separate bill of rights, it did include several provisions protecting specific individual liberties. When those delegates who favored a separate bill of rights failed to impress the convention they tried, with some success, to include in the text of the Constitution some basic protections. These are the guarantee of the writ of habeas corpus, prohibitions against bills of attainder or ex post facto laws—all from Article I Section 9—and the preservation of jury trials, found in Article III Section 2.

Another factor in the decision not to provide a bill of rights was that the delegates were confident that the best protection of human rights was the "soundness of sense and honesty of heart" of citizens in a "virtuous" republic. Since the people were the ultimate source of governmental power, so long as they remained responsible, freedom-loving, and involved, their rights would be safeguarded. A closely related notion was that the protection of individual liberties was implicit in the nature of things and needed no express guarantee. As Noah Webster saw it, the Constitution might as well provide: "That everybody shall, in good weather, hunt on his own land, and catch fish in rivers that are public property ... and that Congress shall never restrain any inhabitant of America from eating and drinking, at seasonable times, or prevent his lying on his left side, in a long winter's night, or even on his back, when he is fatigued by lying on his right."[2]

Finally, some historians have suggested that the real reason the convention did not add a bill of rights is that the delegates were so tired after having labored through the long hot summer that they did not want to stay in Philadelphia any longer.

The Constitution Goes to the States: The Lines Are Drawn

When the Constitutional Convention ended and the Constitution went to the states for ratification it was greeted with shock. Meeting in secret proceedings, the convention had instructions from the Continental Congress only to revise the Articles of Confederation. The new Constitution established an entirely new form of government—a national government—not a mere association of independent states. Some politicians were stunned and infuriated when they read over the Constitution. Their principal point of attack was the lack of a bill of rights. Many of them decried its absence and refused to support the Constitution for this reason. Some who opposed the Constitution for other reasons seized upon the absence of a bill of rights as an appealing, easily understood issue that they could use to good effect in blocking ratification.

The nation quickly split into two camps: the "Federalists," or friends of the Constitution, and the "Antifederalists," who opposed it. Dissenting members of the Constitutional Convention—notably George Mason of Virginia, who published a widely read article called "Objections"—led the Antifederalist attack. Eldridge Gerry of Massachusetts, who had refused to sign the Constitution, actively opposed ratification, while Luther Martin, another dissenting delegate, fought ratification vigorously in his home state of Maryland. Martin claimed that he had composed a bill of rights during the convention but had been temporarily persuaded not to move to include it in the Constitution. These men were joined by others who had not participated in the convention, like Patrick Henry and Richard Henry Lee of Virginia, and Samuel Adams of Massachusetts. They and others argued that a bill of rights was absolutely essential to guarantee the preservation of basic human rights. They did not have the trust in checks and balances written into the unamended Constitution that the Federalists had. Henry, Mason, and the others contended vehemently that the protection of individual liberties should not be left implicit—they should be made explicit in a bill of rights.

The Federalists were led by men who had dominated the convention in Philadelphia; the most prominent of these were Madison and Hamilton. A series of eighty-five essays written by Hamilton, Madison, and John Jay, under the pseudonym "Publius," were circulated to back the Federalist cause in New York, where a close battle over ratification was waged. These essays were compiled and published in one volume titled *The Federalist.* Ably organized and persuasively argued, these essays are among the most authoritative sources for determining the original intent of the Founding Fathers. James Wilson also wrote extensively in support of the Federalist position, as did Francis Hopkinson (though in a somewhat lighter vein). George Washington also favored the Constitution without a bill of rights, but by the time of the ratification struggle he had retired from public life and had returned to the serenity of Mount Vernon.

Why would the Federalists continue to oppose a bill of rights? Madison in particular is respected as an advocate of individual liberty. Given the postconvention outcry for a bill of rights, why would he not agree to include guarantees of personal liberty in the Constitution? Part of the answer is tied to the reasons already mentioned and part to developments after the convention adjourned.

The grand strategy of the Antifederalists was to undercut the Federalists and push for a second constitutional convention to revise, not cast aside, the Articles of Confederation. They argued that this second convention would add a bill of rights and correct the other errors that they saw in the Constitution proposed by their opponents. The Federalists were adamantly opposed to another convention, for they remembered how hard it had been to draw up the document they had. They knew that a second convention would not have the advantage of secrecy that the first had enjoyed. All of the states would know what was being discussed and the debates would be even more acrimonious. The Federalists feared that a new convention before the Constitution was ratified would throw away what progress had been made and could end all hopes of an American union stronger than the "league of friendship" provided for in the Articles of Confederation. Thus they did not necessarily oppose some of the ideas behind a bill of rights, if that is what the people wanted; rather, they objected to the timing. Changing the Constitution before ratification would disrupt the new governmental framework they had so carefully constructed. Antifederalists, of course, knew this perfectly well and were not above using the bill of rights issue to defeat their Federalist foes.

While the fear of losing the ratification struggle motivated the Federalists and they expressed this fear in the debates from state to state, the most prominent Federalist argument against a bill of rights was that it would be unnecessary. To have a provision for freedom of the press, observed James Wilson, was not needed because Congress had no power over the press anyway. Wilson took his reasoning one step further and argued that a bill of rights would not only be unnecessary but actually destructive. He contended that if a list of rights were added to the Constitution it would imply that the powers not expressly reserved in the list were given to Congress. An attempt to list the things that Congress could not do would imply that it had power to do everything not on the list.

Federalists like Wilson saw a bill of rights as "the government shall not do X, Y, Z," leaving the government free to do everything not on that list. They knew that no one could write a bill of rights so inclusive as to cover all areas of human activity where government should not interfere. They feared that a partial list would have the ironic effect of expanding Congress's power too far, threatening thereby the delicate balance of their new national government.

Ratification of the Constitution

Supporters of the Constitution did everything they could to insure victory in the ratification struggle. They had wisely written into Article VII that ratification would be by specially elected conventions rather than by state legislatures, realizing that the state legislatures had a vested interest in government under the Articles and might attempt to thwart their move. The Federalists also launched a masterful newspaper campaign and pulled off quick victories in a few states. Antifederalists would be hard pressed to stop Federalist momentum.

Some of the smaller, less populous states like Delaware, New Jersey and Connecticut ratified the Constitution early in the contest. They stood to gain by doing so, since the Constitution secured them against being annexed by their larger, more powerful neighbors and protected their interests in interstate commerce, which would now be unburdened by protectionist devices used by one state against another. Most importantly, the smaller states had obtained equal representation in the Senate.

Rhode Island, however, although the smallest state of all, had a more self-sufficient economy and localistic leaders who did not see eye to eye with the Federalists. Rhode Island delayed ratification until May 1790, nearly two full years after the minimum of nine state conventions had voted for ratification and several months after the new government organized under the Constitution had begun operating.

Pennsylvania was the first of the larger states to ratify, on December 12, 1787, after a short but sharp fight. Federalists in Massachusetts also came up against a determined and well-organized opposition. Because they doubted whether the Constitution would pass unless they compromised on some issues, the Federalists there decided in caucus to give in to demands for a bill of rights. They presented a list of articles that would be recommended as amendments to the Constitution. They proposed that Massachusetts ratify the Constitution as it stood but at the same time send the recommended amendments to the new Congress after it convened, where they could be reviewed according to the criteria outlined in Article V of the Constitution. This compromise on the part of the Federalists caused some Antifederalists to shift and vote for ratification, which carried 187 to 168.

Federalist leaders in other states saw the wisdom of the Massachusetts compromise on a bill of rights. Every state that approved the Constitution after Massachusetts did so with the addition of some proposed amendments on the bill of rights issue. This was a shrewd political move, one necessary to secure ratification and, in the long run, to strengthen the Constitution itself. Once the Federalists formulated a device for adding a bill of rights by amendment without impeding the ratification process or calling for another Constitutional Convention, the Antifederalists had the rug pulled out from under them.

Maryland ratified the Constitution on April 28, 1788, with a proposal asking for amendments; South Carolina did the same in May. New Hampshire became the ninth state to ratify, on June 21, 1788, just about nine months after the Convention had adjourned. New Hampshire's ratification met the requirement of Article VII that the "Ratification of the Conventions of nine States shall be sufficient for the Establishment of this Constitution." Technically, then, the new Constitution could go into effect. Nevertheless, few had much hope for the future of the new Union unless the key states of Virginia and New York ratified. These were the home states of Madison and Hamilton, but they were also Antifederalist strongholds.

The Antifederalists, having been shocked into a more coordinated effort by their defeat in Massachusetts, planned and carried out a determined opposition. They countered the Federalists with a modification of their own: instead of ratifying first and adopting amendments later, Antifederalists at the Virginia convention proposed that a call should go out to the other states requesting a new constitutional convention to add amendments prior to ratification. Madison replied for the Federalists that he would accept any reasonable amendments but that they must be subsequent to ratification; he would never consent to them as a condition of ratification. After much debate the motion calling for previous amendments went to a vote and narrowly failed, eighty-eight to eighty. The Federalists quickly called for a vote on ratification. They picked up one more vote and Virginia ratified, eighty-nine to seventy-nine, on June 26, 1788. The Virginians then wrote a list of amendments which covered most of the changes that Henry, Mason, and the other Antifederalists had insisted upon.

The New York convention was in session when word arrived that Virginia had ratified. The New York debate continued on into July 1788. Generally, there was much more emphasis on economic factors in the New York convention than there had been in previous state conventions. The two sides eventually reached the same impasse that Massachusetts and Virginia had faced. Again the time came to compromise. New York Antifederalists attempted the same strategy as their Virginia counterparts, but without success. They proposed to ratify the Constitution "on condition" that New York could withdraw from the Union after a certain number of years if the Congress did not add a bill of rights.

"Conditional" ratification did not fail by much. Hamilton took the floor to argue that all amendments must be subsequent to ratification; New York could not conditionally ratify without undermining the Constitution. Madison had written a letter to Hamilton on this subject after the Virginia convention and Hamilton read it to his fellow delegates. Madison considered a conditional ratification worse than rejection and noted that "compacts must be reciprocal. . . . An adoption for a limited time would be as defective as an adoption of some of the articles only. In short, any condition whatever must viciate the ratification."[3] In so arguing Madison applied a doctrine from contract law, comparing ratification to the forming of a contract. One party cannot make a contract that does not really bind him. A conditional ratification would not unequivocally bind New York to the Union of States and therefore would not be a true ratification. Apparently Hamilton's and Madison's words were persuasive enough. New York ratified the next day, July 24, 1788, by a margin of three votes, and added to its ratification a suggested list of amendments.

Madison's argument on conditional amendments is especially important because the courts have subsequently followed this same reasoning in holding that states cannot conditionally ratify proposed constitutional amendments. States must ratify amendments as they are sent to them by Congress. If they attempt to change the amendment or add conditions, the courts have declared that that is not ratification.

With New York's acceptance, the Constitution was guaranteed a strong start. The only states that still had not ratified were Rhode Island and North Carolina. Both expressed a wait-and-see attitude toward the proposed Union and eventually ratified, North Carolina in 1789 and Rhode Island in 1790.

The First Ten Amendments

The first Congress elected under the new Constitution in 1789 was dominated by Federalists, many of whom had promised during their campaigns that a bill of rights would be written as Congress's first official act. But when Congress met for the first time in April 1789, it took up every matter of business other than a bill of rights. Many congressmen justified this seeming breach of promise by contending that they needed to take care of economic problems and organize the government and that a bill of rights would have to wait. If not for the constant pressure of James Madison, now a member of the House of Representatives, the first Congress might never have drafted a bill of rights.

It is ironic that the leading effort for a bill of rights should come from Madison. Madison, it should be remembered, had opposed the motion that the Constitutional Convention add a bill of rights. After the convention had closed he still doubted the need for a bill of rights and opposed amending the Constitution to add one. During the ratification struggle, however, he gradually became convinced that a bill of rights would help gain support for the new government. Moreover, Thomas Jefferson, writing from his post as ambassador to France, helped him see the positive effects of such a bill.

After the Constitution had been ratified, Madison had become a candidate for the Senate, only to be defeated by, of all people, Richard Henry Lee, who had boycotted the convention and opposed ratification. To be thus excluded from the very government he had helped to form must have been a great disappointment to Madison. He then ran for the House of Representatives and was barely elected over Jefferson's neighbor, James Monroe, another Antifederalist who, twenty-eight years later, would succeed Madison as president. During that campaign Madison had been forced to make many public denials that he would oppose a bill of rights and, in fact, ended up promising to champion that cause.

Committed to seeing his promise through, Madison rose repeatedly to call for a debate on a bill of rights, only to be put down by other representatives, who claimed that "more important business" should be settled. Finally, on May 25, Madison was given the floor to make his plea. He listed his proposed amendments and made a short speech explaining them.

Madison's proposals and his speech are evidence of his remarkable genius. Even though there was a uniform demand for a bill of rights, the specific rights demanded by the different states were anything but uniform. Taken together, the suggestions from the states totaled over two hundred separate, sometimes overlapping, sometimes conflicting amendments.[4] Madison took these proposals, discarded those he deemed unnecessary, combined those that overlapped, and came up with a drastically reduced total of ten.

Congress added two more and sent them on to George Washington, the new president, who submitted them to the states in September 1789. By the time the amendments could be considered for ratification, Vermont had been added to the Union; and prior to their effective date North Carolina and Rhode Island ratified the Constitution. With fourteen states, ratification by eleven was necessary to satisfy Article V, which required that constitutional amendments be approved by three-fourths of the states.

Only ten of the twelve proposed amendments were ratified by the required eleven states. Once again, Delaware was the first state to ratify. Virginia was the eleventh, and the first ten amendments became effective on December 15, 1791. The two rejected amendments were those added to Madison's list by Congress. One contained a formula for apportioning seats in the House of Representatives, while the other was a prohibition against altering the salary of congressmen during their term of office. Neither dealt with personal rights, and both were subsequently enacted by congressional statutes.

Thus Madison is sometimes called the "father" of the Bill of Rights as well as the "father" of the Constitution. While neither was the product of his genius alone, Madison had been instrumental in giving them form. He and the other Federalists had won. In time the Antifederalists became reconciled to their defeat, and many of them served in the national government they had hoped to prevent. The focal point of the battle between the Federalists and the Antifederalists—the Bill of Rights—would in time become perhaps the most important part of the Constitution.

CHAPTER THREE

A General Survey of the American Constitution

The Articles

The Constitution adopted by the delegates to the Philadelphia Convention in 1787 consists of seven articles. The first three articles establish the branches of the federal government—legislative, executive, and judicial—and enumerate the powers held by each.

Article I declares that all legislative powers of the national government are vested in a Congress of the United States. It provides for a bicameral legislature, along the lines of the earlier English and colonial models. One chamber, the Senate, was more aristocratic: its members, two from each state, were chosen by the state legislatures. The other house, more representative of the general populace, was chosen by popular election. The Constitution was changed in 1913 by the Seventeenth Amendment to provide that each member of the Senate should be elected directly by the people of the state rather than by the legislature. This in turn made the Senate more representative of the voting population, since its members were no longer chosen by state legislators. Even with the Seventeenth Amendment, however, the Senate still fell short of Madison's ideal that the legislative branch of the national government should derive its powers from the people. The number of seats in the Senate is keyed to the existence of each state as a state, rather than to the number of people represented by the individual senators.

Probably the most important feature of Article I, implicit in its structure and made explicit by the Tenth Amendment, is the limited scope of federal lawmaking authority. Strictly defined, the national government is a government of enumerated and therefore limited powers. That is, any action taken by the federal government must find justification somewhere within the four corners of the Constitution. State governments have general authority to act in the interest of the health, safety, morals, and welfare of their people, but the governmental authority of the federal government is limited to that which is expressly authorized by the Constitution. Article I Section 8 lists approximately twenty areas where Congress is specifically authorized to legislate. These and a few other provisions contained in other parts of the Constitution (principally the Thirteenth and Fourteenth amendments) constitute the exclusive authority for congressional lawmaking. Unless a congressional statute is built on the foundation of one of these provisions, it is, for that reason alone, unconstitutional.

This general principle concerning the limited scope of federal governmental authority must be tempered, however, with three other observations. The first is that federal lawmaking authority includes not only those powers that are specifically enumerated, but also those powers that are reasonably implied from the enumerated powers. For example, in the landmark case, *McCulloch v. Maryland*,[1] the question was whether Congress has the authority to establish a national bank. Article I says nothing about Congress having the authority to underwrite a national bank. It does, however, authorize Congress "to borrow money on the credit of the United States" and "to coin money." *McCulloch v. Maryland* held that the power to establish a national bank was reasonably implied by these express powers.

The second observation is closely related to the first. Even though Congress is limited to the powers enumerated by the Constitution, several of those enumerated powers, and others implied by them under the doctrine of *McCulloch v. Maryland*, have been interpreted to have a very broad sweep. The most important of these is Congress's power over foreign and interstate commerce. Probably next in importance are its taxing and spending powers. Broad interpretations of these provisions are possible because the most important provisions of the Constitution, such as the commerce clause, are cast in broad, general language.

The final observation is that, so long as Congress acts within its enumerated powers, to whatever extent there is a conflict between state and federal law, federal law prevails. This is because of the supremacy clause contained in Article VI of the Constitution: all properly passed "Laws of the United States . . . shall be the supreme Law of the Land."

Article II deals with the executive branch, vesting the executive power "in a President of the United States of America." It defines the minimum requirements to be eligible for the office, provides for the election of a President and Vice-president, and sets the term of office at four years for both. It also provides for the President's succession in the event of removal from office, or his death, resignation, or inability to carry out official duties. This presidential succession provision was further refined in 1967 by the Twenty-fifth Amendment. A little-known but interesting provision of Article II is the prohibition against either increasing or diminishing the President's salary during the period for which he shall have been elected.

The President is also constitutionally designated as the "Commander in Chief of the Army and Navy and of the Militia of the several States, when called into the actual Service of the United States." The most important of the enumerated presidential powers is his constitutional responsibility to "take care that the Laws be faithfully executed."

Article I vests all legislative power in the Congress. Article II vests all executive power in the President. Article III vests "The judicial Power of the United States . . . in one supreme Court, and in such inferior Courts as the Congress may from time to time ordain and establish." Therefore, the only federal court whose existence is constitutionally protected is the Supreme Court. The only reason that federal courts other than the Supreme Court exist at all is that Congress created them, and Congress could increase or decrease the number of federal courts or abolish them altogether if it chose to do so. Likewise, Congress can alter the number of Supreme Court justices any time it sees fit. Indeed, there have been as few as five and as many as ten, and the number has been fixed at nine only since 1869.

Each of the remaining four articles of the Constitution deals with a more limited range of constitutional issues than the first three. The common feature of the provisions of Article IV is that each deals in one way or another with the relationships among the states in a federal union. Probably the most important provision of Article IV is the "full faith and credit" clause, which reads, "Full Faith and Credit shall be given in each State to the public Acts, Records, and judicial Proceedings of every other State." The effect of this provision is that certain official acts of each state, such as the granting of marriages and divorces and the rendering of judgments by courts, must be honored and enforced in all other states.

Like any other part of the United States Constitution, Article V, which outlines the amendment process, has its share of ambiguity. Some points, however, are quite clear. Amendment of the Constitution must be accomplished by a two-step process. The first step usually occurs at the national, congressional level, and the second at the local, state level. The first step involves a proposal by Congress, the second step an acceptance of that proposal by the states. To those acquainted with basic contract law, there is a rough analogy between offer and acceptance and Article V. The role of Congress in Article V is to set forth the terms of the proposed constitutional amendment. Congress's proposal is then considered by the states and either accepted or rejected.

At each of these steps, Article V provides two alternative procedures. The proposal may be initiated by Congress itself: whenever two-thirds of the members of each house of Congress agree on the terms of a proposed constitutional amendment, the amending proposal is submitted to the states for ratification. The second procedure for amending the Constitution is initiated in the states. Whenever the legislatures of two-thirds of the states request it, Congress is required to call a national convention for proposing amendments. Congress also has a role in the second phase of the process: the ratification, or acceptance of the proposal by the states. Article V provides that Congress may prescribe the means for ratification, including whether it is to be by state conventions or by state legislatures.

Once Congress has made its proposal and has specified the means of ratification, acceptance of the proposed amendment is up to the states. The states may accept either by vote of the state legislatures or by constitutional conventions. By either method, ratification by three-fourths of the states results in the amendment being added to the Constitution.

All amendments that have been passed have been initiated by congressional action. Of the amendments that have been passed, only the Twenty-first was submitted to the state conventions rather than the state legislatures for ratification.

The Amendments

As has been stated, the first ten amendments, adopted in 1791, were proposed by Congress as part of a generally understood commitment to make the adoption of a bill of rights a first order of business following the adoption of the new Constitution.

In a strict sense, the Bill of Rights consists of the first eight amendments rather than the first ten. These first eight deal with explicit personal freedoms such as freedom of speech, freedom of religion, jury trial, protection against unreasonable searches and seizures, and the like. The Ninth Amendment, by contrast, does not specify any particular individual guarantee but, rather, asserts that "[t]he enumeration in the Constitution, of certain rights, shall not be construed to deny or disparage others retained by the people." The Tenth states that "[t]he powers not delegated to the United States by the Constitution, nor prohibited by it to to the States, are reserved to the States respectively, or to the people." Both the Ninth and Tenth amendments deal with issues of governmental power, but they differ from the first eight amendments in that they contain no specific guarantees of individual liberties.

Over the history of our Bill of Rights there has been a great disparity in the extent to which the various provisions have been brought into play as protectors of individual liberties. The most active have been the First, Fourth, Fifth, and Sixth. Four of the amendments—the Fourth, Fifth, Sixth, and Eighth—provide protections for the criminally accused. The Fourth Amendment deals with a single subject: unreasonable searches and seizures. The popular mind most frequently associates the Fifth Amendment with a single provision: the privilege against self-incrimination. Actually, the Fifth Amendment contains five important individual guarantees. One of them, the prohibition against taking private property for public use without just compensation, is not a protection for the criminally accused. Another, the "due-process clause," provides both criminal and noncriminal protections. The Sixth Amendment contains several provisions, whose common feature is the right of the criminally accused to a fair trial.

The First, Second, Third, and Seventh amendments all deal with individual rights other than those of the criminally accused. The First Amendment is by far the most important, viewed either historically or from the attention that it has received in constitutional litigation. The Second, Third, and Seventh amendments have not figured prominently in our constitutional history to date. The Second, dealing with the right of the people to keep and bear arms, has been addressed by the Supreme Court on only three occasions. The Supreme Court has never interpreted the Third Amendment's prohibition against the quartering of soldiers in private homes. The Seventh Amendment guarantees the right of jury trial in civil cases brought in federal courts where the amount in controversy is greater than twenty dollars. It is a curious provision in that it is the only one in the entire Constitution that ties an individual guarantee to a specific dollar amount.

Of the remaining amendments, Eleven through Twenty-six, the Fourteenth is the only one that occupies a position of importance comparable to the First, or to the first three articles of the Constitution. This is because of two of the provisions of the Fourteenth Amendment: the equal-protection clause and the due-process clause. Of the remaining fifteen amendments, one-third—the Twelfth, Twentieth, Twenty-second, Twenty-third, and Twenty-fifth—deal with the selection of the President and Vice-President, their terms of office, and their succession. Four amendments—the Fifteenth, Nineteenth, Twenty-fourth, and Twenty-sixth—enlarged the number of people who can vote. Two amendments, the Eighteenth and Twenty-first, deal with Prohibition and essentially cancel each other out. Of the remaining four, the Eleventh overturns a judicial decision dealing with sovereign immunity, the Thirteenth abolishes slavery, the Sixteenth authorizes a national income tax, and the Seventeenth provides for direct election of senators.

Against the background of this general survey, we now examine some of the more important constitutional principles and constitutional structure and how these affect the affairs of American citizens. The balance of Part I deals with the powers of government.

CHAPTER FOUR

The Fundamentals of Separation of Powers: Separateness and Sharing

The term "separation of powers" cannot be found anywhere in the Constitution. Neither can the phrase frequently associated with it, "checks and balances." Both concepts are clearly present, but they are different from each other and have different historical backgrounds.

Historical Roots of Separation of Powers and Checks and Balances

The separation of powers involves more than just a division of labor among the branches of government. Its primary purpose is to prevent concentration of power in any single person or group, thereby assuring that law will be both general and prospective. Laws should be general in the sense that they apply equally to all citizens and prospective in that they do not punish acts that were innocent when committed.

The Founding Fathers' idea that there should be a separateness among the powers of the three branches of government—that each branch possess powers that the others could not exercise—was rooted principally in English experience. It was an idea that had been expressed in the House of Commons as early as 1645. John Lilburne, a Leveller leader during the English civil wars, had been called before the House of Commons in what was essentially a judicial proceeding. He protested that the Committee of Examination, which was to hear his case, could not try him unless it were a court, and that if it were a court it must be bound by the same rules as other courts. Thus Lilburne asserted that "rule first stated in 1645, that legislators should not be justices, for they would then execute the law as well as make it."[1]

Later, Lilburne's argument went even further. Just as legislators should not be judges, neither should they be administrators. For if Parliament, which made the laws, could also "execute the law, they might do palpable injustice and maladminister it." In that case, to whom could the injured persons turn for justice? Surely not to Parliament, the very source of the wrongdoing; the members of Parliament would "vote that man a traitor and destroy him."[2]

English parliamentary government today is not a good example of separation of powers. The English prime minister, who is the chief executive officer, is also a member of Parliament; and the House of Lords, one of the two houses of Parliament, constitutes the highest English court. In the mid-seventeenth century, however, the combination or separation of English governmental powers was a more open question. Though the separation-of-powers seeds failed to take root in English soil, that is where they were first nurtured. Their most notable fruit is in the American Constitution. The Founding Fathers brought to the Constitutional Convention their conviction that "the accumulation of all powers—legislative, executive, and judiciary in the same hands ... may justly be pronounced the very definition of tyranny."[3]

While the ideas about separation of powers came from the Founding Fathers' English heritage, the concept of checks and balances was drawn directly from their own experience in self-government. Jefferson argued from Virginia's experiences that a separation of powers was not likely to last unless barriers were erected to prevent the flow of power to the legislative branch. He proposed, therefore, that a system of checks and balances should be adopted to assure the continued separation of powers among the three branches of government.[4] Though Jefferson was not present at the convention, many who were shared his views.

The Federalist noted that the "great security against gradual concentration of the several powers in the same department, consists in giving to those who administer each department the necessary constitutional means and personal motives to resist encroachments of the others."[5]

The Concepts in Operation

The overriding objective of separation of powers and checks and balances is to prevent any branch of government from exercising unrestrained power. The checks and balances provided by the Constitution attempt to accomplish this objective by giving each of the branches powers that moderate and offset those of the other two branches. Although the Founding Fathers hoped that theirs would be a republic of "virtuous citizens," they were not naive in this respect. As Madison noted in *The Federalist,* Number 10, they had to build a solid, seaworthy ship of state because "enlightened statesmen will not always be at the helm."

Most American citizens have a general understanding of checks and balances. The President, for example, can veto congressional legislation. The Congress, in turn, can override this veto if two-thirds of both houses concur. Both the executive and the legislative branches enjoy significant checks over the power of the judiciary. Congress controls the kinds of cases that federal courts can consider and, with the exception of the Supreme Court, controls the very existence of federal courts. The enforcement of judicial decisions is dependent on the executive branch. The judicial branch in turn exercises checks over both of the other branches. The courts can declare unconstitutional the decisions of either Congress or the President.

As effective as these checks and balances are, I believe that the most important structural feature of the Constitution is the separateness of the principal powers of each individual branch—a feature whose fundamentals are simple, and yet whose implications are profound.

The Constitution vests in each of the three branches an important primary governmental responsibility. Each branch has supreme authority over its area of responsibility. For Congress, it is lawmaking; for the President, law enforcement; and for the courts, interpretation of the laws, including interpretation of the Constitution itself. This does not mean, however, that the separateness is complete. The separate responsibilities of two of the branches, lawmaking and law interpretation, are shared among all of the branches. But the ultimate authority over the enactment, the enforcement, and the interpretation of the laws rests, respectively, with the Congress, the President, and the Supreme Court.

Probably the most important of the powers of government is that which belongs to Congress, the power to make law. Congress's lawmaking power means that it has the authority to make the major policy decisions confronting our nation. These are the kinds of decisions that affect every American: how high taxes should be; whether to balance the budget; how much to spend for defense and how much for welfare programs; what to do (economically and otherwise) about clean air and clean water.

Once Congress makes its laws, however, the congressional function ceases. The Constitution leaves the interpretation of those laws to another branch—the courts—and their enforcement to yet another—the President. The President's enforcement authority rests on the words of Article II that the President "shall take care that the Laws be faithfully executed."[6] The judicial authority to interpret the laws is found in Article III, which vests power in Congress to give the federal courts jurisdiction to decide cases or controversies involving the Constitution and the laws of the United States.[7]

The powers of the three branches to make the laws, to interpret them, and to enforce them are not separated by rigid or neatly defined barriers. In fact, all three branches engage to one extent or another in at least the two functions of lawmaking and law interpretation. We will consider first how the executive and judicial branches engage in lawmaking. This will be followed by an examination of legislative and executive involvement in law interpretation.

Executive and Judicial Lawmaking

The role of the executive and judicial branches in lawmaking can be illustrated by considering one of our most important laws, the Sherman Antitrust Act of 1890. Section 1 of the Sherman Act states: "Every contract, combination in the form of trust or otherwise, or conspiracy, in restraint of trade or commerce among the several states, or with foreign nations, is declared to be illegal."

Congress made a policy decision in 1890, therefore, that "restraint of trade" in interstate and foreign commerce is illegal. But what is included within the prohibition against restraint of trade? Does it include agreements among retailers to fix prices? Does it include a manufacturer's discontinuance of one of his distributors? Does it include efforts by a large retailer of electrical appliances to induce its suppliers not to sell to the retailer's competitors? The answers to those questions are not apparent on the face of the statutory prohibition against restraint of trade.

Those issues and others require identification of the kinds of practices that constitute unlawful restraint of trade. They are issues of important national policy, and the resolving of policy issues is what lawmaking is all about. Who makes these decisions? The answer is that under our separation of powers system those policy decisions may be made by the executive branch, by the courts, or by Congress. Ironically, even though conventional understanding teaches that policy decisions—and therefore lawmaking—are for Congress, the branches that have been most active in filling in the blanks of the meaning of restraint of trade have been the executive and the judicial branches. They perform this function as a necessary requirement of their reponsibilities to enforce the laws (in the case of the executive) and to interpret them (in the case of the judiciary).

An example should make this clear. Assume that a manufacturer of large diesel trucks concludes that its products can compete more effectively against other brands if the manufacturer requires that its distributors not compete with each other. Accordingly, the manufacturer assigns to each distributor a geographical territory within which that distributor may sell and prohibits each distributor from selling in another's territory. In other words, the manufacturer prevents its distributors form competing with each other. One may sell only in Colorado, one may sell only in Utah, and so on. Is this a restraint of trade prohibited by the Sherman Act?

Enforcement of the Sherman Act is vested partially in the Antitrust Division of the Justice Department, which is part of the executive branch. Remembering the facts described in the preceding paragraph, assume that the Antitrust Division concludes that the manufacturer's imposition of such territorial restrictions on his distributors' freedom to compete with each other constitutes a restraint of trade. In reaching this conclusion, the Justice Department has made law. It has made an official governmental decision concerning what shall be unlawful as a restraint of trade. It has done so pursuant to its responsibilities to enforce the law. That is, in order to prohibit restraints of trade, as it is required to do by the Sherman Act, the Justice Department was required to make a decision concerning what a restraint of trade is.

Assume further that the manufacturer disagrees with the Justice Department, and the matter is then brought into court. The prime responsibility of the courts is to determine the meaning of law. In the case of the Sherman Act, this means defining what is meant by restraint of trade and, in our hypothetical case, whether a manufacturer's territorial restrictions on his distributors qualify as a restraint of trade. The courts have before them a lawsuit involving two adverse parties, the United States Government on the one side and the truck manufacturer on the other. In order to do its job, the court must decide whether these territorial restrictions constitute a restraint of trade. There is no way that the court can resolve the case before it, therefore, as it is required to do, without making an important policy decision: whether territorial restrictions imposed by a manufacturer or a distributor are legal or illegal. Is this lawmaking? Of course it is. Whether the manufacturer's conduct is legal or illegal and whether our national policy should prohibit or permit the imposition of territorial restrictions on dealers by manufacturers depends on a judicial decision. The judicial decision, therefore, is the very essence of lawmaking, because it involves determining legality or illegality and choosing between policy alternatives in an area of national importance. The earlier policy decision by Congress—prohibiting restraints of trade—does not answer the question concerning these dealer restrictions.

This does not mean, however, that the separation of powers principle has been violated. In that regard, three facts must be noted. The first is that it was Congress itself that placed both the executive branch and the courts in a position where they were not only authorized but required to make policy choices and therefore to make law. Congress deliberately chose to pass an antitrust law whose prohibition was cast in such broad terms that further definition was inevitably required. Second, the only reason either the executive or the judicial branch engaged in filling in the blanks of Congress's broad prohibition against restraint of trade is that they were required to do so in order to fulfill their own constitutional responsibilities to enforce and to interpret a law passed by Congress. Third, the final policymaking authority still rests with Congress. In the event Congress disagrees with the policy results reached either by the executive branch or by the courts, Congress can take the matter into its own hands and its judgment will prevail. Thus, if the courts declare that the territorial restriction is not a restraint of trade, Congress can pass a statute specifically prohibiting any transaction in interstate or foreign commerce in which a manufacturer limits the territory within which a distributor may sell that manufacturer's product. If Congress passes such a statute, its word is final. It cannot be changed by the President or the Supreme Court (or lesser courts). It can be changed only by Congress itself.

Legislative and Executive Law Interpretation

Interpretation of the laws is the central function of the courts. Almost two centuries ago in the landmark decision, *Marbury v. Madison*, the United States Supreme Court held that the "laws" subject to judicial interpretation include the United States Constitution.[8] This is what is meant by judicial review: the power of the courts to review the acts of other branches and departments of government to determine whether they measure up to the standards imposed by the Constitution, and to invalidate those acts in the event that they do not. In *The Federalist*, Number 78, Alexander Hamilton had argued that judicial review was implicit in the Constitution since "the interpretation of the laws is the proper and peculiar province of the courts." The merits of judicial review will be discussed in Chapter 18. The important point for present purposes is the most fundamental one: that the determination of constitutionality is a judicial function.

This does not mean, however, that the other branches do not deal with issues of constitutionality. Congress, in deciding whether to pass statutes, constantly takes into account the views of its members concerning the constitutionality of proposed laws. For two years I served as an official of the executive branch. During that time my responsibilities required that I make decisions several times a week based on my judgment concerning constitutional issues. Thus, in both Congress and the executive branch, constitutional issues enter into official governmental decisionmaking and action. But just as the final authority over policymaking through statutory enactment is vested in Congress, the final word on constitutionality is vested in the courts. Let us suppose that Congress passes a statute it believes to be constitutional. As assistant attorney general I decide to take a certain position in litigation because of my views concerning constitutionality. In both cases, however—the constitutionality of the congressional statute and the correctness of the government's constitutional position in litigation—the courts have the final say.

Mr. Justice Stewart, in a concurring opinion in the *Pentagon Papers Case*,[9] referred to the core powers of the separate branches as being "unshared." In my view, that is not an accurate characterization. The core functions of at least two of the branches—lawmaking by Congress and constitutional interpretation by the courts—are shared. They are not, however, shared equally. Congress enjoys a primacy over statutory policymaking, and the courts enjoy a primacy over constitutional adjudication. It is a primacy that is reflected in the ultimate power of those branches in the event of a conflict with the others. It is not a primacy that excludes all participation by the other branches.

CHAPTER FIVE

The Separation-of-Powers Dynamic

Efficiency and Arbitrariness

One branch of the federal government makes the laws, a second branch enforces them, and a third branch interprets them. It is the kind of system that must give efficiency experts fits.

In the first place, the lawmaking function – the power to make policy choices that affect every American – is spread among 535 separate individuals and between two separate governmental bodies, the United States Senat҄ and the House of Representatives. Each one of these 535 individuals is a separate power center, each costing the American taxpayers over a million dollars a year for their staffs and other expenses. Of even greater concern from an efficiency standpoint, once a majority of these high-priced legislators have agreed on something, why should we ask someone else what they really meant? If there is some doubt about what they meant, why not ask them, rather than turn to a completely separate group of government officials?

Worst of all, what if the courts make a mistake and fail in their attempt to determine what Congress meant? The inefficiency is then compounded, because the expensive, cumbersome process must begin all over again: million-dollar-a-year policymakers correcting what another branch of government incorrectly thought they meant the first time around.

Probably even more inefficient is separating policymaking from policy enforcement. It is Congress that determines what it wants done. Why turn over to someone else the job of carrying out the congressional will? The objective of law enforcement ought to be maximum fidelity to the legislative intent. Given that objective, the most effective way to achieve it would be through some entity that is part of Congress itself, or at the very least is directly responsible to Congress. Instead, we have a system under which the policymakers must content themselves with passing the laws, and then take themselves out of the picture. In many instances, this results in executive-branch attempts to remake congressional policy under the guise of law enforcement. Examples of this are provided by Richard Nixon's impoundment of funds appropriated by Congress and by HEW's interpretations of Title IX of the Civil Rights Act of 1964. Members of Congress may react by collectively attempting to enact new legislation or by individually attempting to persuade federal bureaucrats to enforce the statute the way that they, the congressmen, would like. These processes are time consuming, cumbersome, and costly. And it all comes about because the enforcement of law and policy—as well as the interpretation that necessarily accompanies enforcement—are constitutionally separated from the governmental entity that makes that law and policy.

The only way to construct a system that would be more inefficient, even in theory, would be to create more branches of government with a further splintering of governmental powers among them. And yet, though the inefficiency of separation of powers is obvious, it is equally obvious that, in a large sense, separation of powers was intended to be inefficient. The reason is that any system of government—in any country, in any century—involves a necessary choice between two competing values. They are efficiency, on the one hand, and checks against arbitrary exercise of governmental power on the other. It is impossible to have both.

In theory (though, I am convinced, only in theory) the best form of government is rule by an enlightened despot. That kind of government could be the ultimate in efficiency. If a policy needed to be adopted, the king would adopt it; he could do it with dispatch, because he need consult no one. If there was a question about what the king meant, one could ask him and he would explain. And there would be no slippage between policymaking and policy enforcement, because the king would do his own enforcing. There would be no check against arbitrary exercise of power, but there would be no need for such a check. Since our hypothetical king was an enlightened despot, he would refrain from any misuse of his power.

The problem with that theoretical model is that such an enlightened despot, if he has ever existed, has been an extraordinarily rare historic phenomenon. Recently I asked one of my historian friends to give me some examples of monarchs under whose reign the people prospered because of efficiencies resulting from all powers being vested in a single individual. His response: Napoleon, Frederick the Great, Louis XIV, Peter the Great, and Catherine the Great. I then asked him to give me some examples of monarchs who subjected their people to great suffering because they enjoyed absolute, unchecked power. He thought for a moment, smiled, and then responded: Napoleon, Frederick the Great, Louis XIV, Peter the Great, and Catherine the Great. In each case, the contrasting circumstances existed at different periods of the individual monarch's reign. In no instance was the monarch capable of using his or her uncontested power only for good, resisting the temptations for misuse.[1]

The important point is that inefficiency is a necessary cost for the avoidance of tyrannical rule. Viewed in those terms, the product is worth the price. In selecting separation of powers and checks and balances as our constitutional cornerstones, the Founding Fathers opted close to one extreme end of the spectrum between efficiency and structural barriers to governmental arbitrariness.

How is it, then, that separateness provides a check against arbitrary exercise of government power? As discussed in Chapter 4, the separation is not always marked by fine bright lines. Thus, it would not be accurate to conceptualize the three branches' circles of authority as completely isolated from each other, as illustrated by the diagram below.

Rather, the more accurate illustration is provided by the following.

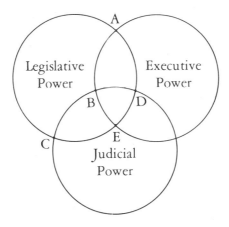

Within that part of the legislative circle that lies above and to the left of points A, B, and C, Congress's power is exclusive. It is that part of the congressional power circle within which there is no overlap with the other branches. Within that area is contained, for example, Congress's final authority over statutory policymaking, illustrated by the Sherman Act example discussed in Chapter 4.

The area bounded by points A, B, and D represents overlap between Congress's lawmaking powers and the executive's powers of law enforcement. The impoundment cases are illustrative. The impoundment issue arose when Congress passed a statute that so much money would be spent for certain purposes. President Nixon then refused to spend it. Was the President's refusal a proper exercise (or nonexercise) of his law-enforcement powers, or was he in effect usurping Congress's authority to make law? This issue fits within the overlap area bounded by points A, B, and D.

Assume that Congress passes a law limiting federal funds available for abortions. Persons adversely affected by the law challenge it in court on constitutional grounds. In considering the constitutional issues, are the courts properly exercising their authority to interpret the Constitution, or are they simply remaking congressional policy? This is an issue which fits within the overlap area bounded by points B, C, and E.

The most sensitive area of interbranch power overlap lies in the center of the three circles, the confluence of powers (in the triangle marked by points B, D, and E). Disputes in this area are rare, but when they arise they are usually of "nerve center constitutional significance."[2] They involve judicial efforts to resolve issues concerning the competing claims to power of the other two branches. The most frequent interbranch power disputes are between Congress and the President. Almost all of these disputes are eventually resolved by negotiation, thereby confining them to the area bounded by points A, B, and D in the diagram. Occasionally, however, the issue finds its way into court, thus bringing into play not only the competing claims of Congress and the President but also the mainstay power of the courts: judicial review.

Probably the most famous case involving the overlapping powers of all three branches was *Youngstown Sheet & Tube Co. v. Sawyer*, the steel seizure case.[3] During the Korean War, President Truman, without authorization by Congress, seized the nation's steel mills in order to prevent an impending strike from adversely affecting the war effort. The Supreme Court held the seizure unconstitutional. According to the Court, the President's action represented a policy decision. It was not a policy decision concerning the enforcement of the laws, which is the rightful responsibility of the President; rather, the President had made a substantive decision as to what policy alternative was in the best interest of the country. The Court ruled that such decisions properly fall within Congress's sphere of responsibility, and not within the President's. Since the President had acted without congressional authorization in an area that properly belonged to Congress, his action was unconstitutional.

In the steel seizure case, the President intruded into an area of governmental authority that properly belonged to Congress. The effect of that intrusion is demonstrated by the diagram below. This diagram, a modification of that previous, is useful in illustrating the separation-of-powers dynamic. It also illustrates why the powers of the three branches can operate—and I believe that over the long run they usually do operate—as an automatic, mutual check.

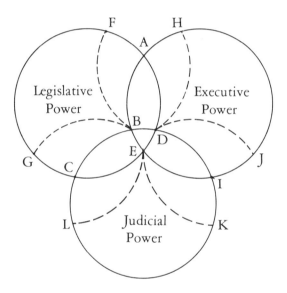

The area bounded by points A, B, and F represents the intrusion in the steel seizure controversy by the President into the policymaking domain of Congress. The intrusion had two effects: it expanded the power of the President, but it also diminished the power of Congress by shifting a legislative responsibility from Congress to the President.

The impoundment controversy is another example of an attempt by one branch of government to expand its powers at the expense of another. The President's decision not to spend money for programs that had been approved by Congress was an attempt to expand the area of overlap between congressional and presidential powers from A, B, and D to A, B, D, and F. The increment in asserted presidential power is represented, as in the steel seizure case, by A, B, and F. In both cases, what had formerly been considered an unshared power of Congress was diminished.

Another example is provided by judicial policymaking, under the aegis of deciding litigated cases. To whatever extent the courts make policy in areas that properly belong to Congress, they do so at the expense of congressional legislative power. The resulting enlargement of judicial power and diminution of congressional power is represented by the area B, C, and G.

Congress is also capable of intrusions into the domain of other branches. The Supreme Court held in *Buckley v. Valeo*, for example, that the bringing of lawsuits to vindicate public policy is exclusively a function of the executive branch.[4] Accordingly, it held unconstitutional a congressional statute giving the Federal Elections Commission (which was composed in part of congressional appointees) the authority to bring lawsuits for the purpose of enforcing a federal statute. This represented an attempted expansion of congressional power at the expense of the executive, represented by the area A, D, and H.

In my view, the most frequent attempts by one branch to expand its own jurisdictional turf at the expense of another branch are invasions of the legislative power by the executive branch (A, B, and F), of the legislative power by the judicial branch (B, C, and G), and of executive power by Congress (A, D, and H). There are, of course, three other possibilities: invasion of executive power by the courts (i.e., by judicial interpretation of an administrative regulation) (D, I, and J); invasion of judicial power by the executive (i.e., refusal to enforce a judicial decree) (E, I, and K); and congressional invasion of judicial power (i.e., passing legislation that does not make general policy but rather attempts to resolve disputes between particular individuals) (C, E, and L).[5]

In some cases, the branch whose powers are invaded takes no immediate steps to resist. This was true in the steel seizure case. Also, some historians have argued rather persuasively that over the years presidents have expanded their power to involve our nation in war, with a corresponding diminution in the powers of Congress and expansion within the A-B-F area.[6]

My own view is that, while there are some instances in which one branch has not immediately and vigorously resisted intrusions into its governmental powers, over the long run the invasion has not been taken lightly. Few instincts are more firmly embedded in the psyche of the governmental officer than the preservation of his own governmental territory. As shown by the diagram, attempts by one branch to expand its powers necessarily result in the diminution of the powers of one or the other branches. Sooner or later, the likelihood of resistance is high. In the impoundment cases, the resistance was almost immediate. With respect to the war powers, while Congress's reaction time was slow, Congress did react. Congress ultimately passed, over the

President's veto, the War Powers Resolution of 1973, which goes so far in asserting congressional authority as to raise serious questions concerning its constitutionality. And even with respect to the steel seizure case, though Congress did not react, the steel companies did.

Most, if not all, attempts to expand presidential power at the expense of another branch can be expected to meet vigorous resistance – usually by the branch whose powers are invaded, or, as in the steel seizure case, by private parties. This has the effect of bringing the merits of the competing branch's claims before some forum – Congress, the courts, or the public. It also assures that there will be an eventual consideration and determination of those merits, so that any attempt at usurpation will not be accomplished by default.

The separation-of-powers dynamic works, therefore, for the same reason that the free enterprise system works: it depends on the self-interest of persons affected. Any distortions will adversely affect important interests of powerful people, who will take reactive measures. I believe that historically it has prevented, and over the long run will always prevent, any gross shifts in the allocation of powers among the three branches.

Morality

Public opinion is probably the most important single variable in the operation of the separation-of-powers dynamic. The people are the ultimate source of all governmental power. The people hold the only power greater than that of the government officials directly involved in the struggle over the boundary lines that mark their respective spheres. Given the uncertainty of where those boundary lines are and the lack of precedent to support either position, the inevitable tendency of those involved in the struggle is to look to the views held by the public at large.

This means that in a very real sense the ultimate power is vested not in any of the three branches, but in the people of the United States. This power is exercised not only at the voting booth every even-numbered year, but on a continuing basis. President Franklin Roosevelt's court-packing plan, for example, involved an attempt to expand the power of the President at the expense of the courts. The plan was to give President Roosevelt the authority to appoint an additional justice to the Supreme Court for every member on the Court over seventy years old who did not retire. The main reason it failed is that the American people in general disagreed with it, and Congress, which had the power to block Roosevelt's move, sensed this. Madison was right; under the U.S. Constitution, the people are the ultimate source of governmental power.

I believe that the separation-of-powers dynamic has another effect that is not discussed by political science or law textbooks. It is that separation of powers is an effective enforcer of morality. Such a moral force is brought about by (1) the continuing, dynamic struggle among the three branches for power, where increases in the power of one branch are frequently accomplished at the expense of another, and (2) the fact that one of the most important factors ultimately determining shifts of power among the branches is the will of the people, or at least government officials' perceptions concerning the will of the people.

Moral standards among government officials vary from the highest to the lowest. By contrast, an intense concern over jurisdictional turf protection is a virtually universal characteristic among government officials. There is a close relationship between these two facts. Even those who have no morals recognize that the extent of their governmental authority depends in no small degree on the acceptability of their conduct in the eyes of the public. Whatever their inherent moral tendencies, therefore, there exists a natural and compelling inducement toward morality because of the relationship between the public perception of the governmental servant and the amount of power that he enjoys. Moreover, the general public—or at least a substantial segment of it—demands morality in its governmental representatives. Although they may wink at some peccadilloes, they for the most part draw moral lines across which the wise politician does not step. This is true of governmental institutions as well as individuals in government. Lack of public confidence in the morals of a public person will diminish not only the power of that individual but also that of the branch of government in which he serves. Because adding to or subtracting from the power of one branch usually has an opposite effect on the power of another, the impact is visited not only on the individual and his branch of government but on the other branches as well. A series of recent examples will illustrate.

Richard Nixon's overwhelming victory in 1972 gave him four more years as President. Because of the Twenty-second Amendment (prohibiting more than two terms for President and Vice-President), during that second four-year term he did not have to worry about running for reelection. The purpose of the Twenty-second Amendment was to curtail the power of any particular chief executive. My suspicion, however, is that in most instances it will actually have the ironic effect of increasing presidential power. The reason is simply that a second-term President and everyone else in the country will know that for four years the nation will have a chief executive who does not have to cultivate a constituency. There can be both good and bad consequences in this, depending largely on the willingness of the President to follow the admonitions of constituents and the dictates of his conscience. The important point for the present discussion, however, is not whether the power of a president during his second term is used in the public interest or against the public interest. However he uses it, a second-term President will ordinarily enjoy a greater measure of power than a first-term President.

So what does all of this have to do with the relationship between separation of powers and morality in government? Recall the beginnings of Richard Nixon's second term. He showed every sign of becoming one of the strongest Presidents in history and of arrogating to his office powers that it had never before enjoyed. Then came the Watergate disclosures. Day after day the American people watched and read and listened. Each new press release seemed to bring additional revelations of official disregard for basic principles of honesty and morality. For each new disclosure there was a corresponding decrease in confidence in the President. Inevitably, this diminution in public support for the President translated into diminished presidential power. Within a year and a half after the auspicious beginnings of his second presidential term early in 1973, Richard Nixon was forced to resign. He had plummeted from a position of strength matched by only a handful of men in our history to the greatest disgrace that has ever been suffered by an American President.

Regardless of how public officials feel concerning the importance of their own morality, the public whom they serve has certain expectations. When those expectations are violated, as they were during the Watergate era, public confidence is withdrawn, and with it the power of the officeholder.

Richard Nixon was not the only victim of the Watergate tragedy. There was also an effect on the Presidency itself. I witnessed this phenomenon as a member of the Ford administration, which succeeded the Nixon Presidency. One of the major struggles during President Ford's administration revolved around controls that many, inside and outside government, felt should be imposed on American intelligence activities, and the extent to which those controls should be vested in either the executive or the legislative branch. Each time that executive-branch officials in the Ford administration attempted to withhold highly sensitive secret information from congressional committees, on the grounds that those committees had not taken adequate security measures to protect it, they were met with the metaphors of Watergate: "stonewalling," "cover-up," "imperialism in the White House." These retorts were effective. Watergate had left its legacy, and part of that legacy was a diminution in the ability of the executive branch to withstand intrusions by Congress into an area that should have belonged to the executive: protection of official governmental secrets.

I am confident that, over time, the separation-of-powers dynamic will establish a long-range equilibrium and the executive branch will regain its former stature after Watergate fades from memory. This process has been greatly accelerated by a series of revelations during the summer and fall of 1976 concerning the sexual improprieties of several key congressmen. The most notorious was the Wayne Hays–Elizabeth Ray affair, but it was only one of several. Individual immorality not only diminished the power of the individual—recall the speedy end to the congressional career of Wayne Hays—but also had an effect on Congress as an institution. No longer were congressional investigators so anxious to accuse executive branch representatives of "covering up," "stonewalling," or other forms of immorality.

It is true that some individuals have been able personally to weather the storm of public reaction to immorality, at least in the sense that they managed to stay in office. Adam Clayton Powell was reelected to Congress after numerous revelations of dishonesty and other impropriety, including the diversion of public funds for his own use.[7] Congressman Diggs of Michigan was reelected to Congress after he had been convicted of a felony,[8] and Congressman Daniel Flood of Pennsylvania after he had been indicted.[9] It should not be assumed, however, that even in those cases public knowledge of immorality had no effect on the wrongdoers' power. Congressman Hays held a seat that was considered "safe" prior to disclosure of his wrongdoing, but the margin of safety proved insufficient. Even more important, though Powell, Diggs, and Flood stayed in office, the effect on their power was direct and immediate. The House of Representatives for the 90th Congress excluded Adam Clayton Powell from taking his seat. The United States Supreme Court eventually determined that in taking this action the House used a procedure that was constitutionally impermissible, but Congressman Powell never again assumed a position of authority comparable to what he had once enjoyed.[10] Congressman Diggs, though reelected, lost the chairmanship of the House District of Columbia Committee and the House Subcommittee on African Affairs.[11] Similarly, Congressman Flood, though reelected, was forced to give up his chairmanship of the House Subcommittee on Labor and Health, Education, and Welfare Appropriations.[12]

These examples demonstrate that official immorality adversely affects official power. I am convinced that they also demonstrate that the debilitating effect is visited not only on the individual, but also on the branch of government in which he or she serves. Since increases or decreases in the power of one branch result in an opposite impact on the power of another, official immorality also affects the distribution of powers among the three branches of government.

Is There a Fourth Branch?

The Constitution provides for three branches of government. The most frequent and the most important contacts that many people have with the federal government, however, do not involve Congress, the President, or the courts. Rather, their dealings are with one or more of the vast complex of departments, agencies, and bureaus that carry on so much of the federal government's actual business. We refer to them collectively as the "bureaucracy."

The Constitution contains some language indicating that its draftsmen envisioned governmental entities in addition to the three branches created by the first three articles. Article II Section 2, for example, states that: "[The President] shall appoint Ambassadors, other public ministers and Consuls, Judges of the Supreme Court, and all other Officers of the United States, whose Appointments are not herein otherwise provided for, and which shall be established by Law." Beyond any doubt, however, the Founding Fathers did not envision a federal bureaucracy so extensive or so powerful as our federal government has developed. What is this "bureaucracy"? How, if at all, can its existence be reconciled with the provisions of the Constitution—or with sound government?

The words "bureaucracy" and "bureaucrat" are used in at least two separate senses. In the broader sense, the federal "bureaucracy" means the entire federal government, and "bureaucrat" refers to any federal employee, including members of Congress and judges. The narrower, more accurate meaning restricts the term to two basic governmental prototypes. The first includes the departments of the executive branch, such as the departments of Agriculture, Labor, Justice, Commerce, and so forth, which are presided over by a member of the President's cabinet and are, at least in principle, directly responsible to the President. The heads of these departments and their immediate subordinates are appointed by the President and are subject to dismissal by him at his discretion.[13] The second prototype includes the independent regulatory agencies, the Federal Trade Commission, the Securities and Exchange Commission, the Federal Power Commission, the Civil Aeronautics Board, and the like. These entities are not attached to an executive-branch department. Their chief officers are appointed by the President, but they are neither part of his cabinet, nor subject to his absolute powers of dismissal.[14]

These differences in governmental status between executive department and independent regulatory agencies are largely technical. For the average citizen, the more important characteristics are those they share in common. Though their chief officers are all appointed by the President and to varying degrees are considered part of the executive-branch

team, most of them in fact exercise the powers of all three branches—
lawmaking, law enforcement, and law interpretation. They are among
the people who carry on those aspects of the business of government
that affect the average citizen most importantly. For example, they collect our taxes, decide how safe our children's toys should be, prescribe
work or safety conditions that the employer must meet, decide how
much postage stamps should cost, maintain our army and navy, and spy
on our enemies.

Since the bureaucrats are not elected officials, they lack the in-
centives for responsiveness and even responsibility that the citizens can
command from their congressmen—or their President. It is true that
the people at the top are a part of the President's team—at least in the
case of the departments and, to a lesser extent, the independent regulatory agencies. But many people feel that the leadership within a department, agency, bureau, or commission has comparatively little effect
on the attitudes and practices of that vast army of career officials who
really administer the government programs, and that periodic changes
at the secretary and assistant secretary level are just like "changing the
fleas on a dog."

These considerations form the basis for the concern that the federal
bureaucracy really constitutes a fourth branch—one whose powers and
responsibilities are neither recognized nor spelled out by the Constitution, yet one that is more powerful than the other three, exercising
all three powers: legislative, executive, and judicial. The concern is a
legitimate one. It is no wonder that most Presidents within recent
memory, as well as many members of Congress, have vowed to do
something to "cut down the powers of the bureaucracy."

Are the administrative agencies and departments of the federal government a headless fourth branch of government, equal or even superi-
or in power to the other three? In at least one important sense, they are
not. Because the Constitution makes no provision for them, they enjoy
no constitutionally irreducible powers. This means that all of their authority is subject to change or even total elimination by the two elected
branches, Congress and the President. As a practical matter, changes in
the bureaucracy of any notable magnitude are difficult to accomplish,
but the power to make those changes exists in the President and Congress; and to the extent that needed changes have not been made, the
fault does not lie exclusively with the bureaucrats. It lies with those
elected officials who have the power to make the changes but have not
done so. I believe that the reason they have not done so is that, although there is general agreement that administrative agencies and departments do not always perform as we would like them to perform
and that some ought to be eliminated altogether, there is no consensus
as to which agencies ought to be eliminated. Thus, substantial

segments of our society believe that our nation would be better off if the Social Security Administration and the Occupational Safety and Health Administration (OSHA) were eliminated, but that the Federal Bureau of Investigation and the Central Intelligence Agency are absolutely essential to our national welfare. Other substantial segments of our society want OSHA and the Social Security Administration but disdain the FBI and the CIA.

In any event, it is inevitable that administrative agencies, departments, bureaus, and commissions will continue to be part of the American governmental way of life. We may not like the income tax and we may not like the Internal Revenue Service. But some form of taxation scheme is inevitable, as is the reality that the President of the United States—the only elected official of the branch that is charged with executing the laws—cannot be expected personally to perform all the tasks of the tax collector.

The more practical goal, therefore, is not to eliminate the bureaucracy, but to make it more responsive and perhaps to make its judgments subject to closer judicial scrutiny than the judgments of Congress and the President, who must periodically subject themselves to the approval or disapproval of the voters. Changes of this sort—or complete elimination of some pockets of the bureaucracy—can be accomplished by Congress, the President, or both. The likelihood of such reform depends principally on the perception of these elected officials as to breadth and depth of public opinion.

CHAPTER SIX
Federalism

The value of separation of powers is that it divides governmental power among units that compete for it. The result is salutary for several reasons: no entity enjoys all power, and any attempt to expand power is met by resistance from another branch at whose expense the expansion would be accomplished.

The splintering of the powers of government through separation of powers is accomplished along a horizontal plane among the three branches of the federal government. The Constitution also divides governmental powers along a vertical plane, between the federal government and the state governments. The problems raised by this vertical division are treated under the general label of federalism. Separation of powers and federalism have many of the same purposes and effects: both attempt to decentralize and diffuse governmental powers, and both create some inefficiencies. Perhaps the most important similarity between separation of powers and federalism is that, over the long run, public opinion is the most effective single force in controlling the allocation of power between federal and state governments.

There are also differences between separation of powers and federalism. The courts have played a more active role in deciding federalism issues than separation-of-power issues. Because both involve constitutional questions, the courts are the final authority. Nevertheless, while the Supreme Court has decided literally thousands of federalism cases, its separation-of-powers decisions have been comparatively few.

Issues of constitutional federalism fall into two broad categories: (1) constitutional authorization of powers in the national government (mainly Congress) and the necessary impact of this authorization on the powers of state governments, and (2) constitutional prohibitions on the exercise of powers by the states. The net effect of both the constitutional authorizations covered by the first category and the prohibitions covered by the second is the same—diminution of state power. Each category is separately discussed below.

The Expansion of Federal Authority
at the Expense of State Authority

The key to understanding this first category is the difference in the nature and the scope of federal and state powers. The reach of subjects over which the states may exercise their governing power is in theory much broader than the reach of the federal power. State power extends to all subjects with which it is proper for a government as government to deal. State powers are sometimes referred to as "police powers" and they extend to matters of health, safety, morals, and welfare. There are few, if any, subjects that cannot be fitted within such authority.

The federal government does not have police-power authority. Rather, it is a government of limited powers, all of which are specifically enumerated in the Constitution.

Some examples highlight the difference between state and federal governmental powers. Providing a school system (or a system of marriage and divorce laws) properly falls within the police-power definition: health, safety, morals, and welfare. Power over these areas is not specifically granted to the federal government by the Constitution. As a consequence, they fall within the realm of state, but not federal, power.

The other notable point is that within its more limited scope, federal power is supreme and supersedes state power to the extent that the two conflict. This relationship may be depicted by two concentric circles, one located inside the other, as in the diagram below.

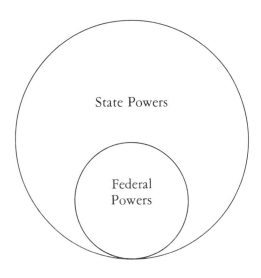

The smaller circle represents the powers of the federal government, the larger circle those of the state governments. Though the state circle is larger, federal power is supreme and preempts state power within the area covered by the smaller circle. Thus, if the circle of federal power is expanded, as shown by the broken line in the following diagram, the necessary consequence is that the nonpreempted portion of the state's power circle—and therefore the effective area in which states may govern—is correspondingly diminished.

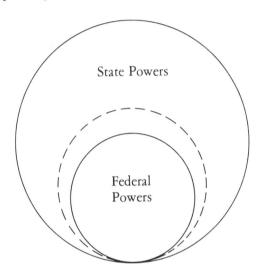

This is in fact what has happened on a rather continuous basis through our nation's history. The main vehicle for expansion has been the provision in Article I Section 8 of the Constitution, often referred to as the commerce clause: "The Congress shall have Power ... to regulate Commerce with foreign Nations, and among the several States." The governing principle concerning the regulation of commerce is that Congress has authority to regulate not only interstate commerce itself, but also those activities that "affect" commerce. The case of *National Labor Relations Board v. Jones & Laughlin Steel Corp.* illustrates the broad application of the interstate commerce clause.[1] States have the power to regulate labor relations under their police-power authority and there is nothing in the Constitution specifically authorizing Congress to regulate labor relations. Congress is authorized, however, to regulate interstate commerce and because of this has moved into the regulation of labor relations. Does Congress's commerce clause power give it any authority to do this?

The *Jones & Laughlin* case tested the constitutionality of the National Labor Relations Act of 1935. The purpose of that act was to prohibit unfair labor practices, to provide for collective bargaining, and generally to control relationships between employers and employees. The Jones & Laughlin Steel Corporation was accused of engaging in "unfair labor practices" by firing some of their employees who had engaged in union activity. These unfair labor practices were in violation of the National Labor Relations Act. The issue in the case was whether Congress had the constitutional authority under the commerce clause to empower the National Labor Relations Board "to prevent any person from engaging in any unfair labor practice . . . affecting commerce."

Obviously, the relationships between the employer and the employees were highly localized. The employees' union activities, and the employer's firing of those employees because of their union activities, occurred only at the particular plant in Pennsylvania where those employees worked. Neither the union activities or the discharges involved transactions across state lines. The Supreme Court held, however, that the governing test to determine the extent of Congress's authority was not whether these activities were themselves interstate transactions, but rather whether they "affected" interstate transactions. One of the purposes of the National Labor Relations Act was to diminish industrial strife, including strikes, boycotts, and the like. Though a strike at the Jones & Laughlin plant would be a highly localized event, occupying at most a few square miles located exclusively within the state of Pennsylvania, the Court reasoned that such a strike would have profound effects on interstate commerce. If the Jones & Laughlin plant were shut down, the importation of iron ore from Michigan and Minnesota, limestone from West Virginia, and coal from other parts of Pennsylvania would come to a halt. So would the shipment of iron and steel from the plant to many other parts of the country.

The *Jones & Laughlin* decision did not give Congress blanket authority to regulate labor disputes. Labor disputes that are strictly local and have no effect on interstate commerce still lie outside the congressional reach. But the great majority of labor issues were moved by the *Jones & Laughlin* case from the exclusive jurisdiction of the states to the exclusive jurisdiction of Congress. As a consequence, national power was enlarged and state power diminished, as depicted by the diagram. The areas of enlargement of federal power and diminution of state power are identical. Both are represented by the area between the small solid-line circle and the broken-line circle.

The case generally considered the most extreme example of the Supreme Court's upholding Congress's commerce-clause power (on the ground that interstate commerce is "affected" even though not directly involved) is *Wickard v. Filburn*.[2] Mr. Filburn raised wheat on his farm in Ohio. Some of the wheat he sold to buyers in Ohio and other states. Some, however, he fed to his own livestock on his own farm. The issue in the case was whether the acreage allotments set by Congress's Agricultural Adjustment Act could be applied to the wheat consumed by Mr. Filburn's livestock. The Supreme Court held that Congress had authority to impose the acreage allotments under its commerce-clause powers.

The usual first reaction to *Wickard v. Filburn* lies somewhere between astonishment and disbelief. The wheat not only had not crossed a state line, but it had never even left Filburn's farm. Does the holding mean that Congress, pursuant to its commerce clause authority, could regulate tomatoes grown in a family's backyard and consumed solely by the family? Probably not. The rationale of *Wickard v. Filburn* was that, while Filburn's wheat consumed by his livestock had not actually moved in interstate commerce, home consumption by American farmers was one of the most important elements entering into the price of wheat shipped in interstate commerce. This fact—the effect of home consumption on interstate pricing—was substantiated by the record in *Wickard v. Filburn* and would appear to be crucial to the Court's holding. That fact would distinguish the backyard tomato hypothetical. It certainly demonstrates the lengths to which the commerce power may extend under the "affecting commerce" rationale announced in the *Jones & Laughlin* case.

The commerce clause has been by far the most fruitful source of enlarged congressional authority. Two others, however, warrant brief mention. These are the taxing power and the spending power. Article I Section 8 of the Constitution provides that "the Congress shall have power to lay and collect taxes, duties, imposts and excises, to pay the debts and provide for the common defence and general welfare of the United States." The Supreme Court has held that this provision does not give general welfare power to the United States. The reference to welfare is limited by the earlier phrase "to pay the debts." Thus, Congress has a welfare-type power only when it is linked to a spending program.

These principles are illustrated by two 1937 cases, *Steward Machine Co. v. Davis* and *Helvering v. Davis*, in which the Supreme Court sustained the constitutionality of both the unemployment compensation and the old age benefits provision of the Social Security Act.[3] Welfare matters are generally viewed as being outside the circle of federal governmental power. But in the case of the Social Security Act, the old age benefits and the unemployment compensation schemes were nevertheless upheld because they involved expenditures of federal funds. The holding in these Social Security Act cases has great potential reach because a vast array of welfare and other police-power programs involve some kind of federal spending for general welfare purposes.

Congress's power to tax is usually exercised in tandem with its power to spend, as in the Social Security cases. It can be exercised independently, however. *United States v. Kahriger* upheld the constitutionality of a congressional statute that imposed a tax on persons engaged in certain kinds of gambling activity.[4] The legislative history of that statute made it quite clear that the purpose of the statute was not to raise revenue but, rather, to penalize interstate gambling. Nevertheless, because the tax produced revenue the statute was upheld as a proper exercise of Congress's power.

Whenever, as in the cases just discussed, the scope of federal power expands, whether under the commerce clause, the taxing clause, or the spending clause, there is a corresponding diminution in the extent to which the police powers of the states exceed enumerated federal powers. As illustrated by the diagram above, the size of the states' power circle remains the same; but since the preempting federal circle is enlarged, the unpreempted area necessarily decreases. As with the separation-of-powers principle, therefore, the expansion of the power of one governmental entity is accomplished at the expense of another.

Constitutional commerce-clause issues may also be presented by state and local governmental taxation schemes. The general concept is that not only regulation but also taxation by the states may impede the free flow of goods and services across state lines. This is true of many kinds of state taxes, including sales taxes, income taxes, privilege or transaction taxes, and even property taxes (especially imposed on the rolling stock, airplanes, railroad cars, and so on, used for interstate transportation). The Supreme Court cases dealing with this problem run into the hundreds—maybe thousands—and their holdings are not always consistent.

Direct Reduction of State Powers by Constitutional Prohibitions

The most important constitutional prohibitions on the exercise of state powers are the guarantees of individual liberties contained in the First and Fourteenth amendments. Those limitations are also applicable to the federal government. Thus, neither the states nor the federal government may pass laws that, for example, unduly infringe on speech or religion or that violate certain standards of fairness or equality.

The Constitution also affirmatively limits the powers of state governments through the commerce clause. It is a limitation that does not depend upon the exercise of congressional powers. Many state police-power regulations have some inhibiting effect on the movement of goods and services in interstate commerce. If the resulting burden on interstate commerce becomes sufficiently severe, the state regulation may be unconstitutional—as a violation of the commerce clause—for that reason alone.

One of the difficult questions is to decide by what standard the existence of an unconstitutional burden on interstate commerce is determined. This is an issue with which the courts have struggled for almost two centuries. There are hundreds of Supreme Court decisions on this subject, reaching back to the landmark case of *Gibbons v. Ogden*, which held unconstitutional the attempt by the New York legislature to grant to Robert Livingston and Robert Fulton the exclusive right to operate steamboats in New York waters.[5]

The current standard is illustrated by the leading case, *Southern Pacific Co. v. Arizona*, which held unconstitutional Arizona's "long train" law.[6] Arizona statutes prohibited the operation within its borders of any passenger train in excess of fourteen cars or any freight train in excess of seventy cars. None of the states surrounding Arizona had such a law. As a result, the two interstate railroads operating within the state were forced to alter the length of their trains just to accommodate Arizona. The stated objective of the long train law was safety: short trains were purportedly safer than long trains. An Arizona state trial court determined, however, that there was serious question whether shorter trains in fact yielded any net safety benefit. There was some evidence that longer trains actually decreased safety risks because they reduced the number of trains and therefore the number of potential accidents.

The Supreme Court held this Arizona law unconstitutional. The relevant standard for determining constitutionality in burden-on-commerce cases, the Court held, is a balancing test. On one side of the balance scale is the state's interest in its police-power objective and the extent to which that interest is achieved by the state law under consideration. Balanced against the state's police-power objective is the extent of the burden on interstate commerce. In many instances this balancing test will be difficult for a court to apply. In the *Southern Pacific* case, however, it was fairly easy, and the *Southern Pacific* facts provide a good illustration of the balancing approach. The burden on interstate commerce was undeniably severe. Compliance cost the state's two interstate railroads about one million dollars a year (and those were 1940s dollars). Moreover, the effect of the law was to control railroad traffic all the way from Los Angeles to El Paso. On the other side of the balance scale, the safety benefits were negligible if they existed at all. Under those circumstances, the *Southern Pacific* balancing test clearly indicated a decision in favor of the railroads.

The *Southern Pacific* case presents a legitimate federalism issue. It involves the extent of state power, and the confining feature is the federal Constitution. The *Southern Pacific* issues differ from the issues discussed earlier in this chapter in that in *Southern Pacific*, unlike *Jones & Laughlin*, a decrease in state power is not accomplished by a corresponding increase in federal power.

The diagram below demonstrates the first problem prototype, as exemplified by the *Jones & Laughlin* case.

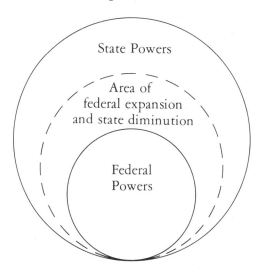

The broken line represents the expansion of federal authority that occurred as a result of the *Jones & Laughlin* decision. The area of both state and federal authority was necessarily changed; the size of the state's circle remained the same, but the unpreempted portion of that circle diminished in the same amount as the federal circle increased. The next diagram demonstrates the second problem prototype, as seen in the *Southern Pacific* case.

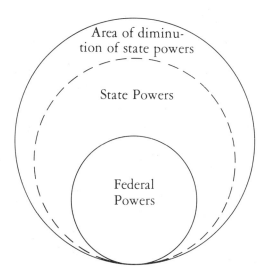

Once again, there is a diminution in the size of the state's power circle. The area of diminution is represented by the space between the large solid-line circle and the broken-line circle. This time, however, there is no corresponding increase in federal power. The federal power circle remains unchanged.

Inter-Sovereign Respect and Relations

Another significant federalism issue concerns the power of either the state or federal governments to regulate or tax the activities of the other. The leading case is *McCulloch v. Maryland* which, as noted above, is also the leading case establishing Congress's implied powers. A second issue in *McCulloch* was whether the state of Maryland had the authority to impose a tax on the obligations of a bank owned by the United States. Building on the famous dictum that "the power to tax is the power to destroy," the Supreme Court in *McCulloch* held that states do not have the power to tax instrumentalities of the United States.

Cases subsequent to *McCulloch* have further developed the law concerning the respective powers of state and federal governments to tax or regulate each other. The power of the state governments over the federal government can be simply stated: it is unconstitutional for states to attempt to tax or regulate any branch, department, or instrumentality of the federal government. This prohibition rests on two separate propositions: the first is federal supremacy, and the second is the inconsistency of regulation by one government in a federal union of the activities of another.

Turning to the issue of the federal government's power to tax or regulate state activities, considerations of supremacy pose no impediment, leaving only issues of intersovereign respect in a federal system. The federal government may not tax "governmental" state functions—that is, functions that relate to the operation of a state in its sovereign, governmental capacity. The federal government may impose taxes, however, on "proprietary" activities, those activities in which the state is in effect carrying on some kind of commercial business. In *United States v. New York*, for example, the Supreme Court upheld a federal tax on New York's business of bottling and selling mineral water.[7]

More important than federal taxation of state operations is the extent to which the federal government may regulate state activities, pursuant to its commerce-clause powers. Prior to 1976 the cases established a rather broad area of potential commerce-clause regulation of state activities by the federal government. In *United States v. California*, for example, the Supreme Court upheld the applicability of the federal Safety Appliance Act to a railroad operated by the state of California.[8] And in *Parden v. Terminal Railway*, the Court held that a workman injured while working on a railroad belonging to the state of Alabama could bring a damage suit against the state under the Federal Employer's Liability Act, which authorizes injured employees of interstate railroads to sue their employers for physical injury.[9] The doctrine of sovereign immunity—which, under the Eleventh Amendment to the Constitution, normally prohibits damage actions against sovereign states without their consent—was held to have been effectively waived by Alabama's voluntary entry into the railroad business, knowing that that business was extensively regulated by Congress.

A major doctrinal limitation on Congress's power to regulate state government activities would appear to have occurred in the Supreme Court's 1976 decision in *National League of Cities and Towns v. Usery*, which held unconstitutional Congress's extension of the Fair Labor Standards Act, which set minimum wages for employees of state and local governments.[10] The Court reasoned that attempts by Congress to dictate the wages that must be paid by state and local governments represented an interference by one sovereign with the affairs of other sovereigns that could not be countenanced by basic principles of constitutional federalism. For example, the state might conclude that its interests in combatting unemployment warranted hiring larger numbers of otherwise unemployable people at lower salaries. It is the kind of decision that lies at the core of the choices that a state makes in exercising its sovereign powers. Yet it was foreclosed by Congress's statute mandating minimum wages to be paid by state government. It was, therefore, a constitutionally impermissible intrusion by the national government into the sovereign prerogatives of the states.

The holding and rationale in *National League of Cities and Towns v. Usery* may reach beyond the setting of minimum wages. It casts a long shadow, for example, on the railroad cases discussed above. At the very least it has greatly strengthened the principle of state sovereignty and the deference that one sovereign within a federal system owes to another.

Over the history of our nation—reaching back before 1776 and continuing to the present—there has been no more persistent (nor more important) group of problems than those that pertain to federalism. The original settlement of America was by colonies. From that time forward the search for a proper balance between state and national powers has endured. The principal motivation for the 1787 Constitutional Convention was a perception shared by many that the Articles of Confederation had given too much power to the states and too little to the national government. The Great Compromise that made the Constitution possible was a compromise over concerns of federal-state power. During the period prior to the Civil War, the Supreme Court introduced the concept of "dual federalism," which held that states are supreme within certain spheres of governmental activity, so that even the commerce clause could not be used as a justification for national intervention into state affairs. Clearly the most important federalism development after 1787 was the adoption of the Fourteenth Amendment, which had the effect of swinging the pendulum toward the national government and away from the states (see the discussion in chapters 14 through 16). Over the century since the adoption of the Fourteenth Amendment it is probably safe to say that there has been a substantial and rather steady shift of power from state and local governments to the national government.[11]

Federalism in all its ramifications is of course a constitutional issue. There is none more important. It is important not only because it allocates power among governments but also because the very process of allocation prevents excessive concentration in any government. Federalism thereby provides a protection for individual rights. Much more important than who is right and who is wrong on any given federalism issue, therefore, is that the centuries-old struggle must continue and that neither side should be allowed to completely prevail. In the pull and haul over state powers versus federal powers, each must remain strong enough to continue as a viable competitor. The history of our nation over the last century teaches, I believe, that if there is a danger in this respect, the risk is on the side of federal infringement of state powers.

PART TWO
Constitutional Protections of Individual Rights

Introduction to Part Two

The introductory comments to the study of constitutional law appearing at the beginning of this book suggest that the entire field could be considered under two large headings: the powers of government, and the protection of individual interests against the exercise of those powers. Part I treats the first of these subjects; Part II is devoted to the second.

An alternate view of constitutional law is that it consists not of two subjects, but of only one: the protection of individual interests. In support of this view, it might be contended that the only reason to give government any power at all is to secure individual interests and that the principal purpose, if not the sole purpose, of federalism and separation of powers is to prevent any component of government from having sufficient power to abuse individual interests.

Whatever the comparative merit of these two views, three matters are clear. The first is that, regardless of whether the Constitution has other purposes, its most important purpose is the securing of individual interests. The second is that there is a close relationship between our constitutional structure allocating the powers of government and the protection of individual interests. The third is that some sections of the Constitution (such as those discussed in Part I of this study) secure the interests of the individual in different ways than others (such as those discussed in Part II). The constitutional provisions treated in Part I secure individual interests against the powers of government indirectly by diffusing the powers of government. The constitutional provisions we examine in Part II deal with the issue directly rather than indirectly, by positive prohibition against governmental conduct. The provisions discussed in Part I deal principally with what government can do; the provisions discussed in Part II prescribe what government cannot do.

For purposes of the discussion in Part II it is helpful to distinguish between "interests" and "rights." The term "interest" in this context refers to what the individual would like—what is in his interest to have—regardless of whether he is legally entitled to it. A "right," by contrast, is an interest to which an individual is entitled because of a guarantee contained either in the Constitution or some other legally recognized source. Thus, a person may have an interest in having government reduce his taxes and build a freeway with an exit adjacent to land that he holds for commercial development. Neither of these is a right because neither carries any legal entitlement. The same person may also have an interest in being compensated for property that the government takes from him for governmental purposes, and this interest is a right because it is guaranteed by the Constitution.

CHAPTER SEVEN
Constitutional Guarantees for the Criminally Accused

Some may ask why a civilized society should extend any rights at all to criminals, who by their conduct have made themselves enemies to the group and have forfeited any right to protection. Should we not concentrate on protecting the victims of criminal conduct rather than the perpetrators?

Those who are established to be criminals are in fact deprived of many rights. It is only those accused of crime to whom the Constitution gives the full range of its protections. Central to our constitutional guarantees is the principle that until an accused is proven to be a criminal beyond a reasonable doubt he continues to enjoy most of the privileges available to people generally. Why should this be?

Assume that a man is caught in the act of murder. The public is outraged at the crime. To many, it seems ridiculous to pretend that he is "innocent until proven guilty." "Everyone knows he did it," they say. "Why should we go through a trial and appeals and all that, when he might get off on a technicality?" But what "everyone knows" sometimes proves false. Without inquiry we might not know that the man acted in self-defense or under an insane delusion. And there is a possibility that the witness to the act may be mistaken as to identity.

Assume, however, that in the theoretical case there is no doubt of the man's guilt. Perhaps in his case there would be no immediate harm in doing away with his rights and summarily condemning him. But consider the precedent that is set. Society is condemning a man without a trial, without forcing the state to prove to a jury of ordinary citizens that the man is guilty. What could happen the next time a crime occurs and the evidence is not quite so overwhelming? Will our system deal with the one defendant as it did the other? Who draws the line between those cases so clear that the accused should have no constitutional protection and those cases that may involve innocent persons falsely accused, who should receive every protection?

The only solution is to draw the line at the point where all persons, no matter how good or bad or how serious the crime or how clear the case, have all the protections of a fair trial. To draw the line anywhere else puts all of us in danger of losing our own constitutional rights to zealots who have no doubt of their rightness. As distasteful as this reality may be to some, the rights of every American citizen are inseparably bound in the same package as those of the nation's worst criminals.

Any system operated by mortals is capable of sending innocent people to jail or to the gallows, either through innocent mistake or through intentional abuse of official power. Assurance against either the inadvertent or the intentional breach cannot be reserved for some and not for others. That is, the Constitution cannot guarantee that the innocent person be fairly treated without giving the same guarantees to the guilty, because by hypothesis the objective is to segregate the innocent from the guilty. Until the system has done its work, we cannot distinguish one from the other. Any system run by fallible human beings must therefore make some choices between two competing objectives: identification and punishment of those who have committed crimes, and assurance that innocent people will not be punished for crimes that they did not commit.

History and our experience should remind us that the tension between these two objectives is not just theoretical. Our common experience with traffic offenses should have taught us that policemen, too, can make mistakes. Our constitutional system has drawbacks, but are they as serious as those of other systems that place a higher degree of reliance on the fact that an individual has been accused of crime by those in governmental authority? The lessons of the Spanish Inquisition and the Star Chamber should not be forgotten. In more recent times, we can note the results of criminal systems in Iran, Idi Amin's Uganda, and many of the Communist countries. The teachings of those comparisons should be clear: if we are going to make some mistakes, it is better to make them in favor of human life and freedom. In the trade-off between protecting the individual and protecting society, we will require that, before our government kills a person or locks him up, certain conditions must first be satisfied. This is, in fact, the judgment reflected in the American Constitution.

Criminal Protections in the Body of the Constitution

Most of the protections extended by the Constitution to persons accused of committing a crime are found in the Fourteenth Amendment and in the Bill of Rights, specifically the Fourth, Fifth, Sixth, and Eighth amendments. Several important provisions, however, are found in the main body of the Constitution. These include the habeas corpus and jury-trial guarantees, and the prohibitions against bills of attainder and ex post facto laws.

Article I Section 9 states: "The Privilege of the Writ of Habeas Corpus shall not be suspended, unless when in Cases of Rebellion or Invasion the public Safety may require it." Today we often take for granted the writ of habeas corpus and fail to remember how important this right is to our liberty. The framers of the Constitution considered habeas corpus to be of the highest value; it was often called "the Great Writ of Liberty, the most important writ of all."[1]

During early English history the king had the power to imprison a person and throw away the key. There was no guarantee that a person would ever get a trial or a chance to prove his innocence. In Magna Charta, written in 1215, the English barons wrested from King John the promise that "[N]o free man shall be seized or imprisoned, or stripped of his rights or possessions ... except by lawful judgment of his equals or by the law of the land."[2] This right came to be known as habeas corpus, a Latin term meaning "you have the body." Many people think that habeas corpus has something to do with the body of the victim of a crime. In fact, the "corpus" referred to is the body of the accused. The writ is an order from a court, commanding the person holding the accused in custody to produce the body of the accused before a magistrate and state the legal grounds for the detention. If the judge finds that the accused is unlawfully detained the prisoner will be set free. Thus the writ of habeas corpus means that before any person can be imprisoned for more than a very short time an impartial judge must determine the validity of the imprisonment.

The framers considered habeas corpus important because it placed control of the power to imprison in the hands of the judiciary, the branch of government least likely to abuse this power. The Supreme Court has observed this of habeas corpus:

Its root principle is that in a civilized society, government must always be accountable to the judiciary for a man's imprisonment: if the imprisonment cannot be shown to conform with the fundamental requirements of law, the individual is entitled to his immediate release.[3]

The writ of habeas corpus can be applied for whenever a person is in custody of a government officer. Custody does not only mean jail; in recent years a person on parole or out on bail has come to be considered under sufficient restraints that the courts can intervene to assure that the restraints are justified. Habeas corpus can be applied for at any stage of the criminal proceedings. It can force the police to go before a judge and justify the arrest and detention of a suspect. It is most often used, however, after conviction. If the defendant believes there was some error in law or procedure at the trial, he can request that higher courts review his conviction on appeal. And if for some reason the claim he makes (that his rights were violated in the trial) is not reviewable on appeal, he can use habeas corpus to test the legality of his imprisonment. For example, if a defendant is found guilty on the basis of a confession that he can prove was obtained in violation of his constitutional rights, the higher court will overturn his conviction. Habeas corpus has been used to hear a wide variety of claims—that the court lacked jurisdiction to try the case, that it admitted unconstitutionally obtained evidence, or that the prison conditions were so poor that they violated even a criminal's right to a minimal standard of decent treatment.[4]

Petitions for writ of habeas corpus cause delays in the execution of the death penalty. There are, however, definite limits on use of the writ. A court will seldom hear a petition based on the same ground more than once, and in Fourth Amendment cases the federal courts will not grant a petition if the state courts fully reviewed the alleged error.[5] The trend in recent years is toward limiting the scope of habeas corpus review. A balancing process is evident: the right of the defendant to a full and fair trial and appeal process is balanced against the competing right of the public and the defendant to a speedy resolution of cases.

Article I Section 9 also states: "No Bill of Attainder or ex post facto law shall be passed." Bills of attainder are legislative acts that inflict some punishment on persons or groups without a judicial trial. However, bills of attainder do not necessarily involve criminal proceedings and no bill of attainder cases to reach the Supreme Court have involved legislative determinations of criminal guilt.[6] Accordingly, bills of attainder are discussed in the next chapter. The prohibition against ex post facto laws applies only to retroactive changes in criminal law; it does not reach retroactive changes in laws dealing with other than criminal matters. Four categories of retroactive change are precluded by this constitutional provision: (1) making an act criminal that was not criminal at the time it was committed; (2) changing the severity of the crime (for example, from a misdemeanor to a felony after the act was committed); (3) retroactively increasing the potential punishment, as from five to eight years; and (4) making it easier to convict after the crime was committed.

The right to a jury trial is guaranteed both in Article III ("The Trial of all Crimes, except in Cases of Impeachment, shall be by Jury") and in the Sixth Amendment ("In all criminal prosecutions the accused shall enjoy the right to a speedy and public trial, by an impartial jury"). Even though Article III and the Sixth Amendment speak of "all crimes" and "all criminal prosecutions," there are many criminal proceedings for which a jury is not used. There are several reasons. First, the courts have interpreted the Constitution to require jury trials only for "serious crimes." It is difficult to draw the line between serious crimes and petty ones, but the courts have devised a rule based on the penalty. If the possible punishment is more than six months in prison and a fine of $500 or more, the defendant is entitled to a jury trial. Though Article I Section 9 guarantees that "trial . . . shall be by jury," the Sixth Amendment makes clear that this is a right the accused may waive, either by pleading guilty or by agreeing to be tried by a judge sitting without a jury. Such waiver most often occurs as part of a bargain with the prosecutor, or in the expectation that a judge will be swayed less than a jury by the "gruesome details" of the crime.

The constitutional guarantee of jury trial raises subsidiary issues upon which the Constitution is silent. Does a jury have to consist of twelve people? Does the verdict have to be unanimous? Must the states grant jury trials for violations of state law? On these issues the courts have concluded that (1) states must provide the right to a jury trial for all serious crimes just as the federal government must, because a jury trial is required by the Constitution's due-process guarantee; (2) a twelve-person jury is not essential—juries can be as few as, but not fewer than, six people; and (3) verdicts of full-size juries do not have to be unanimous, though those of a six-person jury must be. Most states require unanimity, but a growing number allow super-majority verdicts (at least 9 or 10 out of 12, for example.)[7]

The Constitution calls for "impartial" juries. The standard for impartiality developed by the courts is that no recognized group of people can be systematically excluded from jury service. For example, a conviction would be overturned if a defendant proved that a black had never served on a jury in a county where there was a recognizable percentage of black residents.[8] The same would occur if few women served. There is no requirement that each particular jury represent every segment of the community, but no recognizable group of otherwise qualified persons can be systematically excluded in whole or in part from jury service.

Not only must the jury be impartial at the outset, but it must remain impartial throughout the trial. For this reason only those jurors are chosen who swear that they are able to base their decision solely on the evidence presented in court. They are cautioned not to discuss the case with outsiders or listen to any comments on the case from anyone outside the court. Neither are they to discuss the case among themselves or make up their own mind until after all the evidence has been presented. It is to preserve their objectivity and freedom from outside influence that jurors in sensational cases are often secluded until the trial is over. In one famous case, the bailiff, within the hearing of the jury, commented: "Oh that wicked fellow, he is guilty." The conviction was reversed and a new trial granted.[9]

The Fourth Amendment

The Fourth Amendment centers on a single constitutional value: protection against unreasonable searches and seizures. The amendment states:

> The right of the people to be secure in their persons, houses, papers, and effects, against unreasonable searches and seizures, shall not be violated, and no Warrants shall issue, but upon probable cause, supported by Oath or affirmation, and particularly describing the place to be searched, and the persons or things to be seized.

Constitutional law regarding the Fourth Amendment consists essentially of a general rule and several exceptions to that general rule. The general rule is that law enforcement officers may not search any persons or private property without a warrant. Search warrants are issued by judges. As a consequence, the general rule that no search or seizure may be conducted without a warrant reflects a judgment that the decision of whether, in any particular case, the search is reasonable should be made by someone other than the police officer who wants to conduct it. This general rule reflects the high value that Americans—and our Enlgish ancestors before us—have placed on the proposition that "a man's home is his castle." As stated by William Pitt:

> The poorest man may in his cottage bid defiance to all the forces of the Crown. It may be frail—its roof may shake—the wind may blow through it—the storm may enter—the rain may enter—but the King of England cannot enter!—all his force dares not cross the threshold of the ruined tenement![10]

The Fourth Amendment protects everyone, not just the criminally accused. Its most important function is to protect the privacy of persons who have not been charged with criminal conduct. The search-warrant requirement means that before the police can conduct a search they must convince a judge that the intrusion into the citizen's privacy is warranted. The judge will not permit a search of the property or person if law enforcement officers lack sufficient evidence that a crime has been committed and that the search will help solve the crime.

Any standard the judge uses in determining whether the required threshold of proof has been established will of course be subject to some leeway in its practical application. The standard the courts apply is that there must be "probable cause" that the search will produce evidence relevant to the crime.[11]

The Fourth Amendment applies not only to searches for evidence of commission of a violent crime but also to inspections in enforcement of health and safety laws. The Supreme Court held in *Marshall v. Barlow's Inc.,* for example, that Fourth Amendment guarantees are applicable to searches by persons enforcing the federal Occupational Safety and Health Act (OSHA).[12]

Despite the general rule requiring warrants, most searches occur without use of a warrant, justified under one of the many exceptions to the rule. Some major exceptions are:

1. A warrantless search may be made in connection with a lawful arrest. The officer making an arrest is allowed to search the person thoroughly and may also examine his immediate surroundings (the area within reach or a little more) to prevent the destruction of evidence or to discover and confiscate weapons that might be used to help him escape or to harm the officer.[13]

2. A warrantless search may be made of a vehicle, which, unlike a house, may be moved and the evidence destroyed before the police would have time to obtain a warrant, provided that the police have "probable cause."[14]

3. The "hot pursuit" exception allows police to pursue a person they are trying to arrest into a private dwelling.[15]

The Fourth Amendment is illustrative of one of the most perplexing problems currently facing our criminal-justice system. It declares that the right to be secure against unreasonable searches and seizures "shall not be violated." It does not say what will happen if those rights are violated.

Assume that a man has illegal drugs hidden in his home. The police break into the home illegally, without a warrant or probable cause, and find drugs. There is no question that (1) the man violated the law by having drugs in his home, and (2) the police violated the Fourth Amendment by illegally entering a private home. Should the police be permitted to use the illegally seized evidence in court? The issue is not an easy one. On the one hand, there is no question about the value of the evidence. The man had the drugs and the evidence proves that he is a criminal. Why should our system turn its back on valid, probative evidence? On the other hand, should the police be allowed to prevail through their own lawlessness? Moreover, if this evidence can be introduced, the police may be encouraged to commit other Fourth Amendment violations, because they know that even though they have broken the law they will be allowed to use the fruits of their unlawful searches.

There are two competing theories concerning the best way to deal with unlawful police conduct in obtaining evidence. One is to deny the law enforcement officers the fruits of their illegal activity by excluding the illegally obtained evidence from the trial of the offender. The other is to leave the defendant to vindicate his rights by suing the policemen. Civil suits against police officers have so far proved inadequate to prevent official violation of constitutional rights. In most instances the criminal defendant is too fearful or poor to bring such suit, and juries are likely to return light verdicts (or none) against individual policemen, who typically lack resources to pay much to a successful plaintiff.

Because such civil suits proved ineffectual and the courts were faced with continuing illegal police searches, the Supreme Court adopted the exclusionary rule.[16] The exclusionary rule extends to all illegally seized evidence, including confessions obtained in violation of the privilege against self-incrimination and conversations overheard through unwarranted electronic surveillance, as well as tangible seized objects. Since its inception, the exclusionary rule, which has been criticized by many scholars and judges, has suffered from increasing skepticism in the Supreme Court.[17] Proposals for reform have called for abandonment of the exclusionary rule and replacement of it by forceful and effective law allowing civil actions by citizens whose constitutional rights (to be free from unreasonable searches and seizures) have been infringed.

The Fifth Amendment

The Fifth Amendment provides:

No person shall be held to answer for a capital, or otherwise infamous crime, unless on a presentment or indictment of a Grand Jury, except in cases arising in the land or naval forces, or in the Militia, when in actual service in time of War or public danger; nor shall any person be subject for the same offence to be twice put in jeopardy of life or limb; nor shall be compelled in any criminal case to be a witness against himself, nor be deprived of life, liberty, or property, without due process of law; nor shall private property be taken for public use, without just compensation.

Popular impression usually equates the Fifth Amendment with only one of its provisions—the privilege against self-incrimination. "Taking the Fifth" is a well-known phrase, a shorthand expression for asserting the privilege against self-incrimination. Actually, the Fifth Amendment contains five separate provisions. One of them—the guarantee that "private property [shall not] be taken for public use, without just compensation"—is a noncriminal provision. Another, the guarantee that no person shall be "deprived of life, liberty or property without due process of law" and the similar provision in the Fourteenth Amendment are among the most important provisions of the Constitution and have an impact on both criminal and noncriminal matters. The due-process clauses will be discussed in detail in Chapter 16.

The remaining three provisions of the Fifth Amendment deal exclusively with protections for the criminally accused. One is a prohibition against accusation for a "capital, or otherwise infamous crime, unless on a presentment or indictment of a Grand Jury." There are two basic means by which formal criminal charges may be brought in the United States—by the prosecutor alone or by a grand jury (with or without the concurrence of the prosecutor). Under the Fifth Amendment a citizen can be subjected to the expense and trauma of a criminal trial only if a grand jury, a group of citizens selected specifically for this purpose, concludes that he is probably guilty. The states are not required to use the grand jury, and even federal defendants often waive this right.

A fourth guarantee of the Fifth Amendment is that no person shall "be subject for the same offence to be twice put in jeopardy of life or limb." Most Americans have at least a general understanding of this "double jeopardy" clause. As with the privilege against self-incrimination, there is an element of gamesmanship about double jeopardy. Once a person has been tried for a crime he cannot be tried a second time for the same crime, regardless of whether he was convicted or acquitted on the first trial. The gamesmanship is borne out most poignantly in those cases where, after being acquitted at the first trial, new evidence of the defendant's guilt is discovered. Even if this new evidence would completely change the verdict, the defendant cannot be retried. As is the case with other constitutional protections, the prohibition against double jeopardy may result in the escape from punishment of a few people in our society who have committed crimes. But it appears to reflect a common sense recognition of the great strain a criminal trial imposes on an individual defendant and his family. It says, in effect, that a person need not endure that experience more than once for the same offense. In those instances where the government, for whatever reason, was not able to present its case well enough the first time and thinks it could do better the second, the government's failure should not result in the individual being put through the ordeal again.

Double jeopardy precludes a second criminal proceeding either for the same offense or a "lesser included offense." That is, if all the elements of the second offense were included within the first, double jeopardy would apply. For example, first degree murder might include manslaughter as a lesser included offense, so that acquittal for murder would preclude a second trial for manslaughter. By contrast, conviction for failure to reduce speed does not necessarily preclude a subsequent trial for manslaughter.[18]

There are also other circumstances in which the double jeopardy guarantee is inapplicable. The first proceeding must have in fact placed the defendant in jeopardy. A person is placed in "jeopardy" for constitutional purposes when the jury is sworn in or, in a nonjury trial, when the first witness is called. If the case is dismissed before those points, the defendant is said to have been exposed to no jeopardy in the first trial and therefore the second trial is not double jeopardy. Also, if the defendant appeals his first conviction and the appellate court grants a new trial, the new trial is not barred by double jeopardy. At the defendant's request the errors in the first trial have resulted in its being considered a nullity; the appellate order for a new trial destroys the jeopardy-creating status of the original trial.

The phrase that made the Fifth Amendment famous—"nor shall [any person] be compelled in any criminal case to be a witness against himself"—has been the subject of extensive constitutional litigation as well as scholarly and popular debate. In rare instances the privilege against self-incrimination protects a person who is innocent in fact but caught up in a web of suspicious circumstances, but it is clear that the privilege against self-incrimination is intended to protect, and does protect, primarily the accused who is in fact guilty.

Why, then, do we have it? The defendant knows better than any other person what his involvement was; why not require him to tell what he knows? The explanation is simply distaste for requiring a person "to be the engine of his own destruction." The drafters wished to avoid the "honest criminal's dilemma," which would result in punishing most surely the criminal who would not lie under oath while allowing those with no scruples to avoid incriminating themselves.

Concern for the person who has scruples about lying to save himself from conviction appears to be reflected in some of the judicial decisions interpreting and applying the privilege against self-incrimination. The privilege applies, for example, only to *testimonial* evidence. After arrest, a defendant cannot refuse to be fingerprinted, or to supply skin, hair, or blood samples, or to try on a jacket worn by the person committing the crime so that the jury can see whether it fits him, or even to give a handwriting sample or speak for identification.[19] In each of these examples the defendant is required to give evidence that may help to convict him, but the evidence is not testimonial. The defendant therefore has no control over the incriminating nature of the evidence. He can control the content of what he says, but he cannot control whether the jacket fits him or whether his blood, hair, skin, voice, or handwriting samples match those of the offender. Whether his blood is AB negative—the same type found under the fingernails of his victim—is certainly of concern to him, but it does not pose the dilemma because there is nothing he can do to change his blood type.

The privilege against incriminating oneself is not limited to criminal proceedings. Moreover, if there is no possibility that a statement could be used in a criminal proceeding against a person, he may be required to testify even though it amounts to a confession of criminal conduct. These principles can be illustrated by a single example.

Assume that a state bar association, through its ethics committee, is investigating charges that a lawyer misappropriated a client's funds to his own uses. In a formal, transcribed hearing the lawyer is asked to state under oath whether he used the client's money to buy a car that is registered in his wife's name. Can he refuse to answer on Fifth Amendment grounds? The answer is that he probably can. The state bar cannot prosecute him for embezzlement, but if he answers the ethics committee's question truthfully, his answer can be used in a criminal court to support an embezzlement prosecution. It is for this reason that he can refuse to answer: not because his answer might contribute to his disbarment, but because it might lead to criminal prosecution and conviction.

Assume, then, that the lawyer refuses to testify and the bar association lacks other evidence against him. Does this mean that the bar association is powerless to discipline him? Not necessarily. The Fifth Amendment would probably prevent the bar from disciplining him for invoking his constitutionally guaranteed privilege. What the bar can do is attempt to persuade the local prosecutor to commit himself not to use the lawyer's testimony or any other evidence derived from it in any embezzlement prosecution against the lawyer. If the prosecutor agrees, then the bar association can require the lawyer to answer the question and can use his response to disbar him. If the lawyer still refuses, his refusal to answer a proper question can be used as a basis for discipline. And if he testifies falsely, he will have exposed himself to a perjury prosecution.

In a criminal trial the privilege against self-incrimination does not completely insulate the defendant from the consequences of his decision not to testify, so long as the prosecution has enough other evidence of guilt to justify the judge letting the case go to the jury. If the judge concludes that the evidence of guilt is so weak that no reasonable jury could find the defendant guilty, the judge will himself acquit the defendant by directing a verdict in his favor. But if there is enough evidence of guilt to warrant submitting the case to the jury, the defendant's failure to testify will almost always hurt him. The jury will be told they should not hold the defendant's silence against him. Nevertheless, the defendant is in the courtroom. Evidence has been presented that he committed the crime. Almost inevitably, the jurors will think,

"He knows whether he did it or not. If he didn't, why doesn't he say so? The fact that he knows and says nothing means that he must have done it."

Unfortunately, this nearly inevitable inference drawn by jurors, always unjustified under the Constitution, is often clearly unfair to an accused because it leads to a false assumption of guilt. In many cases the defendant's lawyer has concluded that he will not be an effective witness. And if the defendant has previously been convicted of a crime, that damning fact may often be shown by the prosecutor to impeach the defendant's testimony. Thus, even though the defendant is innocent of this particular offense, he may be reluctant to testify because his testimony will open the door for the prosecutor to inform the judge and jury of his previous convictions.

The juror's inference from the defendant's decision not to testify is one instance in which our system fails to avoid penalizing the truthful person. Faced with the dilemma of either lying or convicting himself and with the likelihood that jurors may draw negative inferences from his failure to testify, the criminal who has no regard for truth will take the stand and lie. The truthful defendant must face the dilemma.

What about confessions? If a defendant has confessed to the commission of a crime, does the use of that confession in his criminal trial violate his privilege against self-incrimination? For many years, the constitutional rule was that confessions were admissible so long as they were "voluntarily" given—that is, so long as there was no evidence of undue coercion in exacting the confession. In *Miranda v. Arizona*, the Supreme Court held that the voluntariness test did not afford sufficient protection for the self-incrimination rights of the accused.[20] The famous "Miranda" rule, requiring that certain warnings be given to a person accused of committing a crime, is therefore rooted in the self-incrimination provision of the Fifth Amendment. The consequence of failure to give the warning is that the government may not introduce into evidence any confession obtained without the warning. Even if the warning is given, the confession will still be excluded if it was obtained by coercion.

The Sixth Amendment

The Sixth Amendment states:

In all criminal prosecutions, the accused shall enjoy the right to a
speedy and public trial, by an impartial jury of the State and district
wherein the crime shall have been committed, which district shall have
been previously ascertained by law, and to be informed of the nature
and cause of the accusation; to be confronted with the Witnesses

against him; to have compulsory process for obtaining witnesses in his favor, and to have the Assistance of Counsel for his defence.

The common denominator of all Sixth Amendment provisions is the right to a fair trial. Two of the guarantees deal with the time and place of trial. The time guarantee—"the accused shall enjoy the right to a speedy . . . trial"—is based on a common sense premise that the burden of official accusation the defendant must bear is magnified by lengthening the time period between the accusation and his opportunity to prove his innocence. The constitutional provision, however, has been loosely interpreted, so that any time requirements likely to be imposed by the legislature are almost certainly within the Constitution's bounds.

The Sixth Amendment also guarantees that the trial be held in the "district wherein the crime shall have been committed." This prohibition against defendants being tried outside the district where the crime was committed was a product of the bitter colonial American resentment against the transporting of colonists to other British colonies or across the ocean to England for their criminal trials—particularly as the result of Parliament's passing of the "Murder Act" in May 1774, one of the infamous "intolerable acts" that precipitated the War of Independence.

In addition to these time and place guarantees, the Sixth Amendment secures five rights to the criminally accused, all of which relate to the conduct of the trial. The trial must be public, so that the defendant's friends can see that justice is done. The defendant also has the right to be informed of the nature and cause of the accusation. This provision simply incorporates into the Constitution the common sense principle that one who is accused of a crime should be entitled to know with some precision what acts he is accused of committing so that he can prepare his defense. This can be accomplished by supplying the accused with either a copy of the grand jury indictment, as required in federal cases; or a copy of the criminal complaint; or information, as is the practice in those states where an indictment is not used. In any instance, the relevant document describes the acts that the defendant is alleged to have committed and the criminal laws alleged to have been violated. Lack of sufficient specificity in the indictment or the complaint may be grounds for a determination that this Sixth Amendment guarantee has not been satisfied and that the criminal case cannot proceed against the defendant until the indictment or complaint has been amended or supplemented.

The right of the defendant "to be confronted with the witnesses against him" again reflects the Founding Fathers' grievances against English criminal practice. English law at one time permitted criminal convictions to be based on written testimony or "depositions" of wit-

nesses. These depositions were simply read into evidence in the criminal
trial. Several unjust consequences followed from that practice. First, the
accuser was allowed the luxury of making his accusation without having to face the accused. An even more serious consequence was the
complete insulation of the witness from having to answer for any inconsistencies or falsehoods contained in his deposition. Since the witness was not present in the courtroom, it was not possible to cross-
examine him, either to point out inconsistencies or even to clarify what
he meant. Finally, once a written deposition was prepared, it could be
used even if the witness had subsequently recanted his story. The most
famous case illustrating the unfairness of criminal trials without the
right of confrontation and cross-examination is the trial in which Sir
Walter Raleigh was condemned to death, during the reign of James I,
on the written deposition of a single witness who, prior to the trial,
had renounced his story.[21]

The Sixth Amendment's right of confrontation is founded on fundamental notions of fair play and justice that have very deep roots in civilized society. The Roman law on this issue is reflected in the book of
Acts. When Paul was accused at Jerusalem, the Roman procurator
(prosecutor) told his accusers: "It is not the manner of the Romans to
deliver any man to die, before that he which is accused have the accusers face to face, and have license to answer for himself concerning the
crime laid against him" (Acts 25:16). Similarly, Felix, the Roman governor of Caesarea, after reading the letter of accusation gainst Paul, announced: "I will hear thee ... when thine accusers are also come"
(Acts 23:35).

The final provisions secured by the Sixth Amendment relate to the
ability of the defendant to present his side of the case at his trial. They
consist of the right "to have compulsory process for obtaining witnesses in his favor, and to have the assistance of counsel for his defense." In order to appreciate the importance of these guarantees, it will
be helpful to review the means by which the American legal system
tries to determine truth and render judgment between two competing
positions in either a civil or a criminal case. The system that we employ
for that purpose is called the adversary system.

The fundamental underpinning of the adversary system is that the
search for truth between two opposing positions—whether between
prosecution and defense in a criminal case or between plaintiff and defendant in a civil case—is for the person or group who must decide to
consider the opposing positions as they are advanced by professionals
representing both sides. The role of the lawyer is essential to the effective operation of this system. The lawyer's task is not to decide who
should win and who should lose. Rather, the lawyer's task is to do the
most skillful job possible of marshaling, presenting, and urging the

significance of the facts that support his client's side of the case. As a matter of strategy, the good lawyer knows the strengths of his opponent's case; but he cannot fulfil his assigned role properly if he tries to present the other side. That is the job of the opposing lawyer. Neither is it the lawyer's task to make the ultimate decision concerning who should prevail; that is the job of the judge, or the jury, or both.

A bedrock premise of the adversary system is that, if both sides are adequately presented, truth will win over error. As expressed so eloquently by John Milton in a slightly different though related context:

> And though all the winds of doctrine were let loose to play upon the earth, so truth be in the field, we do injuriously by licensing and prohibiting, to misdoubt her strength. Let her and Falsehood grapple; who ever knew truth put to the worse, in a free and open encounter?[22]

It is not always the case, of course, that truth prevails. So long as fallible humans fill the roles of the adversaries, and also the roles of the ultimate decision makers, truth will sometimes lose. But the faith of the adversary system is that the search for truth is better served by its procedures than by those of any other system.

The importance of the Sixth Amendment's guarantee of the right to counsel in a criminal case follows from these basic postulates of the adversary system. In many countries the primary responsibility for development of the evidence rests not with the lawyer, but with the judge, and the prime responsibility of all participants in the litigation process runs to determination of "the truth." Under the adversary system, reaching the truth is also the ultimate objective; but it is accomplished by assigning to skilled professionals the responsibility of representing opposing viewpoints.

The defendant in a criminal case should be entitled to a lawyer who will assist him in the preparation and presentation of his case. The person accused of criminal conduct faces the stigma of a criminal label, the loss of his liberty, and perhaps even loss of his life. Accordingly, our Founding Fathers concluded that death or imprisonment will not be permitted unless the accused has had the assistance of a skilled professional who will help him work his way through the adversary system and present his case in its most favorable light. Lawyers are not all of equal ability; but so long as the lawyer is minimally competent, the defendant's right to the aid of counsel is satisfied.

The remaining Bill of Rights guarantees for the criminally accused are contained in the Eighth Amendment, which prohibits excessive bail, excessive fines, and "cruel and unusual punishment." Until a person has been tried and found guilty, there has been no determination that he has committed a crime and therefore no justification for his imprisonment for punishment. If, however, there is a likelihood that if permitted to remain free pending his trial he will hide, leave the jurisdiction, or for some other reason not appear for his trial, then the government is justified in imprisoning him in order to assure that he will be present for his trial. The Constitution may be open to the interpretation that if bail is granted it must not be excessive, but that bail can be denied entirely if the judge feels the public safety would be endangered by permitting the defendant to be released.

To give assurance that the defendant will in fact be available for trial, bail may consist of a sum of money or a money bond, which will be forfeited in the event that the defendant does not appear for trial. The defendant may be a person of such stability in the community that the likelihood that he would not appear for his trial is remote, thus justifying releasing him, pending trial, "on his own recognizance," which means his own assurance that he will appear at the appointed time for his trial. Alternatively, the defendant may be released into the custody of some respected citizen who is willing to take the responsibility of having the defendant present for trial. Or the defendant may be put under any other reasonable restriction.

It is quite clear that the principal, if not the exclusive, original purpose of the prohibition against cruel and unusual punishment was to prevent the imposition of physical torture. Imposition of such criminal punishment was well known at the time the Constitution was drafted. It was not until 1814 that Parliament put a stop to the practice, as punishment for high treason, of hanging the guilty person by the neck and then cutting him down and disembowelling him while he was still living. In what must rank as one of the all-time leading understatements, Blackstone in 1758 described this practice as "very solemn and terrible." Other practices involved cutting off the ears, whipping, splitting the nose, or branding the cheek. Since these were not ever used as punishment for federal crimes, there has been no decision as to whether they would be "cruel and unusual"; but it appears that they would if instituted today.

The major recent issue has been whether capital punishment is by its nature cruel and unusual, so that all executions for the commission of a crime are a violation of the Eighth Amendment. The Supreme Court has held that execution does not in every case fall under the Eighth Amendment ban against cruel and unusual punishment. It has held that the disproportion between the death penalty and some crimes is so great as to make that punishment "cruel and unusual" in some cases.

CHAPTER EIGHT
Constitutional Standards for Noncriminal Guarantees: Absolutes, Balancing, and Weighted Balancing

We come now to the area where the Constitution affects most Americans most directly. In any of its functions, the Constitution may affect the interests of individual Americans. For example, as citizens in a participatory democracy, we all have an interest in preserving the allocation of governmental power between state and federal governments and among the three branches of the federal government. The existence or nonexistence of a certain governmental power can have great significance to a person who would be adversely affected by the exercise of that power. And even though most of us will never be accused of committing a serious crime, we all benefit from the constitutional protections afforded those who are. There is a direct benefit from provisions such as those of the Fourth Amendment, which protect those who have not been accused of crime, and an indirect benefit from the civilizing assurance that our society takes very seriously the deprivation of life, liberty, or property and that such deprivation will be accomplished only after certain safeguards have been guaranteed.

It is as a protector of individual interests in the noncriminal area, however, that the Constitution reaches most people in a direct and significant way. The reason is based on a fundamental relationship between government and the people who are subject to its powers. Quite literally, anything that government does will have some adverse effect on the interests of some persons subject to its governance. Consider three examples: the building of a new park, raising city employees' wages, and the adoption of a governmental policy to employ more women and members of ethnic minorities. In each case, the interests of many people would be furthered by what government has done. Each of these decisions, however, will have some adverse effect on the interests of some individuals. Some may object to the presence of a park near their homes because of the increase in noise and the loss of privacy; others, who hold a different view concerning parks, may feel injured because the park was not located closer to where they live. The increase in governmental salaries may attract additional employees into government service, to the corresponding detriment of private employers. And the affirmative action programs place equally qualified white male applicants at a disadvantage. Moreover, to the extent that any of these programs cost money—and all of them do—there is an adverse effect on taxpayers' interests.

There is no need to multiply the examples. It is sufficient to observe that literally anything that government does—maintaining a navy, repairing the streets, hiring teachers, delivering the mail, cleaning up the air that we breathe or the water that we drink, granting patents or copyrights, collecting taxes, fighting wars, or putting out fires—is going to hurt some person in some way. It is possible that there might be some exceptions, but I know of none. A friend once suggested, as exceptions, passing marriage laws and keeping dead dogs off the highway; but in my opinion these are not exceptions. When a state passes marriage laws, it necessarily draws dividing lines, defining, for example, who may be married or not. Any time any dividing lines are drawn, some persons will be adversely affected; marriage laws are no exception. And some method has to be provided for disposing of those dead dogs; almost certainly, this will result in some kind of harm to someone.

It would be unfair to characterize this conflict as a conflict between government on the one hand and the individuals on the other. In a democracy or a republic, almost all governmental action represents an attempt to advance the interests of individuals and groups. The real conflict, therefore, is between the interests of some individuals, usually a majority, and interests of other individuals, usually a minority. The decision to favor one group is made by governmental servants, elected or nonelected, who are charged with the responsibility of representing all interests of the people they serve. In making their judgment, they have presumably taken into account the issues on all sides of the competing interests and have conscientiously performed their assigned task.

The conflict is inevitable. Still, in resolving the conflicting interests the relevant government officers are doing the job that must be done by someone. This, in fact, is the essence of governmental policy-making—choosing between competing objectives of different groups. Since the conflict is inevitable, and since the governmental decision will always adversely affect someone, in the great majority of instances these adverse effects are simply regarded as part of the price we pay for living in a civilized society.

There are some exceptions here, however. Some instances in which the interests of an individual adversely affected by what government has done are of such a nature, or are of such importance, that the Constitution protects the individual interest. It accomplishes this by invalidating the governmental decision. This is what is meant by holding that a law or program is unconstitutional. It necessarily means that the normal process of governmental decisionmaking—legislative weighing of competing policy interests and making a choice between them—is displaced. For example, assume that the residents of a particular community have complained to members of the city council about missionaries who go door to door distributing literature and requesting an opportunity to hold religious discussions with family members. The city council responds by passing an ordinance prohibiting that kind of activity. In adopting that ordinance, the city council is engaging in lawmaking by choosing between competing policy interests. The competing policy interests are the privacy of the homeowner and the religious proselyting interests of the door-to-door missionaries. In this example, the city council's choice will be disallowed by the courts. One of the competing sets of interests—the religious interests of the individual missionaries—is protected by the United States Constitution.

This raises the question of the standard by which conflicts between governmental decisions and constitutionally protected interests are to be resolved. The anti-tracting ordinance considered above is unconstitutional, as a violation of the freedom-of-religion guarantee contained in the First Amendment.[1] Does this mean that any time the person attacking a law relies on a particular constitutional provision, he is assured a victory? The answer is no.

In approaching this problem of resolving the conflict between constitutionally based individual interests on the one hand and societal interests as determined by society's official representatives on the other, three basic approaches are theoretically available. The first is an absolutist, or per se approach, under which the conflict would always be resolved by selecting one set of interests—either those of the government or those of the individual. This approach can be illustrated by a balancing scale. One side is so much heavier than the other that the weighted side will always win, no matter how weighty the interest on the other side.

Private
Interest

GOVERNMENT
INTEREST

ABSOLUTIST STANDARD

In this case the government interest will always prevail, but the scales could be weighted the other way so that the individual interests will always win.

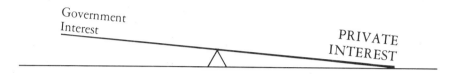

A second approach, at the opposite end of the spectrum, is a true, evenhanded balance of the competing objectives, weighing the constitutionally based interest against the governmental interest.

Government Interest — Private Interest

EVENHANDED STANDARD

In this approach both interests start off equally, and the interest that is the strongest on the facts of each individual case will prevail.

The third approach represents a middle ground between the other two. It involves a balancing of the competing interests but is not an evenhanded, fifty-fifty balance, with the decision favoring the side of the balance scale that weighs slightly more than the other. Rather, it is what might be termed a weighted balance. Under this approach, the competing interests on both sides will be taken into account but a presumption will be indulged for one side or the other. As a consequence, the interests in whose favor the scales are weighted will prevail unless the relevant considerations in the particular case strongly favor the interests on the other side.

WEIGHTED-BALANCING STANDARD

Weighted balancing differs from the straight-balancing approach in that, before the merits of the particular case are considered, a presumption is made favoring either the government's side or the individual's side. It differs from the absolutist approach in that the presumption can be overcome. The side favored by the premerits weighting will win in most cases, but not all. Thus, the government interest could start out favored, but if the private interest is strong enough it can overcome the preweighting.

Obviously, this approach could start with the scales favoring the individual interest. Then a strong governmental interest would be required to overcome the advantage enjoyed by the private interest.

From this brief review of the three available standards, two conclusions should be apparent. First, selection of the relevant standard will usually determine the issue of constitutionality and, therefore, who wins in the competition between governmental interests and individual interests. Second, the responsibility for selecting the relevant standard and applying it must be vested with some governmental entity. These tasks involve the interpretation of the Constitution. Under our separation-of-powers system, the responsibility for interpreting the Constitution is vested in the courts. Sometimes the courts explicitly state the standards they are following and sometimes they do not. Whether articulated by the court as a "standard" or not, however, any court necessarily bases its decision on an assumption concerning the comparative weights to be given to the interests of government, on the one hand, and those of the individual, on the other.

The absolutist approach is the easiest to apply. There is no need to inquire concerning the peculiarities of the individual case because (by hypothesis) they are irrelevant. All cases that fall within a category covered by the absolutist approach will always be treated the same; either the governmental decision will always be upheld or the individual interest will always be vindicated, depending on which side the absolutist approach favors. The absolutist approach is characteristic of totalitarian governments. In such governments the favored interests are those of government rather than the individual. This does not necessarily mean, however, that an absolutist standard favoring government implies totalitarianism. Remember that in a democracy most governmental decisions are made by the people's chosen representatives or by those who are responsible to those representatives; hence government interest is often referred to as the "public interest," even though they are not always the same. In this circumstance, an absolutist approach favoring government in certain areas simply implies that in that area we are willing to abide without question by the judgment of those governmental servants. Applied in favor of the individual, the absolutist approach would mean that whenever any governmental action adversely affects *any* interest in speech or religion (assuming those were the interests favored by the absolutist approach) the governmental action would always be held unconstitutional.

In some cases the courts have approached—indeed, they may have reached—an absolutist standard favoring legislative decisions that come into conflict with asserted constitutionally protected interests. Consider, for example, the Supreme Court's statement in *Williamson v. Lee Optical Co.*: "The Oklahoma law may exact a needless, wasteful requirement in many cases. But it is for the legislature, not the courts to balance the advantages and disadvantages of the new requirement.[2]

Some scholars and judges have advocated an absolutist approach on the individual's side of the balance scale, at least in the First Amendment area. The leading advocates of this position have been Professor Donald Meiklejohn, and Justices Black and Douglas of the United States Supreme Court.

It can be argued that in some cases the absolutist approach has been applied. The quotation from *Williamson v. Lee Optical* is illustrative. Even if the absolutist standard has slipped into one or two cases, however, it is clear to me that it is not the prevailing standard in any area of constitutional law.

The straight balancing approach has already been illustrated by the *Southern Pacific* case, discussed in Chapter 6. In *Southern Pacific* the Supreme Court balanced Arizona's health and safety interests against the constitutional protection of interstate commerce from undue burdens.

It is my opinion that the approach the courts have followed in the overwhelming majority of cases has been the intermediate one, a balancing approach that weights the balance scales either in favor of the individual or the government. The result is that in the particular case one side or the other will have more than a fifty-fifty burden to overcome. Put another way, one side will have to overcome a presumption favoring the other side. Sometimes this premerits weighting favors government, and sometimes it favors the individual. In some kinds of constitutional categories (most notably substantive due process, discussed in Chapter 18), the weighting at one time in our history strongly favored the individual; now it strongly favors the government. In most instances the judicial decision—which side to give the premerits weighting for cases falling within a particular constitutional category—will be determinative of most cases in that category. The substantive due-process cases are again illustrative. During the earlier period when the weighting favored the individual, the majority of substantive due-process cases were in fact decided in favor of the individual and against the government; and today, with the weighting favoring government, the overwhelming majority of substantive due-process cases, at least those dealing with economic matters, are being decided in favor of the government.

Against this general background the remaining chapters in Part II are devoted to a consideration of the noncriminal individual interests secured by the Constitution.[3]

CHAPTER NINE

Noncriminal Guarantees in the Main Body of the Constitution

The most important constitutional guarantees of individual liberties and interests are found in the First and Fourteenth amendments. Before turning to these, however, it is helpful to review briefly three guarantees of individual interests contained in Article I. They are the commerce clause, the prohibition against bills of attainder, and the contract clause.

The Commerce Clause

The commerce clause limitations on state power are usually considered in connection with the powers of government, specifically federalism, but the commerce clause is also involved with the accommodation of governmental and individual interests. The individual interest is an economic interest in keeping the channels of interstate commerce free from undue impediments imposed by the various states. The *Southern Pacific* case, for example, involved a conflict between Arizona's interest in health and safety and the economic interests of the railroads, which were forced to pay a million dollars a year to comply with the state's regulation.

During the period of the Articles of Confederation, trade between states was often as complicated and burdensome as between nations, largely because of trade barriers imposed by individual states. The need to change this and regularize trade among the states is generally considered to have provided one of the principal reasons for the Constitutional Convention of 1787. The history of interstate commerce under the Articles of Confederation was summarized by Justice Jackson, writing for a majority of the Supreme Court in *Hood & Sons v. DuMond*, as follows:

> When victory relieved the Colonies from the pressure for solidarity that war had exerted, a drift toward anarchy and commercial warfare

between states began. "... each State would legislate according to its estimate of its own interests, the importance of its own products, and the local advantages or disadvantages of its position in a political or commercial view." This came "to threaten at once the peace and safety of the Union." The sole purpose for which Virginia initiated the movement which ultimately produced the Constitution was "to take into consideration the trade of the United States; to examine the relative situations and trade of the said States; to consider how far a uniform system in their commercial regulations may be necessary to their common interest and their permanent harmony" and for that purpose the General Assembly of Virginia in January of 1786 named commissioners and proposed their meeting with those from other states.[1]

The result of the Constitution-makers' work was also described by Justice Jackson in *Hood & Sons*:

> Our system, fostered by the Commerce Clause, is that every farmer and every craftsman shall be encouraged to produce by the certainty that he will have free access to every market in the Nation, that no home embargoes will withhold his exports, and no foreign state will by customs duties or regulations exclude them. Likewise, every consumer may look to the free competition from every producing area in the Nation to protect him from exploitation by any. Such was the vision of the Founders; such has been the doctrine of this Court which has given it reality.[2]

To the interstate businessman, the commerce clause written into Article I of the Constitution assures the existence of an interstate common market. Because of the commerce clause a merchant in any state knows that the markets of every other state are open to him and that no tariffs, embargoes, quotas, or other undue burdens may impede his access to those markets. The nature of this guarantee is illustrated by *Baldwin v. Seelig*.[3] At issue in *Baldwin v. Seelig* was a New York statute that attempted to increase the financial return to New York milk producers. In addition to fixing a minimum price that had to be paid to New York producers, the statute also prohibited the sale in New York of any milk that had been purchased in another state at less than the minimum price. Mr. Seelig, a Vermont milk producer, challenged the New York statute's constitutionality, and the Supreme Court ruled in his favor. The effect of the statute—as described by Justice Cardozo, the author of the Supreme Court opinion—was that if milk purchased out of state was brought into New York by the purchaser, then the purchaser "may keep his milk or drink it, but sell it he may not." The rationale was that the commerce clause guarantees to all milk producers in all states the unencumbered right to come into New York and compete in that state. Mr. Seelig has a right to compete for the milk business in New York or any other state at any price he wants to set. It is a right assured by the commerce clause of the Constitution.

Eight years after *Baldwin v. Seelig*, the Supreme Court held in *Hood & Sons v. DuMond*, cited above, that New York could not require a Pennsylvania milk purchaser to obtain a license for the privilege of buying milk produced in New York. The teaching of *Baldwin v. Seelig* and *Hood & Sons v. DuMond*, taken together, is that no state may keep its own productive capacity for its own consumers, and no state may keep its own markets for its producers.

Bills of Attainder

Article I contains two separate prohibitions against bills of attainder. Section 9, which deals generally with limitations on congressional power, provides that "no Bill of Attainder or ex post facto Law shall be passed"; and Section 10, which limits state lawmaking power, similarly provides that "no state shall . . . pass any bill of attainder."

What is a bill of attainder? Simply stated, it is a legislative determination of guilt or imposition of penalty. The underlying concept is that the determination of criminal guilt or innocence and the imposition of penalties for individual wrongful conduct are strictly judicial functions. Thus, the classic example of a bill of attainder would be a law passed by Congress or a state legislature declaring that persons identified by the legislature are criminals without having their criminality determined by a judicial trial.

Congress and the state legislatures apparently understand the central concept of the prohibition against bills of attainder, because our actual experience with the bill of attainder clauses has not involved any legislative attempt to declare criminality. The cases that have come before the Supreme Court have established, however, that the ban on bills of attainder also reaches legislative attempts to deprive persons of benefits because of adverse conclusions reached by the legislature concerning those persons. This is illustrated by the leading case of *United States v. Lovett*.[4] That case involved a congressional appropriation bill to which the United States Senate had attached a rider providing that no part of the money appropriated in that bill should be used to pay the salaries of five named persons (one of whom was Mr. Lovett) employed by the State Department. The United States Supreme Court held this provision unconstitutional as a bill of attainder. While the congressional act did not declare Lovett and his colleagues to be criminals, it nevertheless inflicted on them a detriment—and therefore a legislatively determined punishment—because of what Congress had perceived to be improper conduct on their part.

Why were the Founding Fathers concerned about bills of attainder? Probably because the legislature is not bound by rules of evidence, nor by other protections that assure the rights of the criminally accused. Moreover, since the legislature is a political branch, it is more susceptible to political pressures that should play no part in determining whether a person should be punished as a criminal. Both in the English experience and the colonial experience, the Founding Fathers had adequate examples of the injustices that can result from the legislature's attempts to deal with the issue of guilt or innocence.

The Contract Clause

Article I Section 10 of the Constitution—the general Article I provision limiting state power—provides that "no State shall . . . pass any . . . Law impairing the Obligation of Contracts." This prohibition against laws that impair the obligation of contracts applies only to the state governments; it does not affect the federal government.

There are two situations to which this prohibition against laws impairing the obligation of contracts (usually referred to as the "contract clause") applies. The first situation is one in which the state attempts to abolish its own contracts, thereby reneging on a deal to which the state is a party. The second situation involves state legislation that changes the nature of contracts entered into by private parties after the contracts have been made.

It is fairly clear from the history of adoption of the contract clause that its principal purpose, if not its exclusive purpose, was to prevent the states from making changes in private contracts. Nevertheless, the most famous case decided under the contract clause, *The Trustees of Dartmouth College v. Woodward*, involved a state modification of one of its own contracts.[5]

The applicability of the contract clause to private contracts has always presented something of a dilemma. The constitutional prohibition against impairing the obligation of contracts is absolute; on its face, it recognizes no exceptions. If it were literally applied, however, it would consume a broad range of state police-power authority. Many state laws, enacted pursuant to the state's police powers, in fact have an adverse effect upon, and therefore "impair," the contractual arrangements of some persons. This is true, for example, of minimum wage laws, mortgage moratorium laws, building codes, and laws limiting the number of hours that people in certain trades may be required to work. Power to pass these and other laws that in fact impair contractual arrangements has been sustained by the courts. One rationale is that when any contract is entered into the contracting parties recognize that the state may exercise its police powers and affect their contract. Yet that rationale, if applied literally, would effectively nullify the contract clause. As a consequence, the contract clause and the state police powers stand in eternal potential conflict with each other. Either has the potential to render the other practically meaningless.

Prior to 1977 it appeared that the contract clause was on its way to extinction. Two recent cases would indicate, however, that the pendulum may be swinging back. The first of these cases is *United States Trust Co. v. New Jersey.*[6] The Port Authority of New York and New Jersey is a political subdivision of those two states which operates the port facilities and other facilities serving both states. In 1962 this bistate authority issued some municipal bonds. Like any other municipal bonds, these constituted a contract between the issuing authority and the bondholders, since the issuer agreed to certain covenants (contractual obligations) in consideration of the purchase of the bonds. Included among the covenants undertaken by the port authority was a limitation on its ability to subsidize rail passenger transportation from revenues and reserves. In 1974 the legislatures of the two respective states passed statutes repealing this 1962 covenant. The Supreme Court held the repealing statutes invalid because they violated the constitutional prohibition against state impairment of the obligation of contracts. The opinion suggests that the contract clause allows the states greater leeway to interfere with private contractual obligations than to change their own contractual obligations.

One year later, in *Allied Structural Steel Co. v. Spannaus*, the court held unconstitutional, as a violation of the contract clause, Minnesota's Private Pension Benefits Protection Act.[7] That act imposed on employers who had established an employee pension plan within the state of Minnesota, and who then terminated the plan or closed their Minnesota office, an obligation to pay a "pension funding charge" unless their pension funds were sufficient to finance full pensions for all employees who had worked at least ten years. The law, therefore, changed the contractual obligations already entered into between the employer and his employees. The Supreme Court held that the law violated the contract clause.

Unlike the *United States Trust Co.* case, the *Allied Structural Steel* case involved a modification of private contractual arrangements. Neither of these cases has definitively resolved the built-in conflict between the contract clause and the state police powers, though their undeniable effect is to give greater vitality to the contract clause. The current approach, under *United States Trust Co.* and *Allied Structural Steel*, appears to be essentially a balancing approach. On the two sides of the balance scales are (1) the importance of the state's police power objective and whether that objective can be achieved through other means not violative of the contract clause, and (2) the extent to which contractual obligations have been impaired. As the Court observed in the *Allied Structural Steel* opinion, "the severity of the impairment measures the height of the hurdle the state legislation must clear."[8]

The Elusive Distinction between Compensable Taking and Noncompensable Regulation

Several provisions in the Constitution afford protections to property interests. One of these is the contract clause, just discussed. Another is the controversial substantive due process provision, which will be treated in Chapter 15. A third is the guarantee contained in the Fifth Amendment that "private property [shall not] be taken for public use, without just compensation."

There are some black and white circumstances to which this guarantee against governmental taking without compensation is clearly applicable. If the federal government wants to build a post office or widen a road, it has the right to take private property for either purpose. This is called the power of eminent domain. But the Constitution guarantees that the propery owner will be paid just compensation.

At the other end of the spectrum, it is equally clear that not every governmental action that has some adverse effect on people's property values entitles the owners to compensation. Assume, for example, that the post office is constructed right across the street from land whose value is cut in half because of the location of the post office. Or assume that the government abandons a highway that formerly ran in front of a service station and that, because of the abandonment, the service station no longer has commercial value.

The potential examples are almost endless. Pursuant to their governmental powers, both state and federal governments regulate in many ways. Many of those regulations have the effect of diminishing property values. At some point the diminution will be of such a nature and extent that government is required to pay for it. The dividing line between those diminutions—values for which government must pay and those the Constitution permits without payment—is difficult to identify, and the articulation of helpful standards in this area has proven to be an almost insuperable task for both judges and constitutional scholars.

There are two basic approaches to this problem. One focuses on the literal language of the constitutional guarantee, which says that compensation must be paid where private property is "taken." Under this approach the road-widening and post office construction cases would require compensation, but the passing of a building code would not. Government need not pay unless there is actual taking of the property.

A distinction keyed to the "taking" requirement of the Fifth Amendment would be the cleaner theoretical approach and easier to apply. It has the additional advantage of focusing on the literal language of the Constitution. However, this approach may not always be adequate. Assume, for example, two individuals, Smith and Jones, each of whom has an equal amount of money to invest. Smith invests his in General Motors stock and Jones purchases some land fronting on a lake near a growing metropolitan center. The day after Smith and Jones make their investments, the local zoning authority zones Smith's property to prohibit the construction of any buildings. Technically, there has been no taking. The land still belongs to Smith; it does not belong to any government. Yet there is something fundamentally unfair about the way government has treated Smith. It may be that this lakefront property should be maintained in its pristine state, for the benefit of all citizens. But whatever one's view may be on that issue, it is difficult to sustain the proposition that Smith is under any more obligation to pay for that societal benefit than is Jones. If the community as a whole is to benefit, then the community as a whole should pay the cost.

The approach that appears to have prevailed does not draw a rigid line between those governmental actions that in fact consitute a taking and those which do not, though the decisions are not entirely consistent. The leading case is *Pennsylvania Coal Co. v. Mahon.*[9] During the late 1800s, the Pennsylvania Coal Company and other coal companies operating in northeastern Pennsylvania followed a practice of selling land that they owned subject to the coal companies' right to remove the coal under the land, without any liability for damages. The land on which the Mahon's home was located was subject to such a deed, executed in 1878. In the early part of the twentieth century, the coal mining areas of Pennsylvania experienced a serious problem of "surface subsidence"–the collapse of the surface over which coal had been mined. After lengthy consideration of the matter, the Pennsylvania legislature enacted in 1921 a statute known as the Kohler Act, which prohibited the mining of anthracite coal in a way that would cause the subsidence of people's homes.

The Supreme Court held the statute unconstitutional in an opinion written by Justice Holmes. The coal company argued that prohibiting the mining of the coal amounted to a taking of their property. If the Court had followed the rigid view that the constitutional guarantee against taking prohibits only those governmental acts that involve actual takings, the Mahons would have won. The test, under the *Pennsylvania Coal* opinion, does not turn exclusively on the narrow question of whether there has been an actual taking; rather, the central issue is one of a degree: "The general rule at least is, that while property may be regulated to a certain extent, if regulation goes too far it will be recognized as taking."

This test of whether government has gone "too far" is not susceptible to precise guidelines, and its predictive value on a case-to-case basis is not very great. Its offsetting virtue is that it offers more protection for private property interests than the less flexible distinction based on whether there has or has not been an actual taking.

CHAPTER TEN
The First Amendment: Freedom of Speech

The First Amendment protects the very core of interests that are important to every American. It is the home of the rights of free expression: freedom of speech, freedom of the press, freedom of religion, and freedom to assemble and petition the government for redress of grievances. These liberties to express one's views freely are largely taken for granted. But one who has lived or traveled in foreign countries and who has witnessed the consequences of criticism of government officials in many parts of the world gains a new appreciation for the rights of free expression.

Freedom of speech and its kinfolk—freedom of the press and freedom to assemble and petition the government—are important not only in their own right, but also because they preserve so many other democratic values. As discussions in the earlier chapters dealing with governmental structure have shown, public opinion is the principal force behind the separation-of-powers dynamic. It is also the most effective allocator of power between federal and state governments. The effectiveness of public opinion in the allocation of governmental power rests in substantial part on the fact that the free expression of views is constitutionally guaranteed.

This chapter will deal primarily with freedom of speech. However, the linkage between freedom of speech and freedom of the press goes beyond the simple fact that both guarantees appear back to back in the First Amendment. The constitutional promise of a free press has primarily involved applying general principles of free speech in the media context. The principles discussed in this chapter, therefore, are discussed under the label of free speech, but they largely involve free-press principles as well. There are also some areas that affect the press in a particular way. Those are treated in Chapter 11.

The constitutional guarantee of free speech and free press consists of only fourteen words: "Congress shall make no law ... abridging the freedom of speech, or of the press." The free speech—free press guarantee is simple and unqualified. The lack of any limitation has been used by advocates of an absolutist First Amendment standard in support of their position. The First Amendment, it is contended, is the clearest possible area where the framers must have intended strict construction to apply. "No law" must mean "no law."

I have never been persuaded by the absolutist approach, even in the First Amendment area. The evidence that the framers intended such a literal reading of the First Amendment is not conclusive. Defamation and obscenity laws, for example, were in existence at the time the Bill of Rights was adopted, and there is no proof that the framers intended to abolish either. The overwhelming majority of Americans would be quite uncomfortable with an absolutist approach to the First Amendment. It would mean, for example, that no government, state or federal, would have any power to exercise any control over pornography, since pornography involves the use of words and other forms of expression. It would also mean that all defamation laws would be unconstitutional. A literalist, absolutist approach to the guarantee that government shall make no law abridging the freedom of speech would foreclose all governmental power to act in the interest of the majority of its citizens, protecting them from any utterances, writings, or other expressional attempts, no matter how vile and no matter how offensive.

Given the importance of the First Amendment, it is surprising that no freedom-of-speech case reached the Supreme Court until after the First World War, when our republic was more than a century and a quarter old. The initial freedom-of-speech cases arose out of the First World War and involved governmental efforts to control subversive speech. During the intervening six decades, freedom of speech has been one of the most active areas of constitutional adjudication.

In general, the approach that the Court has developed toward free-speech cases has been to weight the balance scales in the individual's favor—that is, in favor of the free-speech interests. Out of the large number of free-speech cases that have come before the courts, individual exceptions to this approach can be identified. But it is quite clear to me that, in their total effort to pour content into the free-speech guarantee, the courts have generally placed a sizable burden on governmental efforts to limit the right of free speech or free expression.

This general concept of a weighted balance in favor of speech interests has been variously expressed. Sometimes the courts state that government regulation in this area will be countenanced only when it is supported by a "compelling state interest." At other times, other words are used. But whatever the language, the approach is essentially the same: as a general rule, the Constitution places a high value on speech and expression interests; and, in going about their task of accommodating governmental interests and individual interests, the courts will weight the balance scales heavily in favor of individual interests where matters of free speech and free expression are involved.

The most helpful way to analyze the complex body of constitutional law dealing with free speech and expression is to examine those categories of cases in which the courts have departed from this general rule. As we proceed through these various categories, it will be helpful to bear in mind that they are exceptions or modifications of the general rule that abridgments or regulations of speech can be accomplished only where there is a compelling state interest, or where the state can overcome a strong weighting of the scales in favor of permitting the speech or expression.

For convenience' sake, these categories can be discussed under four headings, which are best stated as questions. Who is involved in the activity that raises the speech issues? Where is the speech taking place? How is the person attempting to communicate? What is he saying? It would be an oversimplification to refer to these categories as the who, where, how, and what exceptions to the general rule, because the concepts are more sophisticated than that. Nevertheless, for analysis purposes, the breakdown of some of the exceptions into these categories can be helpful.

Who Is Involved?

In the great majority of cases, the persons who speak or who are the target of the speech have no bearing on the applicable constitutional standard. There are at least two instances, however, in which the applicable standard may differ, depending on who is involved.

In *Miami Herald Publishing Co. v. Tornillo* the Supreme Court invalidated Florida's right-of-reply statute because it violated the First Amendment's free press guarantee.[1] The invalidated statute had required any newspaper that attacked a political candidate to afford that candidate a right to equal space in the newspaper for reply. The *Miami Herald* case demonstrates the general principle discussed in Chapter 8: In the great majority of instances, the conflict between governmental and individual interests is actually a conflict between the interests of two groups of individuals, with government having made a policy decision to prefer one of those sets of interests. Indeed, in the *Miami Herald* case both sets of interests were based on free expression. On the government's side, it was an interest in assuring that all political candidates had equal opportunity to make their views known, and on the individual's side the right of the newspaper to express its own views as it saw fit, unfettered by governmental requirement or interference.

The *Miami Herald* case held that the right-of-reply statute was unconstitutional because of its inhibiting effect on the editorial right of the newspaper to determine the content of what it printed, unhampered by governmental requirements. Contrast that holding with the Court's earlier decision in *Red Lion Broadcasting Co. v. Federal Communications Commission.*[2] The *Red Lion* case upheld the constitutionality of the Federal Communication Commission's "fairness" doctrine that requires radio and television stations to present full discussion of public issues and to assure fair coverage for each side. The commission had interpreted this rule to require broadcasters to allow reply time for individuals attacked on their programs. The Supreme Court sustained the FCC regulations as constitutional. Why should federal government regulations requiring reply time be valid while five years later state regulations requiring reply space were held invalid? The characteristic that reconciles these two cases is probably the "who" factor. In one case the requirement was imposed on a broadcasting company, and in another on a newspaper. Why should this make a difference?

In order to avoid undue interference by radio and television stations with each other's signals, the number of authorized stations must be limited. The number of persons and groups who would like to operate radio or television stations far exceeds the number that can be operated. As a consequence, the scarce right of access to the public airways is limited and allocated by the Federal Communications Commission. This is why it is not unreasonable to impose on those few who receive the benefit of FCC licenses a requirement different from other media forms that do not owe their existence to a government license. As the Court observed in the *Red Lion* case: "Where there are substantially more individuals who want to broadcast than there are frequencies to allocate, it is idle to posit an unabridgeable First Amendment right to broadcast comparable to the right of every individual to speak, write or publish."[3]

There is another instance in which the applicable constitutional text depends on who is involved; it is in the area of defamation of public officials or public figures. The difference is that, in the defamation context, the "who" issue focuses not on who is the speaker but, rather, on who is the target of the speech.

Defamation laws are state laws that permit recovery for injury to reputation. The very existence of defamation laws is of course a limitation on free speech; and if an absolutist First Amendment standard were applied, all defamation laws would be unconstitutional. The First Amendment does not follow an absolutist standard, however; and, in general, the application of defamation laws to award damages for injury to reputation is not foreclosed by the Constitution.

There are two exceptions. The first applies where the plaintiff—the person claiming that his reputation has been injured—is a public official or public figure. The principle is illustrated by the leading case, *New York Times Co. v. Sullivan*, popularly referred to as the *"Times Libel"* case.⁴ This case arose out of a full-page advertisement carried in the *New York Times* in 1962 soliciting contributions for various civil-rights purposes. The ad reported alleged civil-rights violations that had been inflicted on Dr. Martin Luther King and others by certain public officials in the South, including L. F. Sullivan. Sullivan's responsibilities as one of three elected city commissioners in Montgomery, Alabama, included supervision of the police department. Several allegations contained in the ad turned out to be false. The ad alleged, for example, that police had "ringed" the Alabama State College campus (a black institution) and that King had been arrested seven times. In fact, police were deployed to the campus in large numbers on three occasions, but they did not actually "ring" it; and King had been arrested four times, not seven.

Sullivan and others brought suit under Alabama defamation law and recovered a judgment against the *New York Times* and four individuals for five hundred thousand dollars, the full amount claimed by the complaint. The Supreme Court reversed this judgment. The Court did not hold that all defamation recoveries violate the First Amendment, or even that all defamation recoveries by public officials are barred by the First Amendment. It held that defamation actions brought by public officials can be sustained only where those officials prove "actual malice" on the part of the person or entity who allegedly damaged their reputation. Specifically, the test is:

> The constitutional guarantees require, we think, a federal rule that prohibits a public official from recovering damages for defamatory falsehood relating to his official conduct unless he proves that the statement was made with "actual malice"—that is with knowledge that it was false or with reckless disregard of whether it was false or not.⁵

This limitation on the right of defamation recovery by public officials reflects a judgment that, in a free and open society, the leeway of the ordinary citizen to criticize should be larger where the target of his criticism is a public official than where the target is another private citizen. Public officials voluntarily make a decision to enter public life. By their own choice they elect to engage in activity that will lead to discussion and debate of controversial subjects. They should therefore expect a larger measure of criticism than should those who have not made that same judgment. This does not mean that when that criticism harms their reputation they have no right to sue their critics. But it does limit their right to sue to those cases where they can show that the person making the speech or printing the story against them either actually knew that it was false or at least acted recklessly. Consistent with this general philosophy, the Supreme Court has subsequently held that the *Times Libel* rule also applies to "public figures," persons who have voluntarily "thrust themselves into the vortex of public discussion."[6]

What about a private individual involved in a newsworthy event who claims to have been damaged by the press? The Supreme Court dealt with this issue in *Gertz v. Welch*.[7] *Gertz v. Welch* arose out of a defamation suit by Elmer Gertz, a Chicago lawyer, against Robert Welch for falsely calling Gertz a communist. At the time Welch called him a communist, Gertz was representing the family of a man killed by a Chicago policeman. The family was bringing a civil damage action against the policeman. Mr. Gertz had not voluntarily entered public life or thrust himself into the middle of a public controversy; he was simply doing his job as a lawyer. Accordingly, the *Times Libel* actual-malice rule was inapplicable.

The Supreme Court promulgated a different standard for private plaintiffs: "We hold that, so long as they do not impose liability without fault, the states may define for themselves the appropriate standard of liability for a publisher or broadcaster of defamatory falsehood injurious to a private individual."[8] In other words, the states cannot hold publishers or broadcasters liable if they were without fault. This is a lighter burden on plaintiffs than is imposed by the *Times Libel* actual-malice requirement.

Where Does the Speech Occur?

The place where the speech occurs may make a difference in the applicable constitutional standard. In ancient Rome the Forum was a place where all citizens could go to express their views concerning issues of the day. The word *forum* has come to mean a place that provides opportunity for communication. Beginning with the leading case, *Hague v. Committee for Industrial Organization*, the Supreme Court has articulated the concept of a "public forum" guaranteed by the First Amendment.[9] The concept is that there are certain public places to which all individuals may have access for the purpose of exercising First Amendment freedoms, giving speeches, assembling in groups, and holding rallies, religious meetings, and the like. These places are territorial enclaves which can in effect be commandeered by the individual citizen and used by him as a forum for his First Amendment activity. They have been described as constituting "the poor man's printing press."

The opinion in *Hague v. C.I.O.* contains dictum (language not essential to the decision) implying that all publicly owned places might be part of the public forum.[10] Subsequent holdings have clarified that this is not the case. The two public areas most clearly included within the public forum are the public streets and the public parks. The catalogue of public-forum places clearly includes more than just streets and parks, however. It probably extends generally to those public places that have traditionally been regarded as appropriate places for public expression and the exercise of First Amendment freedoms, such as the statehouse grounds.[11] It is equally clear that some public places are not included within the public forum. What are the consequences of including some kinds of places within the public forum and excluding others?

In any case involving First Amendment activity occurring in public places, one of the most important isues will be whether that place constitutes part of the public forum. We know that some kinds of places—parks, streets, and probably statehouse grounds—are included. We know that other places—libraries, jails, military bases, courthouses—are excluded.[12] We also know that the applicable First Amendment standard will vary according to whether the place is or is not a part of the public forum. But what about other places? What about airports? (No, the Supreme Court has never ruled on airports, though some lower courts have.) What about the campuses of state universities? Might it make a difference whether the activity occurs in front of the student union building or in the cafeteria or in a study hall? What about the parking lot in front of the state driver's license bureau? Might it make a difference whether the activity consisted of a religious rally or a protest against the policies of the driver's license bureau? In each case, the question will probably be whether the First Amendment activity is consistent with the purpose for which the public place was intended. To use some obvious examples, a group demonstration that is noisy but not violent is perfectly appropriate on a city street or in a park but inappropriate in a library or courthouse. A religious street meeting that would be protected by the First Amendment if held on a public sidewalk might not be afforded the same protection on a publicly owned bus.

I believe that the impact of the kind of public place selected for First Amendment activity (on the standard of constitutional protection afforded that activity) can fairly be summarized in this way: if the public place constitutes part of the public forum, then the usual high standard of protection afforded by the First Amendment to the individual is applied. That is, the balance scales will be strongly weighted in favor of the individual and against the government. If, however, the public place falls in the category of the courthouse, the library, or the jail, then an additional factor enters into the overall balance. It is a factor that favors the government, but its weightiness will depend on the facts of the individual case. In general, it inquires into whether the activity at issue is appropriate for that particular public place.

It is well established that, even within the public forum, First Amendment activities are subject to reasonable limitations concerning time, place, and manner. Indeed, time, place, and manner restrictions constitute the best recognized category of permissible limitations on First Amendment activity. The city probably cannot prohibit the holding of a parade for purposes of demonstrating in favor of the adoption of a state right-to-work law, but it can require that the parade be held on Saturday morning rather than Friday afternoon during rush hour. Similarly, government may not prohibit the distribution of leaflets, but it may require that adequate assurance be given that the leaflet distribution will not result in the streets being littered.

It should be noted that the exercise of First Amendment liberties is not always dependent on the use of public facilities, so that not all freedom-of-expression or freedom-of-religion cases will involve the public-forum issues. First Amendment exercise may consist of the distribution of handbills or tracts on a door-to-door basis, the printing of literature, meetings held on private premises, and others. It is only when the individual attempts to use public facilities for his First Amendment exercise that the public-forum issue comes into play.

How Is the First Amendment Activity Expressed?

Expression can take many forms. Assume that I have a grievance against the government of the city of Denver, I could express this grievance in many ways. I could organize a parade—complete with banners, chants, and slogans. I could write letters to the editor of the *Denver Post.* I could give speeches outside city hall. Assume, however, that instead of choosing any of these means of expressing my displeasure, I simply stand in front of the Denver city hall with a black arm band on each of my arms. Assume further that I later stand in front of the mayor's office and with great flourish—but without uttering a word—ceremoniously burn a copy of the city charter.

Acts such as arm-band wearing, draft-card burning, or standing or sitting in strategic places are sometimes referred to as "symbolic speech." They are attempts to communicate, but they are not really speech. The attempted communication is not accomplished through words, either oral or written. Does the applicable constitutional standard turn on whether the communication is verbal or nonverbal—that is, on whether any words are used? Is symbolic speech treated differently from pure speech? The answer is yes. Two propositions are clear. The first is that symbolic speech is entitled to some First Amendment protection. The second is that it is not entitled to as much First

Amendment protection as pure speech. Probably the strongest statement for the general principle that symbolic speech is entitled to a lesser measure of protection than pure speech comes from the Supreme Court's decision in the draft-card burning case *United States v. O'Brien.*[13] In upholding O'Brien's conviction for burning his draft card, the Court made the following observations:

> We cannot accept the view that an apparently limitless variety of conduct can be labeled "speech" whenever the person engaging in the conduct intends thereby to express an idea.... This court has held that when "speech" and "nonspeech" elements are combined in the same course of conduct, a sufficiently important governmental interest in regulating the nonspeech element can justify incidental limitations on First Amendment freedoms.[14]

Why should symbolic speech be treated any less favorably than pure speech? In some cases there may be some question as to what the individual is attempting to express—or, indeed, whether he is attempting to express anything at all. Take the examples of my standing with black arm bands in front of the Denver city hall or burning the city charter outside the mayor's office. What am I expressing by these acts? Am I expressing anything? I may be communicating nothing other than the fact that there are strange features to my clothing or that I am burning some papers in a place that is not customarily used for paper burning. On the other hand, under some circumstances, symbolic speech may not only constitute expression in fact, but it may be the most effective possible form of expression. Continuing with the example, assume that, during the week preceding my arm band wearing and charter burning, I had resigned my position as a member of the Denver city council. I resigned because of a dispute with the mayor over an increase in the salaries of city councilmen; I regarded the increases as a breach of campaign promises. Assume further that on the morning of my wordless performance the *Denver Post* carried a front-page story reporting that on that day I would appear at city hall to protest my dismay at the death of responsible city government in Denver. Under those circumstances the black arm bands and the charter burning might be more effective expression than any words I could speak.

Nevertheless, whatever the comparative potential for ambiguity between symbolic speech and pure speech, and whatever their comparative merits generally, the courts have not treated them the same. Indeed, in many symbolic-speech cases the main judicial task has been to determine to what extent pure speech and to what extent symbolic speech elements are present.[15]

When Is the Regulation Imposed?

There is a "when" issue that can have an important bearing on the weight of the burden that government must overcome. The focus of the "when" issue is not so much on when the First Amendment activity occurs as on when the government regulation occurs in relation to the First Amendment activity. The "when" issue is distinctive in one important respect. Most deviations from the general First Amendment approach result in lesser protections to the individual. Application of the "when" deviation actually increases the weight of the governmental burden and therefore the protection afforded the individual.

What, then, is this "when" issue? The label that it bears is "prior restraint." The underlying concept is that it is more harmful to First Amendment interests to prohibit speech, assembly, worship, or other protected activity from ever occurring in the first place than to impose punishments after it has occurred. Assume, for example, that a government prosecutor has reliable evidence that a particular individual is about to deliver a highly provocative—even incendiary—speech and that some public unrest may result. Or assume that the prosecutor's evidence is that a religious group plans to have a religious meeting sharply critical of Baptists in a place where pro-Baptist sentiment is very strong and that the police are not sure they can preserve order. In either of these situations, is the prosecutor entitled to a court order preventing the speech or the religious meeting from occurring?

Probably not. Almost certainly not. Prosecuting a speaker on account of the content of his speech can be accomplished only if the prosecutor satisfies a very heavy burden—by showing a strong governmental interest in punishing people for such a speech. But the government's burden is even heavier if, instead of prosecuting the speaker for what he said, it attempts to prevent him from making the speech at all. Sending the speaker to jail or branding him a criminal because of his speech will have a chilling effect on his willingness to make speeches in the future. It will have a similar effect on the willingness of others once they learn of his conviction. But punishment after the fact is not as detrimental to First Amendment activity as complete prevention of its ever occurring. Punishment after the fact at least permits the speech to be delivered, the meeting to be held. It is less inimical to the exercise of First Amendment interests, therefore, to permit the speaker, or the person who wants to hold a religious exercise, to run the risk of prosecution if he so elects than absolutely to prohibit his speaking or holding the meeting.

In its essence, prior restraint means the same thing as censorship. There is no catch phrase to describe the weight of the burden it imposes on government, but it is the heaviest burden known to constitutional law. The leading prior-restraint case is *Near v. Minnesota*.[16] The *Near* case involved a Minneapolis city ordinance whose effect was to require the publisher of a newspaper to submit certain materials to a governmental board for approval in advance of publication. It was the classic prior-restraint case: the publisher was required to submit his material *before* publication and as a condition to publication. The Supreme Court held the ordinance unconstitutional. A more recent example of this is the *Pentagon Papers Case*, in which the Court held unconstitutional the federal government's effort to prohibit the *Washington Post* and the *New York Times* from publishing excerpts of secret documents concerning the Vietnam War.[17]

If prior restraints carry the heaviest burden known to constitutional law, is it a burden that has ever been satisfied? There is one category of cases in which prior restraints are approved on a consistent basis. That category consists of censorship of movies that are allegedly obscene. Even with regard to movie censorship, the burden imposed on government is a heavy one; but movie censorship is distinct from other censorship in that it occurs on a fairly regular basis.[18] This is not true of pornography censorship generally. Government does not enjoy similar leeway with respect to pornographic books, for example.

Outside the context of movie censorship, prior restraints have been extremely rare. Their theoretical existence has been recognized by judicial dictum. The Supreme Court in *Near v. Minnesota*, for example, observed that "[T]he protection even as to previous restraint is not absolutely unlimited. But the limitation has been recognized only in exceptional cases."[19] The Court's opinion in *Near* also gave what has become a famous example of a prior restraint that might be sustained: prohibiting publication of the location of troop ships in wartime.

In fact, aside from movie censorship, no Supreme Court case has ever sustained a prior restraint. Lower federal courts have sustained at least two, both of which were accompanied by special circumstances. In *Marchetti v. United States,* the Court of Appeals for the District of Columbia enforced an employment agreement by a Central Intelligence Agency agent not to reveal certain kinds of secrets.[20] More recently, a Wisconsin federal district court, in *United States v. The Progressive*,[21] enjoined the publication of certain information concerning technology related to the hydrogen bomb. Aside from the highly sensitive substantive content of the material whose publication was prevented in those cases, each is distinctive in that there was a special legal basis for preventing publication.[22] In each there was a "plus" factor—some legal ground for restraining publication other than the sensitive nature of the material. In *Marchetti*, it was the contract that the agent entered into; the government was simply asking the courts to prevent the agent from breaking his contract not to reveal secrets acquired during his employment as a CIA agent. In the *Progressive* case, the plus factor was a congressional statute–the Atomic Energy Act–which prohibited the publication. Obviously, neither a statute nor a contract can override the Constitution; but in a close case where the material is highly sensitive, a plus factor such as a statute or a contract might make the difference.

The notable thing about these exceptions (movie censorship and the *Marchetti* and *Progressive* cases) is precisely that they are exceptions and that the exceptions are so few.

While most of the prior restraint cases have involved some form of media censorship, the doctrine reaches all across the First Amendment, including freedom of religion. Thus, any attempt by any governmental entity in the United States to prohibit the holding of religious services would be subjected to the intense constitutional searchlight accorded all prior restraints. For that reason, any such law would almost certainly be held unconstitutional.

What Is the Content of the Speech?

Critical examination of the content of the speech to determine whether it is worthy of constitutional protection would be largely inconsistent with the basic free-speech guarantee. The fundamental underpinning of the provision that government shall make no law abridging the freedom of speech is that it is no part of the business of government to decide whether the speech is worthwhile. That decision is for the speaker and for those who listen to him. Similarly, freedom of religion would be a hollow guarantee if the courts were to condition it on a searching, case-to-case inquiry into whether the particular religious belief was really worthwhile.

In the great majority of instances, therefore, the substantive content of First Amendment activity is irrelevant to whether the First Amendment protections will apply. There are nevertheless some categories of speech activity in which the applicable constitutional standard will depend on substantive content. Here are several examples.

Obscenity

The most noted example is obscenity. Obscenity, in my opinion, is the prime candidate for the insoluble constitutional dilemma. I am convinced that government must have some authority to control and prohibit pornographic material. I believe that this is an issue that strikes at the very roots of morality and culture. We spend enormous sums of money to rid ourselves of air pollution and water pollution. We have established a veritable army of state and federal employees whose only task is to improve the quality of our environment. If our physical environment is that important (and I believe that it is) then surely our intellectual and cultural environment—the environment in which our minds and our souls must exist—is at least equally important. It follows that government—both local and national—must be in the business of obscenity control.

It is an insufficient response that the matter is one of individual free choice. The person who prefers to avoid contact with obscenity may be able to diminish his contact, but he cannot avoid it. Moreover, conscientious parents have no more compelling objective than the optimum intellectual, cultural, spiritual, and emotional development of their children. Sizable portions of the family budget and parental time are expended for this purpose. More important than the technical training in special skills that results from these expenditures is that children derive from such opportunities an appreciation of things that stimulate the mind and the spirit. Certainly government has an interest in the welfare of its citizens. It is a proper function, therefore, for government to assist those parents whose objective is to help their children develop an appreciation for things of the mind and things of the soul. The reality is that parents cannot, and should not, exercise constant control over where their children are, what they see and do, and with whom they associate. It should lie within government's prerogative, therefore, to take some steps to control the environment in which its citizens live. The censors cannot be given unlimited power, however. Unlimited powers of censorship could lead—and on occasion have led—to banning everything from parts of the Bible to the great classics of literature.

In our country the problem of controlling obscenity has a constitutional dimension. Like nursery rhymes, like the scriptures, and like books that fall in that vexing gray area that some people would consider pornographic and some people would not, hard-core pornography typically involves speech, or at the very least some form of expression. Because speech and expression are constitutionally protected, the control of obscenity necessarily raises First Amendment issues.

The analytical framework for approaching obscenity cases can be stated fairly simply: obscenity, however defined, is outside the scope of First Amendment protection. The First Amendment protects free speech. Obscenity, even though it uses words or attempts to express something, falls outside the protection of the First Amendment. For First Amendment purposes, obscenity is not speech.

The test is easy enough to express. It is also easy enough to understand, at least in the abstract. The dilemma comes in its application. The key to its application is to define obscenity. Ideally, it should be defined broadly enough to provide an adequate tool for the control of pornography and yet specifically enough that obscenity laws will not be used, as they have in the past, as the censor's weapon against truly worthwhile literature and ideas. There is a tension between those two objectives. Breadth and specificity are necessarily opposites. The tension has led to great judicial difficulty as the courts have attempted to devise a standard that adequately accommodates the conflicting needs of the public for a standard that is sufficiently broad and the need of the individuals potentially affected by the law for a standard that is sufficiently precise and informative.

The Supreme Court held in *Miller v. California* that the basic responsibility for applying the constitutional standard is vested in the jury, subject to review by the courts in the event of serious misapplication of the relevant constitutional standard.[23] And what is that standard? The Court in *Miller* laid down three "basic guidelines for the trier of fact" (that is, the jury) in deciding what is "obscene" for First Amendment purposes. These three guidelines are: (1) "whether 'the average person, applying contemporary community standards' would find that the work, taken as a whole, appeals to the prurient interest"; (2) "whether the work depicts or describes, in a patently offensive way, sexual conduct specifically defined by the applicable state law"; and (3) "whether the work, taken as a whole, lacks serious literary, artistic, political, or scientific value."[24]

Those "guidelines," contained in a jury instruction read by a judge just prior to submitting the case to the jury, fall short of answering all questions that the jury may have concerning a particular movie, book, or photograph. In attempting to accommodate the conflict between the public's need for generality and the publisher's need for specificity, this test tilts toward generality. "Prurient interest" is determined according to "contemporary community standards." The community for these purposes is the local community within which the jury sits. The jury members—as residents of that community—are of course the best judges of what those community standards are. This necessarily means that the First Amendment may have one meaning in Panguitch, Utah, and another in Philadelphia, Pennsylvania; but as the Court observed in *Miller v. California,* "[T]he mere fact juries may reach different conclusions as to the same materials does not mean that constitutional rights are abridged."[25]

What about "private" obscenity involving no one but its consumer? The Court held in *Stanley v. Georgia* that "a state has no business telling a man, sitting alone in his own house, what books he may read or films he may watch."[26] In subsequent cases, however, the Court held (1) that the *Stanley* principle protecting private obscenity does not extend to commercial movies where the individual has a choice whether to pay his money and see the film and where those who choose not to see it are not offended, and (2) the *Stanley* holding does not invalidate government efforts to control the transportation of obscene material intended exclusively for private use.[27]

Fighting Words

Another example of speech that is excluded from First Amendment coverage is "fighting words." There have not been as many cases dealing with this exception as with the obscenity exception, but the core concept is the same: words that are reasonably calculated to start a fight are outside the range of First Amendment protection. Words of that kind are not "speech" for First Amendment purposes. In the leading case, *Chaplinisky v. New Hampshire*,[28] the Court upheld the conviction of a Jehovah's Witness who had called a policeman a "damned racketeer" and a "damned fascist." The words had in fact precipitated a fight in which Chaplinisky was involved. The Supreme Court's opinion observed:

> There are certain well-defined and narrowly limited classes of speech, the prevention and punishment of which have never been thought to raise any Constitutional problem. These include the lewd and obscene, the profane, libelous, and the insulting or "fighting" words—those which by their very utterance inflict injury or intend to incite immediate breach of peace. It has been well observed that such utterances are no essential part of any exposition of ideas, and are of such slight social value as a step to truth that any benefit may be derived from them is clearly outweighed by the social interest in order and morality.[29]

As demonstrated by the discussion of the *Times Libel* case, the Court has subsequently modified its statement that no constitutional protections are applicable to libelous words.

Commercial Speech

At one time, in the early 1970s, the Supreme Court stated that "commercial speech," like obscenity and fighting words, was also outside the protection of the First Amendment.[30] Commercial speech is speech that proposes some kind of a business transaction. It applies mostly to advertisements carried by commercial media such as newspapers, radio, television, and billboards. Today, it is clear that commercial speech does not fit in the same category as obscenity and fighting words. Commercial speech is entitled to some degree of First Amendment protection, though the degree of protection is less than that afforded to speech generally.[31] Commercial speech is speech for First Amendment purposes and courts will therefore balance the competing governmental and individual interests when government attempts to limit it. The scales will not be weighted as heavily on the side of the speaker, however, as they are in the case of noncommercial speech.[32] It is for this reason that commercial speech is another instance in which the applicable constitutional standard is diminished because of the substantive content of what is said.

Subversive Speech

There is a final category of cases that needs to be covered in this general review of constitutional principles dealing with free speech. It is a category that sometimes bears the label "subversive speech." Subversive-speech cases involve the problem of the speaker who advocates the overthrow of government—typically, violent overthrow of government. How does a constitutional system committed to free speech handle that kind of problem? On the one hand, it might be argued that subversive speech should be treated just like obscenity and fighting words—that is, as completely outside the protection of the First Amendment. After all, any government should have the right of self-preservation. The speaker who advocates violent overthrow of the government is attacking not only government as an organization, but also the Constitution itself, including the First Amendment on which he relies. On the other hand, one of the most important differences between our constitutional system of government and totalitarian governments is the very fact that our Constitution guarantees the right to be critical of government. Voltaire's famous statement is relevant: "I disagree with what you say but will defend to the death your right to say it." So also is John Milton's eloquent statement (quoted on page 85) to the effect that truth is able to withstand the onslaught of falsehood and that all truth needs in order to prevail is the opportunity to do battle with falsehood on equal footing. The necessary corollary is that our constitutional system is sufficiently sturdy to withstand the verbal onslaughts of those who advocate its overthrow.

As noted at the outset of this chapter, subversive-speech cases were the first free-speech cases to come before the Supreme Court, just after the First World War. Through the intervening half-century, the Court wrestled with the problem of the appropriate constitutional standard. Along the way the Court's decisions have produced the famous reference to "clear and present danger" and the equally famous dictum that freedom of speech does not include the right to shout "fire" in a crowded theater.[33] Both came from the pen of Justice Holmes.

The test that has evolved turns on the difference between, on the one hand, pure speech, and, on the other, speech advocating that the listener do something, that he engage in some kind of conduct. Assume, for example, that a member of the Communist party gives a speech to a large audience in which he advocates violent overthrow of the government. Even though he is advocating not only that government be overthrown but also that it be accomplished by violent means, the First Amendment will protect him so long as he advocates violent overthrow only as a matter of abstract theory—that is, that violent overthrow is a good idea. He loses his constitutional protection, however, when he advocates that his listeners do something in implementation of what he advocates. At that point, his advocacy crosses over the line between advocacy in the abstract, which is protected, and advocacy of conduct, which is not.

CHAPTER ELEVEN

The First Amendment: Freedom of the Press

What is freedom of the press? In the great majority of cases, freedom of the press means freedom-of-speech principles applied to the commercial media. Many of the free-speech cases and examples treated in Chapter 10 involved the news media. The most effective guarantee of a free press is afforded through the free-speech guarantees that everyone in this country enjoys.

There are some First Amendment issues, however, that have particular relevance to the news media. For example, the *Miami Herald* and *Red Lion* cases, discussed in the previous chapter, dealt with the issue of editorial freedom. Similarly, though the prior-restraint principle applies to all aspects of the First Amendment, the main beneficiaries of this principle have been the commercial media.

Another First Amendment issue having particular applicability to the press is whether there is a constitutionally secured newsman's privilege. What is a newsman's privilege? A hypothetical example will illustrate. Assume that a professional news reporter is conducting a special investigation into narcotics sales within his city. A drug pusher agrees to talk to the reporter only after he exacts a promise that the reporter will not disclose the pusher's identity. The resulting news story attracts widespread interest and attention and generally heightens the community's level of information and concern regarding the city's drug problems. Among those whose attention is attracted by the story, however, are law-enforcement officials. A grand jury subpoenas the reporter and attempts to compel him under oath to reveal the name of his informant and other details concerning narcotics traffic within the city. The newsman refuses to testify, basing his refusal on First Amendment grounds.

The issue is taken into court, where arguments are advanced on both sides. The newsman contends that the total law-enforcement effort is no worse off—and probably better off—if promises such as the one that he made to his informer are honored than if they are not honored.

If not for his promise to conceal the informer's identity, the newsman argues, the informer would never have told anything to anyone. Because of the promise, the police and the rest of the public at least have the substance of the story. Unless that kind of promise is protected by the First Amendment's free-press guarantee, newsmen's sources will dry up and everyone—law enforcement, the news media, and the public in general—will suffer.

In response, the government contends that this is not a legitimate free-press issue. No attempt is being made to control what the newspaper can print; indeed, the stories have already been printed. But this reporter has the name of a person who has information that could lead the police to the arrest and conviction of the major drug traffickers in the city. He should not be permitted to withhold that information, when every day more people are becoming addicted to drugs because of the activities of people whom the reporter's source could identify. Moreover, the reporter's assertion that he would not have obtained the information without his assurance of confidentiality is purely speculative. Absent such a promise, maybe the informer would have talked and maybe he would not have. The controlling fact is that this reporter has information that will lead the police to the arrest and conviction of the worst kind of criminals. He should be required to divulge that information.

In *Branzburg v. Hayes*, the Supreme Court held that freedom of the press does *not* include a newsman's privilege of confidentiality and that, on facts similar to our hypothetical, the reporter can be required to answer the grand jury's questions.[1] The Court reasoned:

> [W]e perceive no basis for holding that the public interest in law
> enforcement and in ensuring effective grand jury proceedings is
> insufficient to override the consequential, but uncertain, burden of news
> gathering that is said to result from insisting that reporters, like other
> citizens, respond to relevant questions put to them in the course of a
> valid grand jury investigation or criminal trial.[2]

News media people have complained that *Branzburg* and other cases in recent years have reflected a hostility toward the press. They have found particularly offensive decisions such as *Zurcher v. Stanford Daily*, which upheld the right of law enforcement officers who had obtained a search warrant for that purpose to search the files of the *Stanford Daily News*,[3] and *Gannett Co. v. De Pasquale*, which upheld a court order barring the public, including the press, from a pretrial hearing on the suppression of evidence.[4] Perhaps the greatest source of alarm in media circles in recent years was the Court's 1979 holding in *Herbert v. Lando*, generally characterized by the media as giving the courts the right to inquire into the newsman's "state of mind" at the time he prepared a news story.[5]

Do these decisions reflect a judicial hostility toward the press? Maybe so, maybe not. That kind of subjective speculation is not very productive. I believe that the real lesson to be learned from *Branzburg v. Hayes, Zurcher v. Stanford Daily, Gannett v. De Pasquale,* and *Herbert v. Lando* is a lesson for professional news-media people. The issues involved in all those cases were media issues—that is, they affected all forms of news media. In each of the cases the interests of all media were identical. This assured that one side of those issues, the media's side, would receive adequate press coverage. But what about the other side? A favorite phrase of media people is "the public's right to know." The public cannot really know unless it is fairly informed concerning both sides. For the great majority of Americans, access to both sides of important public issues can be gained only through the news media. A genuine concern for the "people's right to know," therefore, should translate into an equal concern for setting forth fairly and objectively the arguments on both sides.

This is a particularly acute problem in those instances where all of the media have a collective interest in one side of the issue. Asking the advocate to state his adversary's case as fairly as he states his own is asking a great deal, but I believe that it is an obligation of public trust that ought to be assumed by the media. Unless we hear the antimedia position from the media themselves most of us will not hear it at all. How have the media performed in informing the public concerning positions opposed to those of the media? There have been some exceptions but, in general, they have performed very much like advocates and not very much like the stewards of the public's right to know.

The reaction to *Herbert v. Lando* provides a good example. Some of the media gave a balanced view of both sides of the issue. But the overwhelming majority portrayed that decision as authorizing government to make general inquiry into the newsman's state of mind. For most American citizens, that characterization was the only available "report" of *Herbert v. Lando*. In fact, that characterization was substantially inaccurate. The case dealt with a narrow subissue of the *Times Libel* holding, discussed above. Recall that the *Times Libel* case established a defense in certain kinds of defamation cases: if the defamation suit is brought by either a public official or a public figure, then the defendant will be held liable only if his injury to a plaintiff's reputation was accompanied by actual malice—that is, if he knew that what he said was false or if he acted with reckless disregard for whether it was true or false. By a wide margin, the principal beneficiaries of this *Times Libel* rule are the professional news-media people, precisely because they are the most likely targets of defamation actions by public officials and public figures.

The only issue with which *Herbert v. Lando* dealt was the application of the *Times Libel* defense that is so beneficial to newsmen. It held, quite logically, that a newsman's state of mind at the time he prepared a story was relevant to the question of actual malice—that is, whether he was acting with knowledge of falsity or with reckless disregard for truth or falsity. What the news media should have told their readers, viewers, and listeners, therefore, is that the only time an inquiry into a newsman's state of mind is sanctioned is when the newsman himself, or the corporation for which he works, raises the *Times Libel* defense. It is only when the media defendant in a defamation action raises the *Times Libel* defense in its own interest, and thereby puts malice at issue, that inquiry can ever be made into the reporter's state of mind. Whether the *Times Libel* defense is raised lies exclusively within the newsperson's option. If inquiry into state of mind is objectionable, therefore, this can be avoided by declining to raise the defense to which it pertains.

Perhaps it is unrealistic to expect the media or anyone else to set forth objectively a position that they oppose. I submit, however, that the constitutionally guaranteed free press and the public's confidence in it would be greatly enhanced if the media would treat those media-nonmedia issues with at least the same degree of objectivity with which they approach public issues generally. On most public issues—arms control, right-to-work laws, foreign aid, for example—if one newspaper or television station takes one position, some other paper or station will take the other side. At the very least, there is the theoretical possibility that the media will take opposite sides. But in those few instances where all media have an institutional interest in the issue, fair exposition of both sides will occur only if the media assume a public-trust responsibility. This does not mean that they must compromise their views, which will naturally favor their own self-interest, but they should remain scrupulously objective in reporting the facts and characterizing the issues. They need not advocate the holding in *Herbert v. Lando*, for example, as being in the public interest, but they should make certain that the public has access to the view that it is in the public interest. This could be done by an objective analysis of both sides of the issue. Probably even more effective would be to invite an able advocate of the nonpress view to express that view.

Over the long run, the beneficiaries of such an approach will include not only the public, but also the media themselves. The public would gain greater trust and respect for the media if they objectively report the facts of the issues, especially those in which they have vested interests.

CHAPTER TWELVE

The First Amendment: Freedom to Assemble and Petition the Government

The First Amendment expressly guarantees the right of the people "to assemble, and to petition the Government for a redress of grievances." The two guarantees need not be coupled in order to bring either into play. Thus, the right of assembly is not conditioned on any objective to petition government.

Freedom of assembly is another freedom-of-expression right. Its First Amendment companion, on which it depends for its effectiveness, is the free-speech guarantee. It also raises some problems of its own. The right to petition government, by contrast, is so intimately tied to free speech that it can properly be considered a subset of free speech. What are the issues with which freedom of assembly is concerned? Under its banner two bodies of constitutional rules have developed.

The Limit of the Freedom to Assemble

Assume that a group has gathered on a street corner where an ardent antiunionist is excoriating organized labor, accusing unions of being the main causes of inflation, unemployment, and racial bigotry. Most of his audience is composed of staunch union members, whose passions are aroused by the speech. Some of them begin to yell back at him. The prevailing mood is one of anger and tension, and it is reasonable to assume that the circumstances could deteriorate to something more serious than an exchange of words. Under these conditions, can the police—consistent with the First Amendment's guarantee of free assembly—stop the speaker and disperse the audience? The answer is probably yes. In each case, what is required is a delicate and often difficult balancing of the competing interests: those of government in maintaining order, and those of the individual in pursuing his constitutionally based freedom of assembly. The performance of the policeman's duties in such a case requires that he have a basic knowledge of constitutional law.

The approach that the courts have taken to this problem is illustrated by two cases, *Feiner v. New York* and *Edwards v. South Carolina.*[1] Feiner's speech occurred on a public street in Syracuse, New York. The evil against which he protested was racial discrimination, and he urged blacks to stand up and fight for their rights. The evidence indicated that the crowd gathered around him had begun pushing, milling, and shoving. There was also evidence that the crowd had begun to spill over into the street. At least one member of the crowd told the police that if they did not stop the speaker, he would. The Supreme Court held that, under those circumstances, the police were justified in stopping the speech and dispersing the crowd after the speech had gone on for about thirty minutes.

Contrast *Feiner* with *Edwards v. South Carolina.* In the *Edwards* case, a group of students assembled at a Baptist church. From there they marched to the statehouse grounds, where they sang songs and chanted. There were no overt signs of unrest. The Supreme Court held that, under those conditions, the arrest of the students violated their constitutionally guaranteed right of assembly. The opinion observes:

> This, therefore, was a far cry from the situation in *Feiner v. New York,* where two policemen were faced with a crowd which was "pushing, shoving and milling around," where at least one member of the crowd "threatened violence if the police did not act," where "the crowd was pressing closer around petitioner and the officer," and where "the speaker passes the bounds of argument or persuasion and undertakes incitement to riot."[2]

The facts of these two cases also illustrate the dilemma of the "hostile audience," or the "heckler's veto." It appears that one of the circumstances justifying the arrest in *Feiner* was the threat by a single member of Feiner's audience that if the police did not stop Feiner from speaking, the listener would. The absence of this kind of audience hostility was also apparently relevant in *Edwards.* It is a bit anomalous that, in the face of the constitutional guarantee of freedom of assembly, the wishes of a heckler who wants to stop the speech should be allowed to prevail over those of the speaker—and perhaps many other members of the audience—who want it to continue. In a sense, perhaps, the heckler is also expressing a point of view. But to the extent that he does so, he expresses it in a manner more analogous to symbolic speech than pure speech, and the effect of his actions may be to foreclose expression by other people. In any event, anomalous or not, the heckler's veto appears to be a part of our current constitutional fabric.

Privacy and the Freedom to Assemble

The First Amendment's guarantee of freedom of assembly has been the basis for another, quite distinct right, characterized by the Court as the right of privacy. "Privacy" as a constitutional-law term has come to represent several different values. The word "privacy" does not appear anywhere in the Constitution, though Justice Douglas pointed out in *Griswold v. Connecticut* that several parts of the Constitution attempt to protect the individual's interest in privacy.[3] Probably the most obvious is the Fourth Amendment, which protects the privacy of the home from unwanted and unwarranted police intrusion. Other examples are the Third Amendment's prohibition against the quartering of troops in private homes and the Fifth Amendment's privilege against self-incrimination, which entitles the individual to keep to himself certain types of information that he chooses not to disclose.

The right of privacy that is rooted in freedom of assembly protects a different value than those embraced by the Third, Fourth, or Fifth amendments. The leading case is *NAACP v. Alabama*, which held unconstitutional an attempt by the state of Alabama to force the local chapter of the NAACP to reveal its membership list.[4] The Supreme Court reasoned that, if the membership in the NAACP were generally known, association members might be deprived of economic, social, and other benefits. This in turn would have a chilling effect on their constitutionally guaranteed right to assemble together as members of the NAACP.

The right of privacy that is rooted in freedom of assembly, therefore, can be characterized as the right to belong to an organization of one's choosing, and to have the fact of that membership revealed only to those to whom the individual chooses to reveal it. Its linkage to freedom of assembly is that general knowledge of membership in certain organizations might discourage such membership and therefore impede the assembly of the members of the organization for a common purpose.

This right of privacy—the right to have one's membership in organizations of his choice remain a secret—prohibits any kind of governmental inquiry into organizational memberships except where there is a compelling governmental interest. It not only protects the sanctity of membership lists but also guarantees against governmental requirements that a person disclose all organizations to which he belongs, or that he disclose whether he belongs to a particular organization. The rule is essentially the same whether the disclosure requirements exist in connection with applications for employment, applications for admission to the state bar, or any other governmental disclosure requirement. This right of privacy extends to all types of organizations—except one.

The one exception is membership in a subversive organization. Government can constitutionally inquire, for example, whether an applicant for employment or admission into a licensed profession belongs or has belonged to the Communist party. Thus, the government's interest in preventing subversive persons form entering certain kinds of governmental employment or obtaining membership in certain professions outweighs the individual's interest in assembling with others who share his views. This does not mean that in all cases the benefit the person desires will necessarily be denied. It means only that government can monitor those sensitive avenues to which subversives may have access and that governmental inquiry into the applicant's subversive association is therefore warranted.

The rule is the same with respect to inquiries by legislative investigating bodies. An investigative committee of Congress or a state legislature may constitutionally subpoena a witness and compel him to disclose his affiliations with the Communist party.[5] Such a committee may not, however, compel a nonsubversive organization to disclose its membership lists.[6] Neither may it compel an individual to reveal all organizations to which he belongs or to state whether he belongs to a particular, nonsubversive organization.

CHAPTER THIRTEEN
The First Amendment: Freedom of Religion

The First Amendment contains two separate guarantees dealing with religion. These guarantees are commonly referred to as the establishment clause and the free-exercise clause. The pertinent language is: "Congress shall make no law respecting an establishment of religion, or prohibiting the free exercise thereof."

The underlying concepts of the two religion guarantees are quite different. The free-exercise clause is analogous to other First Amendment provisions; its function is to secure free choice in religious matters against governmental intrusions. Accordingly, free-exercise problems arise in the standard First Amendment individual-rights context: balancing governmental interests against individual interests, with the scales being weighted in favor of the individual.

The establishment clause has a different thrust. Unlike any other First Amendment provision, the establishment clause deals with structural matters, specifically the relationships between government and religious institutions or religious movements. The metaphor that is frequently used to characterize the establishment-clause function is a wall that theoretically separates church and state. Another term frequently used in connection with the establishment clause is neutrality: in the struggle between believers and nonbelievers, and among the various sects of believers for the hearts and minds of individual human beings, government must remain neutral. It must neither favor nor disfavor religion or irreligion. Neither may it favor any particular church or religious organization over another.

Discussed in Part I is the impact that constitutional provisions dealing with structure can have on individual rights. Similarly, keeping government out of the business of favoring or disfavoring any religious group or view can effectively guarantee individual freedom of religious choice. For this reason, though they proceed from quite different premises, the objectives of the establishment and free-exercise clauses may coalesce in certain cases. This was true, for example, in the prayer cases and the released-time cases, both of which will be discussed below. In other instances, the objectives of the two clauses cut in opposite directions. Indeed, in *McDaniel v. Paty*, discussed below, the Supreme Court was called upon to resolve a conflict between the objectives of the establishment and free-exercise clauses.[1]

We will examine cases dealing with both areas: the establishment of religion, and the free exercise thereof. The establishment clause will be considered first.

The Establishment Clause

The prayer decisions of the early 1960s probably received more public attention and notoriety than any other religion case in this nation's history. The first of these cases, *Engel v. Vitale*, is commonly referred to as the "Regents' prayer" case.[2] The Board of Regents of the state of New York composed a prayer to be recited by children in public schools each day as part of the official ceremony marking the beginning of school. The prayer the regents had composed was: "Almighty God, we acknowledge our dependence upon Thee, and we beg Thy blessings upon us, our parents, our teachers and our Country."[3] The Supreme Court's opinion stated:

> ... [W]e think that the constitutional prohibition against laws respecting an establishment of religion must at least mean that in this country it is no part of the business of government to compose official prayers for any group of the American people to recite as a part of a religious program carried on by government.[4]

The next year, 1963, the Court invalidated two practices employed by the states of Pennsylvania and Maryland as part of their official school ceremonies. In *School District of Abington Township, Pa. v. Schempp*, the invalidated practice was the reading of a passage from the Bible, while in *Murray v. Curlett*, the practice held unconstitutional was the recital of the Lord's Prayer.[5] There was a difference between these cases and *Engel v. Vitale*. The Regents' prayer had been composed by government officials and was largely devoid of real religious content except for acknowledgment of the existence of a Supreme Being. The prayers at issue a year later were Christian in origin and in content.

The Court decided the prayer cases under the establishment clause. The rationale was that by incorporating a concededly religious practice as an official part of its daily school ceremony, government had officially identified itself on behalf of religion. In the *Murray v. Curlett* case it had not only identified itself on behalf of religion, but a particular religion: Christianity.

In fact, we are surrounded by examples of official governmental recognition and approval of a belief in God. Did the prayer decisions prevent the United States Treasury Department from stamping "In God We Trust" on American coins? If it is unconstitutional to recite the Lord's Prayer as part of the official school ceremony, what about reciting that part of the Declaration of Independence that asserts that all men "are endowed by their Creator with certain unalienable Rights"? What about the Pledge of Allegiance, "one nation, under God"? Public schools are not the only governmental entities that employ a formal beginning for the day's activities. At the beginning of each day of oral argument before the United States Supreme Court, the marshal chants a formal phrase that ends with the words, "God save the United States and this honorable Court." (Legend has it that on one occasion the marshal slipped: "God save the United States *from* this honorable Court.")

The Court attempted to clarify that some practices do not come under the constitutional ban. The examples included the use of the phrase "So help me God" in the official oath of office, recital of the Declaration of Independence, the singing of the national anthem, and the Supreme Court's opening ceremony. What is less clear is how the dividing lines are to be drawn. Will the coins have to be reminted? Is all official reference to "Divine Providence" foreclosed? Probably not, but the Court's decision failed to provide the kind of clear guidelines that would seem to be required by its entry into an area of such national sensitivity. On the verbal level, the distinction is between "unquestioned religious exercises" and "patriotic or ceremonial" observances. These are not the kind of word distinctions that give much guidance. We know little more than that official prayers and Bible reading are on the forbidden side of the line but that the national anthem and the Pledge of Allegiance are not.

In retrospect, it was probably a mistake for the Supreme Court to decide the prayer cases. (With some exceptions, the Court has discretion to accept or decline review of a case brought before it; it reviews on the merits less than 3 percent of the cases it is asked to review.) The decisions have been widely misunderstood and deeply resented. They are also impossible to enforce; it is a bit unseemly (not to mention expensive) to station federal marshals in public classrooms to make sure that no one prays. The most serious consequence—and the most unfortunate—was the rather widespread public perception at the time the prayer decisions were announced that they disclosed a Supreme Court attitude of hostility toward religion.

Regardless of whether the Court should have decided the prayer cases, however, a strong case can be made that its holdings—which were limited to official prayers and Bible reading as part of public school ceremonies—are constitutionally sound. Consider the competing interests. To the young atheist or agnostic or Jew—and also to his parents—the recital of the Regents' prayer or the Lord's Prayer presents a real dilemma. Moreover, the dilemma heightens in direct proportion to the depth of the individual's belief. If he recites the prayer he makes a mockery of his belief. If he does not, he may become the object of mockery by his classmates. At the very least they will consider him a bit weird; the cruelty of that consequence need not be explained to anyone who has had experience with elementary-school social relations.

The Maryland scheme permitted the nonbeliever or non-Christian to remove himself from the classroom during the recital, but if anything this only exacerbates his classmates' impression that he is "different" and increases his vulnerability to questions or ridicule. At this cost to the individual, what does the government gain by requiring the recital of a written prayer as part of its opening ceremony? Increase in moral fiber among the members of its student body? Perhaps, but I doubt it. In most cases the recital is a sterile exercise, a rote exercise, a group exercise totally lacking in individuality, spontaneity, or real expression of conviction. To the extent that any students pay attention to the words, some will believe them, some will find them irrelevant, and to some they will be positively offensive. All of this comes about because of a requirement imposed by *government.* This is the very kind of thing the First Amendment was intended to protect against.

The prayer decisions are generally perceived by persons with strong religious beliefs as antagonistic to their interests. This perception is as ironic as it is widespread. To the extent the prayer decisions caused harm, it was symbolic harm only. They stand as a shield against interests that are far more important. The real danger to religious interests posed by what happens in schools is not that the school day will not begin with prayer. It is rather that the schools will attempt through their curricula to inculcate notions that are opposed to the religious values held by some students—and their parents. Included are such issues as abortion, population control, and even atheism. On the question of whether public schools can require such courses, or even offer them (so that individual students like the atheist or the Jew in the prayer cases must remove themselves if they choose not to participate), the prayer cases will be the strongest precedents supporting the position of those who oppose such offerings on religious grounds. In both settings, there is an intrusion on individual religious belief. It is an intrusion that comes about because of official governmental policy and action.

There is a distinction between school prayer and proabortion instruction. The prayer recitation had no curricular content. It was at least arguable that the school officials had not adopted it because of their perception concerning its importance to what their students should learn. This is an important distinction, but it has two edges. Matters that are part of the curriculum have far greater potential for adverse impact on the free religious exercise of the individual and his parents than do mere formal exercises at the beginning of the school day.

In other establishment-clause cases the Supreme Court has held unconstitutional a Maryland statute prohibiting atheists from being candidates for public office.[6] In the released-time cases, *McCollum v. Board of Education* and *Zorach v. Clauson*, the validity of released-time programs was upheld when the religious instruction was held on church-owned property located near the school (as in *Zorach*), but released-time programs held on school property (as in *McCollum*) were declared unconstitutional.[7] The *Zorach* opinion is also of interest because it contains probably the strongest assertion of the linkage—as opposed to a wall of separation—between religious values and American values. The Court in *Zorach* stated:

> We are a religious people whose institutions presuppose a Supreme Being. We guarantee the freedom to worship as one chooses. We make room for as wide a variety of beliefs and creeds as the spiritual needs of man deem necessary. We sponsor an attitude on the part of government that shows no partiality to any one group and that lets each flourish according to the zeal of its adherents and the appeal of its dogma.[8]

In recent years the main focus of the establishment clause has been on the constitutionality of governmental aid to parochial schools. The general trend has been away from the constitutionality of such programs. At the center of this trend had been the development of a three-part test that must be satisfied by any extension of government aid to a church-sponsored school. The three requirements are: (1) the assistance must have a secular purpose; (2) its primary effect must neither enhance nor inhibit any religious interest; and (3) there must be an absence of entanglement between the government that grants the aid and the religious body that benefits from it.

The first requirement seldom poses any problem. The purpose for most parochial-aid programs is not to pour money into the coffers of the sponsoring church, but, rather, to assist the state in discharging its obligation to educate its school-age children. It is much more economical for the state to provide some textbooks and other assistance for children who are educated by a church than to bear the entire educational burden for these children. Government is not being generous; it is being practical.

The second requirement—primary effect—raises a higher hurdle. The effects of government aid to church schools are both secular and sectarian. One effect is to keep church schools in business, which has a substantial beneficial effect on government. When a church school fails, the state schools must absorb the students. Equally obvious is the benefit to the sponsoring church. To whatever extent money is available from nonchurch funds to defray education costs, church funds can be used for other purposes.

There is an interesting interaction between the second and third requirements. The most effective way to assure that the primary effect of the government aid is not to aid the religion, but only the education process, would be to have government inspectors periodically check to assure that government monies are not being used for religious purposes. Government inspections, however, would clearly run afoul of the third requirement that there be no entanglement between church and state.

The feature of this three-part test making compliance so difficult is that, if any single part is not satisfied, the governmental assistance will be held unconstitutional. Some of the forms of governmental aid that have survived constitutional scrutiny are free bus transportation for both public and parochial students, nondenominational textbooks, and government aid for school buildings at the higher educational level. Among the types of assistance that have been held unconstitutional are teachers' salaries, tuition payments or rebates, salaries of counselors and auxiliary personnel, teaching equipment, and supplies. The Supreme Court has given some indication that a relationship exists between the age of the students in the school that receives the aid and the likelihood that the grant will be upheld. The theory is that, since older students are less susceptible to religious indoctrination and influence, there is a correspondingly lesser probability that in fact the use of taxpayer funds will result in advancing church interests.

Historians differ as to what the Founding Fathers intended the establishment clause to accomplish. At least one historian has argued that the Founding Fathers intended to prevent any official acts of government that assisted organized religious groups in any way.[9] This absolutist view of the establishment clause has never been adopted. If it ever were, it would work some rather substantial changes not only in Supreme Court precedents but also in practices common to the American experience. It would not only interdict all released-time religious instruction programs and all federal aid to parochial schools, but it would also make unconstitutional all exemptions of church-owned property from property taxes and the income-tax deduction for contributions made to churches. These in turn would have an enormous impact on the ability of churches to finance their activities, including many significant social, educational, and welfare services that benefit not just their members, but also people in general.

The Free-Exercise Clause

In some ways the free-exercise-of-religion guarantee bears closer marks of kinship to the free-expression provisions of the First Amendment than to its sister religion clause. Like the speech, press, and assembly guarantees, the free-exercise-of-religion clause deals directly with the protection of individual liberties, whereas the establishment clause is a structural provision, regulating institutional relationships between church and state.

Moreover, speech and assembly are central to most religious activity. Consider some of the formal religious practices, for example: worship services, prayer circles, recitation of the Catholic mass, Sunday-school classes, missionary proselyting. All involve some form of speech or assembly or a combination of the two. Consider also the more profound religious experiences, those quiet moments when the human soul achieves a complete sense of communion with God and satisfaction with self. These also involve expression. Words may or may not be involved, but it is the highest, the most refined, and the most satisfying form of expression that mortal beings can experience.

Not many free-exercise cases have reached the Supreme Court. Given the close relationship between free exercise of religion and the First Amendment's expression guarantees, it should be no surprise that almost all of them have involved mixed questions of free speech and free exercise. We will review briefly some of the Supreme Court's more important free-exercise cases.

One of the most eloquent opinions came out of the flag salute case, *West Virginia State Board of Education v. Barnette.*[10] The Barnette family members were Jehovah's Witnesses. They contended that the requirement of the West Virginia Board of Education that all children participate in school flag salute ceremonies violated their free-exercise rights by requiring them to profess an allegiance other than to God. The Supreme Court agreed, though the opinion rests as much on free-speech as on free-exercise considerations. Justice Jackson's opinion for the Court states:

> If there is any fixed star in our constitutional constellation, it is that no official, high or petty, can prescribe what shall be orthodox in politics, nationalism, religion, or other matters of opinion or force citizens to confess by word or act their faith therein. If there are any circumstances which permit an exception, they do not now occur to us.[11]

Twenty-nine years later the Court relied on *West Virginia v. Barnette* as precedent for its holding in the Amish school children's case, *Wisconsin v. Yoder.*[12] Wisconsin law required formal school attendance for all children through the age of sixteen. Members of the Amish faith were willing to have their children receive formal schooling through the eighth grade. Beyond the eighth grade, however, the Amish believed as a matter of religious principle that education was a prerogative of the family and that it should concentrate on Amish values, many of which were derogated rather than enhanced by courses at the high-school level. The Supreme Court upheld the First Amendment right of the parents to educate their children beyond the eighth grade in their own way where their objective was rooted in religious belief.

What if government has not required the individual to act contrary to his religious belief, as in the *Barnette* and *Yoder* cases, but has conditioned the availability of certain privileges or benefits on conduct that the individual finds offensive for religious reasons? The state of North Carolina refused to grant unemployment compensation to any person who would not accept available employment. One applicant for unemployment compensation, Adell Sherbert, was refused because she was unwilling to accept employment in a textile mill that required Saturday work. Saturday work would have involved a breach of her religious belief, since she was a member of the Seventh-Day Adventist Church. The Supreme Court held in *Sherbert v. Verner* that under the circumstances of that case the First Amendment required North Carolina to pay Sherbert unemployment compensation.[13] North Carolina was under no constitutional obligation to pay unemployment compensation benefits to anyone; but, having made the decision to assist unemployed persons, the state could not exclude some people solely because of their religious beliefs.

Contrast with *Sherbert v. Verner* the holding two years earlier in *Braunfeld v. Brown*, in which the Court upheld the constitutionality of state-imposed Sunday-closing laws against the argument by orthodox Jewish merchants that they were forced to close on Sundays, whereas their Sabbath was the preceding day.[14] In neither *Sherbert* nor *Braunfeld* did the law require the person to break his Sabbath; in both cases the law simply made Sabbath observance more expensive. Yet Sherbert won her case, and Braunfeld lost his. How can the two holdings be reconciled? Or can they? Probably the best explanation is that the option into which Mr. Braunfeld was forced by the Sunday-closing laws involved only one day of profits out of six allowed by law. He was not completely precluded from his livelihood. For Adell Sherbert, by contrast, the unemployment benefits were her only income source.

The Supreme Court did not attempt to harmonize its *Braunfeld* and *Sherbert* cases on this or any other basis. If this is the reconciling feature, however, it illustrates well the approach that the Court takes in constitutionally guaranteed individual-liberty cases: balancing governmental interests against individual interests. Since Sherbert's entire income source depended on her willingness to compromise her religious belief, her side of the balance scale was more weighty than was Braunfeld's, who had only a part of his income at stake.

The Sunday closing cases illustrate the tension that sometimes exists between establishment clause and free-exercise clause objectives. In an effort to provide a uniform day of rest, the states that adopted Sunday-closing laws chose the day that is the Sabbath of most churches. Free exercise for adherents of the Sunday-Sabbath religions was thereby facilitated. In the process, however, the cost of those who observe the Sabbath on Saturday was increased. This therefore involved the state in favoring one religious group over another, the very kind of thing that cuts against establishment-clause objectives.

An even more poignant example of the potential tension between the two religion clauses is provided by *McDaniel v. Paty*, which held unconstitutional a Tennessee law disqualifying ministers or other professional religious clerics from serving in the state legislature.[15] The constitutional ground for the holding was the free-exercise clause. The choice forced on Reverend McDaniel by the state of Tennessee was at least roughly analogous to *Sherbert v. Verner*. Important benefits—official public service and office—were available to him only if he was willing to forego his chosen profession, the religious ministry. The chilling effect on his free exercise of religion was obvious. And yet it is clear that this Tennessee law—similar to others adopted by many states during the early days of our country—was solidly grounded on objectives that are consistent with the establishment clause. Its purpose was to preserve the separateness of church interests and governmental interests by insulating from government positions those whose church and state interests might conflict. The reason that free-exercise considerations prevailed in *McDaniel* is that the Court imposed a pre-merits weighting in its favor (and therefore in favor of McDaniel). The Court held that the state law must fall because Tennessee had not demonstrated that its existence was necessary to its purported objective. The fact that the state had the burden of making such a showing is a clear example of pre-merits weighting.

In individual cases, the free exercise clause has benefitted the Jehovah's Witnesses, the Seventh-Day Adventists, and McDaniel, a Baptist minister. There are other people whose interests have been impeded by the free-exercise clause or the establishment clause. Individual citizens have been disappointed at individual decisions, the prayer cases probably being the prime example. But far more important than the impact of any given decision is the total combined effect of the religion clauses. Basically, John Milton was right. Truth needs no special preference, no head start, in order to prevail. All that it needs is a fair opportunity to be fairly considered. This is also true of religious truth, which needs no more than a fair opportunity to present itself in the marketplace of ideas. There is no law anywhere in the world that gives as effective an assurance of that kind of opportunity as does the guarantee in the First Amendment of the United States Constitution that government "shall make no law respecting an establishment of religion, or prohibiting the free exercise thereof."

CHAPTER FOURTEEN
The Fourteenth Amendment:
Equal Protection of the Laws

A Perspective on the Fourteenth Amendment

Probably the most enduring effect of the Civil War on our nation was the adoption of three amendments to the Constitution: the Thirteenth, Fourteenth, and Fifteenth. The Thirteenth and Fifteenth amendments deal with rather specific issues. The Thirteenth made slavery and involuntary servitude unlawful; it was considered necessary because of doubts about the constitutional authority for President Lincoln's Emancipation Proclamation. The Fifteenth prohibited denial of a man's right to vote on account of race, color, or previous condition of servitude.

It is the Fourteenth Amendment, however, that constitutes the great constitutional legacy of the Civil War. Reasonable persons may disagree on the extent to which its effects have been good or bad. But there can be no disagreement on one proposition: of all the amendments to the Constitution since 1791, one stands alone in importance. It is the Fourteenth. Among all amendments, it is rivaled only by the First.

Why is the Fourteenth Amendment so important? Because of two provisions in the first of its five sections. One, the due-process clause, prohibits any state from depriving any person of life, liberty, or property without due process of law, applying to the states what the Fifth Amendment had applied to the federal government. The other, the equal-protection clause, assures that no state shall deny any person equal protection of the laws.

The Fourteenth Amendment's first section contains two other substantive provisions that attracted significant attention at the time of the amendment's adoption. Today they are largely of historical interest. One of these is the amendment's first sentence, which made citizens of the newly freed slaves, thereby overruling the Supreme Court's decision in *Dred Scott v. Sandford*.[1] The other is the provision that no state shall abridge the privileges or immunities of citizens of the United States.

Many contemporary students of the Fourteenth Amendment thought that the privileges-or-immunities clause would be the most important part of the Fourteenth Amendment. It was reduced to relative obscurity, however, by the historic *Slaughter-House Cases,* discussed in Chapter 15.

One of the most important effects of the Fourteenth Amendment was that it made most of the Bill of Rights applicable to the individual states. Prior to the adoption of the Fourteenth Amendment, the Bill of Rights applied only to the federal government. This means, for example, that President Martin Van Buren's statement in 1840 to Mormon church leader Joseph Smith that "your cause is just but I can do nothing for you" was technically correct. The statement was made in response to complaints by persecuted Mormons that officials of the state of Missouri had violated religious freedoms. At that time, however, no federal law had been violated. Until the Fourteenth Amendment became part of the Constitution, the freedom-of-religion guarantees of the First Amendment could exercise no control over actions of the state of Missouri.

This chapter, along with the next two, discusses the Fourteenth Amendment. This chapter treats the equal-protection clause and Chapter 15 the due-process clause. Chapter 16 examines some of the ramifications of the "state action" doctrine, the limitation on the Fourteenth Amendment's substantive provisions to those cases where the *state* has acted—that is, where the state, as opposed to nongovernmental private entities, has effected the deprivation of due process or the denial of equal protection.

The Equal-Protection Clause

The Fourteenth Amendment is the only part of the Constitution that contains the word "equal" or any of its derivatives, or that deals with the concept of equality. "That all men are created equal" was one of those self-evident truths asserted by Jefferson in the Declaration of Independence. But equality was not a value that found its way into the Constitution until after the Civil War.

The language of the equal-protection clause is: "No State shall . . . deny to any person within its jurisdiction the equal protection of the laws." This is one constitutional provision whose history leaves little doubt as to the founders' intent. It was concerned with racial equality. Indeed, in the *Slaughter-House Cases,* discussed in the next chapter, the Supreme Court stated that:

> We doubt very much whether any action of a State not directed by way
> of discrimination against the negroes as a class, or on account of their

race, will ever come within the [equal protection clause]. It is so clearly a provision for that race and that emergency, that a strong case would be necessary for its application to any other.[2]

The *Slaughter-House Cases* were decided just five years after adoption of the Fourteenth Amendment, and the majority opinion in those cases observed that its history was "fresh within the memory of us all."[3]

The elimination of racial discrimination by government has in fact been, and continues to be, the principal focus of the equal-protection clause. It is also clear, however, that—particularly since the late 1960s— the equal-protection clause has had enormous impact outside the realm of racial equality.

The first principles of equal protection of the law can be fairly simply stated. The constitutional guarantee of equal protection consists of one general rule and two exceptions to that general rule. We will consider the general rule first and then the exceptions.

The General Rule: Reasonable Basis

Essential to an understanding of the general rule, and of equal protection generally, are these controlling realities: (1) the equal-protection clause limits what government can do, and (2) most things that the government does affect different people in different ways because some people are treated more favorably than others. Equal-protection problems are potentially raised by this disparity in treatment.

This second point warrants brief amplification. At the very heart of lawmaking is linedrawing, or classification. When lines are drawn, or classifications established, some people are usually treated differently than other people. Necessarily, therefore, any government exercise in lawmaking has the potential of raising an equal-protection issue. Two important conclusions follow. First, application of an absolutist standard favoring the individual in the equal-protection area would invalidate most legislation. And an absolutist standard in favor of government would read the equal-protection clause out of the Constitution. Obviously, therefore, some sort of balancing standard is applied to equal-protection issues. The second conclusion, closely related to the first, is that weighting to be assigned to equal-protection balancing is extremely important, especially in light of the potential application of the equal-protection clause to almost every state law.

The general rule in equal-protection cases weights the balance scales in favor of the government. The rule is that government is free to make distinctions—to draw lines, to treat people differently—so long as the distinction bears some reasonable relationship to a legitimate governmental objective.

This rule is commonly referred to as the "reasonable basis" test. It is also called the "rational basis" test, and it accords a large degree of deference to government. So long as a state acts to achieve one of its authorized objectives, and so long as there is some reasonable linkage between what it has done and the achievement of that objective, the law will be upheld. The possibility that the objective might not be achieved by what the state has done, or that the state might have achieved its objective in another way that a court or someone else thinks is better, is beside the point. So long as there is some reasonable (or rational) relationship between what government has done and the achievement of a proper governmental objective, the law will be upheld, at least against an equal-protection challenge.

This general rule can be illustrated by reviewing the facts of an actual case (and by once again illustrating the concept with some circles). The case is *Massachusetts Board of Retirement v. Murgia.*[4] The Massachusetts Board of Retirement adopted a rule that all members of the uniformed police force must retire at age fifty. Mr. Murgia, a member of the Massachusetts uniformed police who had reached that age, challenged the rule on equal-protection grounds. At the trial, the state presented undisputed evidence that there is a general relationship between aging and decreased physical ability and that the stressful duties of state uniformed police justify an early mandatory retirement age. Equally undisputed was Murgia's evidence: whatever may be the case with most people, he did not fit the general pattern. His reflexes and all of his physical abilities were just as good or better than those of much younger men. For him, therefore, the fact that he had passed age fifty was irrelevant to the only real issue: his physical adequacy to perform the tasks of a uniformed policeman.

Murgia's evidence may support the position that Massachusetts was making a mistake by retiring a qualified policeman. But policy misjudgment is not tantamount to unconstitutionality. What was Mr. Murgia's equal-protection argument? An understanding of the answer to that question can be aided by considering the two diagrams on the facing page.

The circle on the left represents all members of the Massachusetts uniformed police. That same circle is the larger circle on the right, which also shows that within the larger group there is a smaller group representing those who lack the physical abilities to perform adequately the duties of uniformed policemen. Murgia's equal-protection argument can be paraphrased as follows: "The Massachusetts Board of Retirement's objective is to take out of the ranks of the police force those persons who are physically unable to perform effectively. Those persons are represented by the smaller circle. This is a perfectly legitimate objective that raises no constitutional issue. But the undisputed evidence

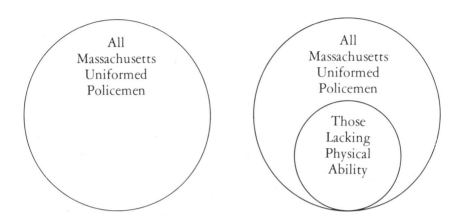

shows that I don't fit in that target group of unqualified persons. I am not in the smaller circle. Persons in my class—within the part of the larger circle that is not covered by the smaller—pose no problem to the efficient operation of the uniformed police; there is no proper basis for the state to dismiss anyone in this class. What the state has attempted to do here is to dismiss some persons in my class—policemen who are physically able—but not all. I am physically qualified; other policemen under fifty years of age are qualified. I have been dismissed; they have not. Massachusetts may discontinue the physically unqualified, but I am not one of them, and the state does not even contend that I am. This kind of discrimination denies me equal protection of the laws."

Murgia's argument seems airtight. Yet the Supreme Court ruled against him. How could this be, if equal protection of the laws means anything at all? Understanding the answer to that question is the key to understanding the reasonable-basis standard, which is the general rule governing equal-protection cases.

It is true that Murgia was qualified—as qualified as many younger members of the police force who were still employed. But Massachusetts or any other state has to have some means of distinguishing those who are qualified from those who are not. There are several means by which this could reasonably be accomplished. One would be to base retirement on individualized physical examinations of each policeman conducted each year or on some other periodic basis. That would be a reasonable procedure, and it would save Murgia. But it is not the only reasonable procedure. Periodic physical exams are expensive. Moreover, while they give some indication of physical ability as of the date of the exam, changes may subsequently occur. And it is undeniable—as the evidence showed in *Murgia*—that physical skills important to a policeman diminish with age. There is no question that use of the Massachusetts system of mandatory retirement at a designated age will eliminate some qualified people. That in fact happened in the *Murgia* case. But other systems also have imperfections; periodic physical exams might fail to screen out some who should be retired.

Even more important, the Massachusetts system—whatever its imperfections—is not arbitrary or capricious; it is a reasonable attempt to solve an important governmental problem. Most of the people who should be dismissed will be dismissed, and their dismissal will occur within a reasonable period of the time their physical abilities begin to deteriorate. Inevitably, this kind of generalized approach will dismiss a few people, such as Murgia, who would not need to be dismissed quite yet; but that kind of imperfection is nothing more than the inevitable consequence of line drawing. Some inequities will always result.

These are the concepts that lie at the core of the reasonable-basis test. Governmental attempts to solve governmental problems will be upheld against an equal-protection challenge so long as they are not arbitrary or capricious, and so long as they are reasonable. The rational (reasonable)-basis test assumes that there may be more than one reasonable way to solve the problem. The choice among available alternatives is for the legislature, city council, administrative agency, or other governmental policymaking entity. Whether another system or another solution might have been selected by the court or by anyone else is immaterial. So long as the government's choice is a reasonable one, reasonably calculated to achieve a proper governmental objective, the choice will be upheld.

In the great majority of cases, application of the reasonable-basis test will result in victory for government. The extent of the deference can be demonstrated by briefly reviewing another Supreme Court case. *Railway Express Agency v. New York* upheld against an equal-protection challenge a New York City traffic regulation prohibiting commercial advertising to be carried on delivery vehicles, but exempting vehicles owned by those firms whose advertising the vehicle carried.[5] Whatever objective the city might have had in prohibiting what it called "advertising vehicles" (several could be hypothesized), it is difficult to perceive how this objective is offended any less by vehicles carrying advertising that promotes the vehicle owner's product. Any difference between an ad for Tide on a truck owned by Procter and Gamble and one owned by Railway Express is not readily apparent. The fact that the ordinance was upheld emphasizes the extent of the deference that the reasonable-basis test affords to governmental policy choices.

As the two exception categories are examined, it is important to remember that they are exceptions and that any equal-protection problem that does not fit within one of the exception categories is therefore subject to the general, reasonable-basis rule. If a problem fits within either exception category the weighting of the scales changes from one that strongly favors the government to one that strongly favors the individual. Outside the realm of one of the exceptions—and therefore within the realm of the general rule—the government will rarely lose. Within the realm of one of the exceptions, the government will rarely win. The issue that will probably control the decision in any equal-protection case, therefore, will be whether the facts of the case place it within either of the exception categories.

The First Exception Category: Nature of the Classification

Classification—drawing lines and making distinctions—is the essence of lawmaking. Classification is also the feature that gives rise to potential equal-protection problems. Two people or two groups are treated unequally when one is treated differently from another because one is classified one way and one another.

The list of possible bases for classification is a lengthy one. The classification in *Murgia*, for example, was based on age; persons over fifty were in one class, and those under fifty were in another. In the *Railway Express* case the basis for classification was vehicle ownership. A vehicle that carried advertising for its owner's product was treated more favorably than a vehicle carrying the identical advertising but owned by someone else.

The first exception category turns on the nature of the classification—the dividing lines by which people are treated differently. The great majority of classification bases leaves the general reasonable-basis rule unaltered and the accompanying deference to government intact.

There are three classification bases, however, that have been held to be suspect classifications. The effect of using one of these suspect classifications for legislative linedrawing purposes is to take an equal-protection case out of the sphere of the reasonable-basis general rule. The Supreme Court has said that using one of these suspect categories subjects the legislative judgment to "close judicial scrutiny," or strict judicial scrutiny. But no matter what the language, determination of this principle dramatically shifts the weight of the balance scale to the side of the individual. What are the three suspect classifications? They are race, national origin, and alienage. Each is briefly discussed below.

Race

The Fourteenth Amendment was born out of a concern over racial classifications. It is appropriate, therefore, that race should be one of the suspect classifications. In the equal-protection area, nothing comes as close to invoking an absolutist standard as does a racial classification. Even here, however, an absolutist standard has not prevailed. At least one racial classification has been upheld; in *Virginia Board of Elections v. Hamm*, the Supreme Court upheld a state law requiring that divorce records reflect the race of the persons involved.[6]

It is in the area of school desegregation that race as a suspect classification is best known and has affected the most important interests. The leading case, *Brown v. Board of Education*, held that "separate but equal" school buildings and facilities are inherently unequal, thereby overruling the Supreme Court's 1896 ruling in *Plessy v. Ferguson*.[7] Even though the buildings, the desks, and the books may be the same, when the state forces black students to go to a school different from that of white students, it stamps them with a badge of inferiority and treats them unequally in a more important way than if they were given books inferior to those used by white students. Whether physically equal or not, separate school facilities for children of different races are a subtle, continuing, and forceful reminder that our society has made a judgment—enforced by the government—that where people may go and what they may do depends on the color of their skin. For the child who is a member of the disfavored class, such a constant reminder inevitably has an adverse impact on his social and intellectual development. Accordingly, separate-but-equal public school facilities violate the equal-protection clause. This same holding has subsequently been extended to other public facilities: swimming pools, buses, parks, libraries, and all others.

It is important to understand the difference between de jure segregation and de facto segregation and the different constitutional treatment afforded to each. Literally these Latin words mean "by right" and "by fact." In the school segregation context, they refer to whether the action of some governmental entity has caused the segregation. That is, if the state legislature, board of education, local school board, or any other official governing body has done anything that contributed to the segregated schools, then the segregation is de jure and the *Brown v. Board of Education* rule applies. De facto segregation occurs in those instances where the segregated schools result exclusively from private, nongovernmental reasons. These reasons may be social (most members of one race prefer a certain neighborhood), economic (many members of a certain race cannot afford some neighborhoods), or other; but the important point is that the segregated quality of the schools comes about because of living patterns that are due to personal decisions not provably influenced by any act of government.

The difference between de facto and de jure segregation is important because the Constitution's equal-protection guarantee does not apply to de facto segregation. Why should this be? The segregation is just as real no matter how it came about, and the continuing reminder to children of both races that all or most of their classmates are of one color is the same. A possible explanation is that the Fourteenth Amendment applies only to action by states. The specific language is, "No *state* shall . . . ." The distinction between de jure and de facto segregation is also consistent with the principle that discrimination violates the Fourteenth Ammendment only if it is purposeful. The fact that discriminatory effects have come about is not sufficient unless some discriminatory intent is also shown.[8]

Once de jure segregation is found, federal courts have a broad authority to eliminate it. The federal courts are not limited to stopping government from encouraging or requiring segregation. They may take affirmative steps to eliminate not only governmental encouragement of segregation, but also the end result: segregation itself. This means that in de jure cases, the Constitution mandates not just desegregation, but integration. It is for this reason that, in some cases where de jure segregation has been found, federal courts have ordered busing to achieve a better racial balance.[9] In the Denver school-desegregation case the Supreme Court held that busing may be ordered anywhere within the school district (which included most of the city of Denver), even though the school board's discriminatory acts had affected only a small part of the district.[10] In the Detroit case the Court held that federal judges do not have authority to order busing across school-district lines.[11] The Court's reasoning was that interdistrict busing would impose a remedy on neighboring districts (the Detroit suburbs) when the only proven acts of discrimination were by the Detroit school district.

National Origin

The Supreme Court has stated on several occasions that classifications based on national origin, like classifications based on race, are suspect and therefore subject to strict judicial scrutiny. It is theoretically possible to have a classification based on national origin that does not also import racial distinctions. Classification lines could be drawn, for example, to mark distinctions on the basis of whether a person was German, Scandanavian, or some other nationality that is dominantly Caucasian.[12]

Probably the most famous national origin cases were those involving treatment of persons of Japanese ancestry—including American citizens—who were in this country during World War II. Shortly after the declaration of war with Japan, President Roosevelt issued an executive order to protect "against espionage and against sabotage." The executive order established a "West Coast Program" for persons of Japanese ancestry. It included curfews, detention in relocation centers, and exclusion from certain designated West Coast areas. One of the Supreme Court opinions arising out of challenges to the West Coast Program contains what appears to be the first Supreme Court reference to race or national origin as a "suspect" classification—*Korematsu v. United States.*[13] It is ironic that, in spite of designating national origin a "suspect" classification, *Korematsu* is one of the rare instances in which the Court has *sustained* classifications based on race or national origin.[14] *Korematsu* held constitutional many aspects of the West Coast Program. However, perhaps the most controversial part of the program, the detention of Japanese naturals, was not at issue in *Korematsu*; in fact, the Supreme Court never did review that portion of the West Coast Program.

The decades since World War II have afforded opportunity for our nation to reflect on whether President Roosevelt made a mistake in issuing his West Coast Program executive order and whether the Supreme Court made a mistake in holding some of its aspects constitutional. Whatever the answers to those questions, today it is clear that national origin, like race, is a suspect classification. Any governmental distinction that is keyed to it will be subjected to close judicial scrutiny, thereby shifting the weighting of the balance scales from the government's side to the individual's side.

Alienage

The third and final suspect classification is alienage. Alienage classifications are those that draw distinctions according to whether the individual is an American citizen. There is language in a number of Supreme Court cases proclaiming that alienage, like race and national origin, is a suspect classification. Supreme Court decisions have invalidated state classifications treating aliens less favorably than American citizens with respect to such matters as welfare benefits, employment in state civil-service positions, financial assistance for higher education, and membership in the legal profession.[15] Most of the cases establishing alienage as a suspect classification have been handed down since the leading case, *Graham v. Richardson*, was decided in 1971.[16]

Since about 1976 the cases appear to have identified two modifications to the rule that alienage is a suspect classification. Since these modifications really amount to exceptions to an exception, their net effect, where they apply, is to place the case back under the general reasonable-basis rule—which means that government will probably win.

The first modification concerns discrimination against aliens by the federal government. The federal government enjoys a rather broad leeway to make classifications favoring citizens over aliens, so long as the discriminatory decisions can be shown to support some legitimate federal governmental interest. The reason is that the Constitution grants to the federal government the power to deal with matters of immigration and naturalization. This power includes a wide range of discretion to make classifications favoring American citizens.[17]

The triggering characteristics of the second modification are not as easily identifiable as those of the first. The apparent focus is on the nature of the task performed by the noncitizen against whom the discrimination has been practiced. In a 1973 case, *Sugarman v. Dougall*, the Court stated that a state might impose citizenship as a qualification for those "important non-elective executive, legislative and judicial positions," held by "officers who participate directly in the formulation, execution or review of broad public policy."[18] It is clearly a modification that pertains to discrimination against aliens with regard to public employment, but it is not certain how broadly across the spectrum of public employment the exception sweeps. Applying this rule, the Supreme Court has upheld two New York statutes, one of which prohibits aliens from serving as members of the state police force while the other forbids certification as a public school teacher of any noncitizen of the United States.[19]

The main significance of these two New York cases is their expansion of the *Sugarman* rationale that a state may prefer United States citizens in those executive, judicial, and legislative positions that involve policymaking functions. Policemen and teachers both occupy significant roles in our society, roles that touch the lives of many people in important ways. But to fit them under the policymaking exception imparts a very expansive interpretation to that exception. The net result is that these cases would appear to have brought about a rather substantial enlargement of state governments' discretion to make classifications favoring United States citizens over noncitizens.

The Halfway Classifications: Sex and Legitimacy

There are two other classifications that have the effect of turning up the constitutional searchlight beyond what the reasonable-basis test requires. They are classifications based on sex and classifications based on legitimacy. Alternatively stated, they involve discriminations against illegitimate children and discriminations against women or men.

Sex and legitimacy are not suspect classifications and the scales are not weighted as heavily in the individual's favor as would be the case if they were suspect classifications. Neither are they governed by the reasonable-basis standard, however. They are intermediate categories, and the level of judicial scrutiny is greater than rational basis but less than strict judicial scrutiny.

It has been argued that sex and legitimacy share a common characteristic linking them to race and national origin. The common characteristic is that each of these four classification bases involves something that the individual can neither control nor alter. As Justice Brennan stated in *Frontiero v. Richardson*: "[S]ex, like race and national origin, is an immutable characteristic determined solely by the accident of birth."[20] There are some problems with this argument. The first is that it proves too much, because it applies to other classification bases such as age. The Supreme Court held in the *Murgia* case that age is not a suspect classification and is governed by the reasonable-basis standard. Moreover, the asserted common characteristics—determination by birth and inability of the individual to change—are not applicable to the third suspect classification: alienage.

In any event, at this writing, classifications based on legitimacy (such as those that permit a legitimate child to inherit on more favorable terms than an illegitimate child) and classifications based on sex occupy a category all their own.[21] It is a category in which governmental judgment is subject to less deference than it would receive under the general, reasonable-basis category but more deference than if it were a full-fledged suspect classification.

Legitimacy

The Supreme Court cases dealing with discrimination based on legitimacy have mostly involved statutes that have made it more difficult for children, because of their illegitimacy, to inherit or receive benefits or to bring suit for damages arising from their parents' deaths. It is not easy to derive any consistent principles from these cases. The Court has not even attempted to articulate a harmonizing rationale. One such rationale that has been suggested would appear to be consistent with the holdings of most of the cases.[22] It is that, where the apparent attempt of the legislature has been to penalize the children for the parents' wrongdoing, the attempt will be unsuccessful. If, on the other hand, the statute does not appear to import a moral judgment, but its objective is simply administrative convenience, it will likely be upheld. What is meant by "administrative convenience" for this purpose? The facts and holding in *Mathews v. Lucas* will illustrate.[23]

The Federal Social Security Act provides benefits not only for the wage earner who made contributions into the Social Security fund, but also for other persons who stand in a certain relationship to the wage earner. In the case of a deceased wage earner, these are known as survivor benefits. Among those entitled to survivor benefits are dependents of the wage earner. *Mathews v. Lucas* involved a provision of the Social Security Act that provided benefits to children who were dependent on the wage earner at the time of his death. Legitimate children were presumed to be dependent. Some illegitimates had to prove dependency on an individual basis, so that a heavier burden was placed on illegitimates than on legitimates. The Supreme Court rejected the argument that this was an unconstitutional denial of equal protection on the ground that "administrative convenience" was served. Why did the discrimination against illegitimate children serve the convenience of the Social Security Administration? If all minor children, legitimates and illegitimates, had been required to prove actual dependency, there would have been no equal-protection issue. It was easier for the Social Security Administration simply to presume that legitimate children were in fact dependent.

Sex

Sex-discrimination issues have occupied a larger share of our national attention in recent years than have any other classifications, with the possible exception of race. Sex-discrimination cases differ from other legislative classifications in that it is more difficult to identify the class affected as a minority, either from the standpoint of voting strength or total numbers. The national debate over sex discrimination has focused more on the proposed Twenty-seventh Amendment to the United States Constitution—the Equal Rights Amendment—than on Supreme Court interpretations of the Fourteenth Amendment's equal-protection clause. The two are not unrelated, however. In at least one case, *Frontiero v. Richardson*, the possible relationship between what the Court did in that case and the proposed Equal Rights Amendment was noted by one of the concurring opinions.[24] This relationship suggests one of the questions that the conscientious citizen or legislator should ask concerning the ERA: how many objectionably discriminatory practices, if any, would be eliminated by the Equal Rights Amendment that are not now prohibited by the equal-protection clause of the Fourteenth Amendment?

In *Reed v. Reed*, the Supreme Court held unconstitutional an Idaho statute providing that, in appointing administrators for decedents' estates, males should be preferred over females.[25] It was not possible from the Court's opinion to determine the constitutional standard by which the case was decided. Two years later, in *Frontiero v. Richardson*, four members of the Court (one less than the majority necessary to make it an official holding of the Court) were of the view that sex should be a suspect classification like race, national origin, and alienage.[26] That view has never prevailed; its high-water mark from the standpoint of vote count was in *Frontiero*. In *Craig v. Boren*, however, the Court held unconstitutional as a violation of the equal-protection clause an Oklahoma statute setting the legal age for consumption of beer containing 3.2 percent alcohol at eighteen for females and twenty-one for males.[27]

It was clearly a classification based on sex. In holding it uncon-stitutional, the Court stated that the constitutional standard for gender-based classifications is that they are subject to "scrutiny." Recall that the standard applicable to suspect classifications is strict judicial scrutiny.

The difference between the "strict judicial scrutiny" to which the suspect classifications are subjected and the "scrutiny" to which dis-criminations based on sex are subjected is, of course, not readily quan-tifiable. Neither, however, accords the broad deference to legislative judgment that results from the reasonable-basis test, as the facts and holdings of both *Reed v. Reed* and *Craig v. Boren* demonstrate. In *Craig v. Boren,* for example, the statute was held unconstitutional notwith-standing the uncontradicted evidence that in the eighteen-to-twenty-year-old category there were over seventeen times as many males ar-rested for driving under the influence of alcohol as females.

It seems fairly safe to generalize from the Court's decisions that any gender-based classification is not likely to survive constitutional chal-lenge if it is based on "archaic and overbroad" generalizations that women should not enter the work force and compete with men, no-tions that "are more consistent with 'the role-typing society as long im-posed' . . . than with contemporary reality."[28]

The Second Exception Category: Fundamental Rights

The second category of exceptions to the reasonable-basis rule has an entirely different focus from the first. The first exception centers on the nature of the classification. The second inquires into the level of impor-tance of the individual interest involved.

It is helpful at this point to recall that all of the constitutional prin-ciples discussed from Chapter 8 forward have involved attempts to re-concile governmental interests with individual interests adversely affect-ed by what government has done. The cases discussed in these chapters demonstrate that the range of individual interests adversely affected by governmental action is wide and varied. In the great majority of in-stances, the constitutional test does not change according to the type of individual interest affected.

There are some individual interests, however, that occupy a favored position. Whenever one of these favored interests comes into conflict with governmental action, then once again the weighting of the bal-ance scales shifts so that these individual interests, rather than the gov-ernmental interests, are favored. Individual interests that fall in this fa-vored category are called fundamental rights.

The earliest Supreme Court decision that articulated the fundamen-tal-rights concept and its accompanying strict standard of review was

Skinner v. Oklahoma.[29] *Skinner* held unconstitutional Oklahoma's Habitual Criminal Sterilization Act, which provided for compulsory sterilization of any person convicted three times of felonies "involving moral turpitude" but which excluded some felonies such as embezzlement. The Court's opinion states:

> We are dealing here with legislation which involves one of the basic civil rights of man. Marriage and procreation are fundamental to the very existence and survival of the race. . . . There is no redemption for the individual whom the law touches. Any experiment which the State conducts is to his irreparable injury. He is forever deprived of a basic liberty. We mention these matters not to reexamine the scope of the police power of the States. We advert to them merely in emphasis of our view that strict scrutiny of the classification which a State makes in a sterilization law is essential.[30]

Neither the phrase "fundamental rights" nor the concept is found in the Constitution. Moreover, the term is not self-defining. What, then, is included? We know that the list includes all First Amendment freedoms, inclusion of which can probably be rationally justified. Guarantees of free expression and free religious exercise constitute the very bedrock of American liberties, for example. The list of fundamental rights also includes the right to vote, not only in federal but also in state elections. The Supreme Court has observed that, in a sense, the right to vote is preservative of other freedoms because it involves the means whereby citizens express their preference for those who will operate their government. The right to vote in "special district" elections, however—municipal subdivisions administering only a limited range of governmental services (such as flood control and water delivery)—is not fundamental, so long as the district's activities have a disproportionate effect on some people (such as the effect of an irrigation district on landowners). Therefore, the right to vote in a special-district election falls outside the exception category and within the realm of the general, reasonable-basis rule.

The fundamental-rights category also includes certain individual interests that are not mentioned in the Constitution but have been held implicit in it. This includes the right to marry, the right to procreate, the right of interstate (though not international) travel, and the right of privacy in sexual matters.[31]

The right of privacy in sexual matters has been the basis for invalidating a Connecticut statute prohibiting the distribution or use of contraceptives. It was also the constitutional basis for the famous holdings in 1973 that state statutes may not prohibit all abortions. As applied to the abortion context, the right of privacy belongs to the pregnant woman, so that statutes requiring the consent of a pregnant minor's parents or the consent of the father of the unborn child are also unconstitutional.[32] The Court has further held that, while government cannot constitutionally prohibit all abortions, neither is it constitutionally required to pay for them.[33] During the first trimester of pregnancy the ban is virtually complete: "[T]he abortion decision and its effectuation must be left to the medical judgment of the pregnant woman's attending physician."[34] During the second trimester but prior to "viability," the state may impose reasonable restrictions related to preservation of the pregnant woman's health; subsequent to "viability," the state's authority to control and prohibit abortions is much broader. ("Viability" is that stage where the fetus "has the capability of meaningful life outside the mother's womb."[35] However, the Court did not attempt to specify at which stage of pregnancy it occurs.) The Supreme Court has ruled that the government is not required to pay for abortions, even for women who cannot afford them, and even where the government would pay the costs of live births for indigent mothers.[36] (The abortion decisions as possible examples of judicial intrusion into the prerogatives of the legislature are discussed in Chapter 18.)

Most people would agree that the right to marry and the right to procreate are very important. Concerning the right to travel, the right of access to contraceptives, or the right to an abortion, some people may consider them very important and others not so important. But none is mentioned by the Constitution.

The proposition that there are fundamental rights also means, of course, that there are other rights, guaranteed by the Constitution, that are not fundamental. This in turn means that some rights guaranteed by the Constitution are more important—and entitled to a greater overall protection—than others. Several important questions are raised by this hierarchy of constitutional values.

First, what is the authority, constitutional or otherwise, for the determination that some constitutional values are more weighty than others? Second, authority aside, is it a good idea for courts to be engaged in that kind of business? What possible standards are there for determining which rights belong in the favored category and which in the disfavored? Since many of the fundamental rights are not mentioned by the Constitution, who determines the standards for their existence and their application? What are the consequences to separation of powers—the allocation to separate branches of lawmaking, law enforcement, and law interpretation powers of government? Part of the next chapter—the part which deals with substantive due process—and all of Chapter 4 are devoted to these and related issues.

Reverse Discrimination

Within recent years, much attention has been placed on an issue that bears a number of labels, including "reverse discrimination," "affirmative action," and "benign discrimination."

Whatever the label, the equal-protection problem is whether and to what extent the constitutional guarantee of equal protection is offended by governmental attempts to rectify past discriminations against a particular class by taking compensating measures that favor members of that group.

Two examples frame the issues. Assume first that a state medical school adopts separate admission standards for whites and nonwhites, so that applicants who are members of a racial minority are admitted with lower college grades and lower scores on the medical-school aptitude test. For the second example, assume that the federal government adopts a policy that favors women for employment in new positions. In both cases there is a preference, an unequal treatment. One class is favored over another. In either case, if the preference ran the other way—in favor of the white medical-school applicant or the male job seeker, it would clearly violate the equal-protection clause. Is the rule the same when government favors a group that has traditionally been disfavored?

This issue is likely to continue for the next decade or so as one of the most important issues of constitutional law. It is also one that attracts great public attention and directly affects the interests of many people. Notwithstanding the notoriety of *Regents of the University of California v. Bakke*, the holding and opinion in that case did not take us very far down the road toward helpful answers.[37] Allan Bakke is a white male who was denied admission to the medical school at the University of California at Davis. He brought suit, contending that his qualifications were superior to those of some of the successful applicants who were members of racial minorities admitted under a special program. Theoretically, the preference was for disadvantaged students, including whites; but no whites had ever in fact been admitted through the special admissions program. Bakke therefore contended that the only reason he was denied admission was because of his race; if he had been black or Indian or Mexican American he would have been admitted. In his view, his was a classic case of governmental (state medical school) discrimination based solely on race. Race is a suspect classification, calling forth strict judicial scrutiny. Under these circumstances, Bakke argued, denial of his medical-school application violated the equal-protection guarantee. In addition to his constitutional argument, Bakke also contended that the Davis medical school's refusal to admit him violated a federal statute, Title VI of the Civil Rights Act of 1964, which prohibits discrimination by educational institutions receiving federal funds.

Regents of the University of California v. Bakke is one of those remarkable cases in which only one justice agreed completely with the Supreme Court's holding. Analysis of the issues in *Bakke* reveals how this came about; it is also instructive concerning several aspects of how the Court does its work. There were two large issues in *Bakke*. The first affected only Allan Bakke: whether he was entitled to admission to medical school, either on Title VI statutory grounds or on constitutional grounds. The second affected virtually every institution of higher learning in the country: whether Davis or any other college or university could take race into account in making its decisions to admit persons from disadvantaged backgrounds on more favorable terms than others. On these issues, four of the justices took the view that under Title VI (without reaching the constitutional issue) (1) Bakke was entitled to admission and (2) Davis (and other colleges and universities) could not take race into account in setting admissions standards. Four other members of the Court were of the view that (1) Bakke was not entitled to admission and (2) race can be taken into account so long as it does not "stigmatize" a particular racial group—that is, so long as it favors the group that has traditionally been disfavored. The final member of the Court was alone in the view that (1) Bakke was entitled to admission, but (2) race could be taken into account as one of many factors considered by a school that attempts to achieve a more diverse student body because it concludes that diversity will enhance the quality of its educational program. The lineup of the Court on the two relevant issues was as follows:

Justices	Issue 1	Issue 2
Burger, Stewart, Blackmun, and Rehnquist	Bakke wins	Race *cannot* be taken into account
Powell	Bakke wins	Race *can* be taken into account
Brennan, White, Marshall, and Stevens	Bakke *loses*	Race *can* be taken into account

On the first issue, Justice Powell joined with four of his colleagues to form a majority of five. On this issue he ruled in Mr. Bakke's favor because, even though race could be taken into account for the limited purpose of achieving a diverse student body, that is not how the Davis program operated. On the second issue, four members of the Court would have gone farther than Justice Powell, but the five votes required for a majority could be found only for the more limited view. Accordingly, there were five votes for Allan Bakke and five votes for at least some racial preference, but they were not the same five votes. The Court's holding in *Bakke* was that Allan Bakke must be admitted to medical school and that institutions of higher education can give some consideration to race in making their admissions decisions. Yet there was only one member of the Court who held that combination of views.

The year following its *Bakke* decision, the Court again faced the issue of "benign" racial discrimination in *Kaiser Aluminum and Chemical Corp. v. Weber.*[38] *Weber*, however, did not involve a constitutional ruling. It held only that private-employment contracts do not violate Title VII of the federal Civil Rights Act of 1964 by granting employment-advancement preferences to minorities who are underrepresented in the company's better paying positions.

In *Fullilove v. Klutznick* the Supreme Court held constitutional a federal law requiring that at least 10 percent of federal funds granted for local public-works projects must be used to procure services or supplies from businesses owned by minority-group members.[39] In the area of governmental preferences for women, the Supreme Court appears to have been a bit more certain in approving governmental favoritism for women so long as it can be established that the purpose of the preference was not to enforce archaic notions about the "proper role" of women but, rather, to compensate them for past acts of discrimination against them. The standard for "benign" sex discrimination is apparently the same as for sex discrimination generally: "Gender-based discrimination must serve important governmental objectives and the discriminatory means employed must be substantially related to the achievement of those objectives."[40]

Because judicial decisions to date on reverse discrimination provide little helpful guidance on the constitutional issue, it is important to consider the competing considerations. Those favoring the individual are fairly obvious. After all, discrimination is discrimination. A person has no control over sex or skin color. For good reasons, government is precluded from using sex or skin color as a basis for discriminating in favor of a white male. Fair play also requires that neither sex nor skin color be employed by government as the basis for disfavoring a white male. The cruelest possible form of discrimination is discrimination that is constitutionally prohibited when it runs in one direction but is permitted, and even encouraged, when it runs the other way.

The arguments favoring government may not be as well known, but they should be. It is easy—part of that argument asserts—for a member of the white, middle-class establishment to contend that opportunity for entry into professional schools, for example, should be based exclusively on merit. How do professional schools measure merit for this purpose? The traditional yardsticks are undergraduate college grades and scores on professional-school aptitude tests. Why is it that members of the majority establishment usually have better grades and better aptitude scores than nonmembers of the establishment? It is because they come out of a family environment that nourishes and encourages high performance in these respects. There will be some exceptions, but in general the children of parents who attended college and professional schools will have a better chance to excel in school because everything about them in their home and family assures them that academic excellence is a value of primary importance. As a consequence, the children who stand the best chance of doing well in school are those whose parents did well in school and who had the benefits of higher education. These same children, once they become parents, will create the same kind of home environment for the benefit of their children.

As a general matter, therefore, those segments of our society that were disadvantaged at one time because of discrimination practiced against them will remain disadvantaged because of their inability as a group to break through the self-perpetuating cycle of educational attainment. The way to break the cycle, at least to a limited extent, is to set aside a limited number of slots in the classes of the professional schools so that at least some minority persons can acquire the education and attitudes about learning that will enable their children to approach the learning process from a better starting point than their parents enjoyed.

There is another consideration. Assume that a state law school has room for 150 students in its entering class. It could fill this class with 150 white, middle- and upper-income-level students, all having the same basic background. What if the faculty should conclude that the study of law would be more effective for all students if there were more diversity among them and that this could be achieved by admitting a dozen people from different backgrounds? Or assume that the state involved has a large Indian population. Most of the Indians live on reservations; there are few Indian lawyers in the state, and most non-Indian lawyers are unwilling to practice their profession on the reservation. Should the state not be permitted the flexibility to decide that, instead of filling all 150 seats at the law school with whites, the state's interests would be better served by admitting a few Indians? If the state is permitted to make that kind of decision, it will increase the likelihood not only that needed legal services will be provided on the reservation, but also that young tribal members will be able to look to Indian professionals as possible role models.

The Federal Government and the Equal-Protection Clause

The only part of the Constitution that says anything about equality is the Fourteenth Amendment ("No state shall . . . deny any person the equal protection of the laws"). But the Fourteenth Amendment contains no provision dealing with Congress or the federal government. Other provisions of the Constitution guarantee individual rights against intrusions by the federal government (most notably the Bill of Rights), but none of these provisions contains an equal-protection clause or even mentions the word or the concept.

Does this mean that the federal government is free to treat its citizens unequally with no constitutional limitation? The answer is no. In *Bolling v. Sharpe*, decided the same day as *Brown v. Board of Education*, the Supreme Court held unconstitutional the segregated system within the public schools of the District of Columbia.[41] The constitutional ground for the holding, obviously, was equal protection. Within the District of Columbia all law is federal law, so that the Fourteenth Amendment was inapplicable. The Court held, however, that the due-process clause of the Fifth Amendment, which is binding on the federal government, includes not only due-process principles (discussed in the next chapter), but also includes protections against governmental denials of equal protection.

Bolling v. Sharpe, and cases that have come after it, have made it clear that the federal government is not only bound by equal-protection guarantees, but also that the extent and the quality of those guarantees are identical to those that are applicable to the states by virtue of the Fourteenth Amendment's equal-protection clause. An interesting question raised by *Bolling v. Sharpe* is this: the due-process clause in the Fifth Amendment (which, the Supreme Court held, incorporates the equal-protection clause of the Fourteenth) is virtually identical to the due-process clause of the Fourteenth Amendment. Does the due-process clause of the Fourteenth Amendment also include equal-protection principles? If it does, why do we need an equal-protection clause at all?

CHAPTER FIFTEEN
Due Process of Law

Most people have heard something about "due process of law." Few people really understand what it means. The due-process guarantee appears in two different parts of the Constitution: the Fifth and Fourteenth amendments. One amendment uses a passive verb and the other an active verb, but their operative language is the same. The relevant words are:

No person shall be ... deprived of life, liberty, or property, without due process of law. [Fifth Amendment]

No State shall ... deprive any person of life, liberty, or property, without due process of law. [Fourteenth Amendment]

In each case, the substantive constitutional guarantee is against governmental deprivation of "life, liberty, or property without due process of law." The difference in the two is that the Fifth Amendment is a limitation on the federal government and the Fourteenth is a limitation on the states.

The due-process clause has been called "the wild card in the Supreme Court's deck." While this is largely a tongue-in-cheek statement, it correctly implies that, of all the provisions of the Constitution, the due-process clause affords the most open-ended opportunity for judicial policymaking.

The due-process clause plays three important roles in American constitutional law: (1) as the vehicle through which some of the provisions of the Bill of Rights are made binding on state governments, (2) as a guarantor against certain governmental actions that have the effect of depriving persons of life, liberty, or property interests, regardless of the fairness of the procedure, and (3) as a guarantor of procedural fairness in civil and criminal trials and trial-type proceedings.

"Incorporation" of Bill of Rights Provisions

In 1833 the Supreme Court held, in *Barron v. Mayor and City Council of Baltimore*, that the Bill of Rights provisions are binding only on the federal government.[1] The adoption of the Fourteenth Amendment, specifically the due-process clause, changed this, though not completely. The Fourteenth Amendment's due-process clause accomplishes what lawyers refer to as an "incorporation by reference." That is, when the Fourteenth Amendment prohibits states from depriving any person of life, liberty, or property without due process of law, it reaches down into the Bill of Rights and makes some of those provisions binding on the states. Among other things, therefore, due process means that no state may imprison an accused criminal without giving him the assistance of counsel to represent him at his trial or having the issue of his guilt or innocence determined by a jury.

Ten justices in the history of the Supreme Court have taken the position that this incorporation is a total one. Under this "total-incorporation" view, all of the provisions of the Bill of Rights were made binding on the states by the adoption of the due-process clause of the Fourteenth. Of those ten justices, however, there were never five on the Court at the same time that the issue was presented. For this reason the total-incorporation theory has never been adopted as the prevailing approach. Rather, the Court has incorporated and made binding on the states only those provisions of the Constitution that rise to a certain level of importance.

The standard articulated by the Court is that the Fourteenth Amendment makes binding on state governments those Bill of Rights provisions that are "essential to a free society" or "implicit in the concept of ordered liberty."[2] Specifically, this has meant that all of the provisions of the First, Fourth, Sixth, and Eighth amendments have been incorporated, along with all of the provisions of the Fifth except the grand-jury indictment guarantee.[3] Grand-jury indictment and the Seventh Amendment provision guaranteeing the right of jury trial in all civil cases involving more than $20 have been held not to rise to the required level of importance.[4]

Incorporation of the Bill of Rights criminal guarantees can be comfortably squared with the language of the due-process clause. Imposing a criminal fine or imprisonment is a deprivation of liberty or property. To accomplish either of these criminal punishments without the important criminal protections afforded by the Bill of Rights is to accomplish it without "due process of law."

Fitting the incorporation of the provisions of the First Amendment within the language of the due-process clause is another matter. Analytically, the due-process clause consists of two parts, each of which must be violated if the constitutional guarantee is to come into play. First, there must be a deprivation of life, liberty, or property. Second, deprivation must be accomplished without due process of law, "due process" meaning proper procedure. The express language of the clause quite clearly says that both the deprivation of life, liberty, or property and an improper procedure are required. It might be argued, therefore, that deprivation of life, liberty, or property without due process of law can occur only where there has been some procedural infirmity–that is, where government has deprived someone of important interests that might be tantamount to life, liberty, or property without affording the person deprived an adequate trial or trial-type hearing in which he could present his side of the case.

The other position takes a broader view of the meaning of due process of law. Under this view, due process of law is not limited to procedural matters. It focuses on the first part of the clause and contends that the constitutional concern is for governmental deprivations of life, liberty, or property and that any such deprivation may be without due process of law regardless of the fairness of the procedure by which those deprivations are accomplished.

If due process reaches only procedural matters–guaranteeing the existence and fairness of trials and trial-type proceedings–then it is hard to see how provisions of the First Amendment can be read into the due-process clause. The guarantees of the First Amendment are very important but, unlike other parts of the Bill of Rights, they have nothing to do with procedure or procedural fairness. For example, assume that a state attempts to prosecute someone for making a political speech on a public street. The defense would not be a procedural one–that is, a defense on the grounds that the state may not prosecute without a fair trial. Rather, the argument would be substantive–that is, the state cannot prosecute at all, because the activity is protected by the First Amendment's guarantee of freedom of speech.

Insofar as the incorporation feature of the due-process clause is concerned, the Supreme Court has never taken seriously the argument that the due-process clause is limited to procedural matters. Among the earliest provisions of the Bill of Rights to be held incorporated were those of the First Amendment. However, the underlying debate– whether due process is limited to procedural matters or whether it extends to substantive protections as well–has far greater importance when the issue moves away from the incorporation problem and into other areas of what is meant by due process of law. And this brings us to the other two roles played by the due-process clause.

Substantive Due Process

The first Supreme Court cases to consider the Fourteenth Amendment reached the Court five years after that amendment became part of the Constitution. The name that these cases bear is *The Slaughter-House Cases.*[5] The *Slaughter-House Cases* were a challenge to a Louisiana law that gave a designated corporation—the Crescent City Live-Stock Landing and Slaughter-House Company—a twenty-five-year exclusive right "to maintain slaughterhouses, landings for cattle and stockyards" within an area of 1,154 square miles, including the city of New Orleans. Excluded slaughterers brought suit to have the law declared unconstitutional. The challengers raised four arguments; three of them were anchored in the Fourteenth Amendment (the fourth was a Thirteenth Amendment argument). The three Fourteenth-Amendment contentions were: (1) that the Louisiana law deprived them of the privileges and immunities of United States citizens, (2) that it deprived them of equal protection of the laws, and (3) that it deprived them of liberty and property without due process of law.

All of the challengers' arguments failed, and the law was upheld. The principal focus was on the privileges-and-immunities issue, and the Court's privileges-and-immunities ruling is the reason the *Slaughter-House Cases* are so famous. The Court held that the privileges-and-immunities clause did nothing more than extend to the newly freed slaves the privileges and immunities that all citizens had enjoyed prior to the amendment and that the amendment had no effect on the privileges and immunities of persons other than ex-slaves. This meant that the clause offered no relief to the slaughterers excluded by the Louisiana law. The effect of the decision was to leave the Fourteenth Amendment's privileges-and-immunities clause in a position of virtual obscurity, a position that it still holds.

The equal-protection and due-process arguments in the *Slaughter-House Cases* were given short shrift. Concerning due process the Court held that "under no construction of that provision . . . can the restraint imposed by the State of Louisiana upon the exercise of their trade by the butchers of New Orleans be held to be a deprivation of property within the meaning of [the due-process clause]."[6]

Unlike its privileges-and-immunities decision, the Court's equal-protection and due-process holdings have not withstood subsequent Supreme Court scrutiny. The expansion of equal protection beyond the black race can be seen from the discussion in Chapter 14. The due-process holding lasted about twenty-five years. Though its probable demise was forecast several years earlier, the coup de grace to the *Slaughter-House* due-process holding was administered in a case called *Allgeyer v. Louisiana.*[7]

The Louisiana statute in *Allgeyer* prohibited marine-insurance companies from pursuing their business in that state unless they had complied in all respects with state law. An understanding of Mr. Allgeyer's challenge to this law will be aided by referring back to the discussion earlier in this chapter of the two different views concerning the meaning of the due-process clause. One view follows a tighter interpretation of due process of law and concludes that the clause deals only with procedural guarantees. The other view contends that the guarantee against deprivation of "life, liberty, or property without due process of law" is not limited to the fairness of the procedure by which the deprivation is accomplished, and that any deprivation is necessarily a constitutional violation. *Allgeyer* took the broader view.

Mr. Allgeyer was convicted for mailing a letter to an insurance company in New York concerning a shipment of goods in accordance with a marine-insurance policy. The New York company was not licensed to do business in Louisiana, so its business transaction in that state was in violation of state law. Allgeyer did not contend that Louisiana's limitation on insurance-contract provisions was unconstitutional because it failed to provide a fair procedure. Procedural issues were wholly irrelevant to his claim. His position can be summarized in this way: "The kind of contract that private parties enter into is a matter for negotiation between them. It is certainly none of government's business. My right to contract involves both liberty and also property. Telling me that I cannot enter into any kind of contractual arrangements that I choose is a deprivation of liberty and property without due process of law. It is therefore unconstitutional."

The Supreme Court agreed with Mr. Allgeyer. It held the Louisiana law invalid as an infringement on freedom of contract, which the Court held was included within the Fourteenth Amendment's due-process guarantee. With the *Allgeyer* decision, the Court ushered in what has come to be known as the "substantive due process era." It was an era that lasted for about forty years, during which a broad variety of state economic and social-welfare programs were invalidated on non-procedural due-process grounds.

The doctrine was not (and is not) restricted to economic issues. In *Meyer v. Nebraska*, for example, the Court struck down a state law prohibiting courses in schools from being taught in any language other than English before the ninth grade, and in *Pierce v. Society of Sisters*, the same fate befell an Oregon law requiring that school children attend public rather than parochial schools.[8] In each case the defect in the law was that it deprived the children and their parents of the liberty to make decisions concerning the children's education.

State attempts to regulate economic activity, however, were the main targets of the substantive due-process cases. The leading case was

Lochner v. New York, which held unconstitutional a New York statute providing that no bakery employee could work more than ten hours a day or sixty hours a week.[9] The legislature had determined that because of the bakers' working conditions, particularly heat and dust, excessive hours of employment were detrimental to the bakers' health. Mr. Lochner was a bakery owner who was fined and convicted for permitting an employee to work in his Utica bakery for more than sixty hours in one week. His position was: "The health of my employees is a matter of concern for them, not the State of New York. Those employees also have other concerns. They have families to feed and bills to pay. If they want to work longer hours because they need more money, that's their decision to make. Whether longer hours hurt their health and whether any injury to their health is worth the extra money are also their decisions. They and I have a constitutional right to contract for whatever term of employment is in our mutual interest. For the State of New York to tell my employees and me that we cannot make those decisions deprives us of liberty and property without due process of law." The Supreme Court agreed with Lochner and held the New York law unconstitutional.

It was the challenge to another New York law, *Nebbia v. New York*,[10] some thirty years after *Lochner,* that began the demise of the *Allgeyer-Lochner* approach to substantive due process. This time the New York statute attempted to set minimum retail prices for milk. The state's objective was to stabilize the return to New York dairy producers. Leo Nebbia was the proprietor of a small grocery store in Rochester, New York. The provision of the New York milk-pricing law with which he came into conflict was one that prohibited the retail sale of a quart of milk for less than nine cents. Nebbia violated the law by selling two quarts of milk and a five-cent loaf of bread for eighteen cents. Nebbia's constitutional argument was similar to those of Allgeyer and Lochner: "This is my milk. I can do with it whatever I want. I can drink it, I can pour it down the drain, or I can give it away. If I want to sell it for less than nine cents a quart, that is my business, because it is my milk. When the State of New York tries to tell me I can't sell my milk for whatever price I choose, the state is depriving me of my liberty and my property without due process of law."

The similarity between Mr. Nebbia's argument and those of Allgeyer and Lochner is readily apparent. Before the Court that decided *Allgeyer v. Louisiana* in 1897, or the Court that decided *Lochner v. New York* in 1905, Nebbia probably would have won. But in 1934 he lost. The new constitutional standard for substantive due-process cases, announced in *Nebbia v. New York*, can be analyzed as consisting of a three-part inquiry:

1. Does the governmental regulation fall within the power of the relevant government to enact?
2. Is the regulation reasonably calculated to further the governmental objective? In other words, is there a reasonable relationship between the governmental end and the means selected by government to achieve that end?
3. Is the regulation either arbitrary or discriminatory?

What really happened in the transition from *Allgeyer-Lochner* to *Nebbia* was a change in the constitutional standard by which conflicting governmental and individual interests are accommodated. For forty years the balance scales were weighted in favor of the individual and against the governmental regulation challenged. The reason that this case involving an eighteen-cent sale is such a landmark is that it shifted the weighted balance from one that favors the individual adversely affected by the governmental decision to one that favors the governmental decision. The Court in *Nebbia* did not describe its result in this way. Indeed, the Court has never described its decisions in terms of weighted balancing. Weighted balancing accurately describes the Court's approach to most constitutional cases, however, and the switch from *Lochner* to *Nebbia* provides an apt illustration. From the mid-1890s to the mid-1930s the courts were very willing to overturn legislative judgments on the ground that they substantively deprived persons of liberty or property.

Nebbia did not restrict the due-process clause to the position that it protects only against procedural deprivations, but the due-process clause as of *Nebbia* still has substantive significance. But whereas prior to *Nebbia* substantive due-process attacks were comparatively easy to sustain, anyone attacking an economic regulation today on substantive due-process grounds is faced with a much weightier burden.

The *Nebbia* opinion reflects a constitutional standard that is highly deferential toward the legislative judgment. Its language and its effect are similar to the reasonable-basis test considered in the preceding chapter. The current substantive due-process test allows state lawmakers about the same deference that they enjoy under the general rule governing equal-protection problems. The requirement is simply that there must be a reasonable likelihood that the legislation under attack will achieve an objective that falls within the state's police powers.

Procedural Due Process

Recall the operative language of the due-process clauses: "No person shall be ... deprived of life, liberty, or property, without due process of law." Substantive due-process doctrine concentrates on the first half of the clause: What is an unconstitutional deprivation of life, liberty, or property? It assumes that some such deprivations are violative of the due-process clause regardless of procedural protections.

Procedural due-process problems can arise in both the criminal and also the civil context. The criminal cases do not as frequently present problems concerning what is the life, liberty, or property interest with whose deprivation the individual is faced. Rather, the issue usually is: What kinds of procedural protections must be afforded an individual as a matter of constitutional right before government is entitled to impose a criminal fine, imprison him, or even put him to death?

In substantial part, the meaning of procedural due-process in the criminal context has already been discussed in connection with the incorporation issue. That is, due process of law means that no government may impose a criminal penalty without providing those Bill of Rights protections that rise to such a level of importance that they have been "incorporated" into the due-process clause of the Fourteenth Amendment. This means that no government, state or federal, may impose serious criminal penalties without affording all of the Bill of Rights criminal protections except for grand-jury indictment. (The federal government is required to indict by grand jury unless waived by the defendant, not because it is included within the package of protections embraced by due process but because, as a Bill of Rights guarantee, grand-jury indictment is directly binding on the federal government.)

The protections provided the criminally accused by the due-process clause are not limited to the package of Bill of Rights guarantees that it incorporates. The guarantee that no state shall deprive any person of life, liberty, or property without due process of law means in general that the criminal process must be fair. It includes such guarantees as the requirement that criminal conviction be established beyond a reasonable doubt, the obligation of the prosecutor to disclose evidence that might be helpful to the defense, the prohibition against identification lineups in which the accused is the only person in the lineup of his size, race, or sex and the prohibition against joinder with other defendants whose mere presence in the same trial might be prejudicial to the accused.[11]

Analysis of procedural due process in the civil context is aided by separate consideration of the parts of the due-process clause. First, what kinds of interests rise to the level of life, liberty, or property for Fifth and Fourteenth amendment purposes; and second, what kinds of procedural protections are sufficient to satisfy the provision that the deprivation not be without due process of law? Each of these issues is separately examined below.

The Meaning of "Property" for Due-Process Purposes

The types of interests that rise to the level of "liberty" or "property" for Fourteenth Amendment due-process purposes have never been satisfactorily defined. Some general guidance can be derived, however, from the facts and holdings of some Supreme Court cases. In *Sniadach v. Family Finance Corporation*, the Court held that wage garnishments, prior to judgment, are unconstitutional.[12] Even though the wages had not yet been paid, they had been earned; and, prior to a judicial trial, there had been no hearing in which the wage earner was given the opportunity to show that in fact his creditor was not entitled to this property interest in his wages. In *Goldberg v. Kelly*, the Court further held that a state could not constitutionally discontinue welfare benefits without affording a hearing to the welfare recipient.[13] What was the "property" interest in *Goldberg v. Kelly*? The Constitution imposes no obligation on any state to provide welfare benefits. How, then, can it be a violation of due process for the state to discontinue benefits—with or without a hearing—that it is under no obligation to grant in the first place? The Court has given no definitive answer to that question, but I believe that the key to its answer may be contained in a comparison of two cases, handed down two years after *Goldberg v. Kelly*, involving the rights of state university professors to a hearing prior to termination. *Board of Regents v. Roth* held that a nontenured professor at a state university could be terminated without a hearing.[14] However, in a companion case, *Perry v. Sinderman*, the Court strongly suggested that a tenured professor at a state college could not be dismissed without a hearing.[15]

I believe that the harmonizing principle coming out of *Goldberg v. Kelly*, *Board of Regents v. Roth*, and *Perry v. Sinderman* is this: when the only interest of which the individual has been deprived is an expectancy—something that the individual would like to have but on which he can lay no claim more solid than the fact that he would like to have it—then his interest does not rise to the level of "property" for Fourteenth Amendment due-process purposes. Where, by contrast, his interest is based on some legally cognizable source, such as the welfare statute in *Goldberg v. Kelly* or the contract of tenure in *Perry v. Sinderman*, there is a sufficient plus factor to take the interest out of the expectancy category and raise it to the level of property for due-process purposes. The contract is probably easier to understand as a property-type interest, but the statute in *Goldberg v. Kelly* also gives to the welfare recipient something more concrete than a mere expectancy. That is, while New York (the state whose statute was at issue in *Goldberg*) is not obligated to provide welfare benefits, once it makes the decision to do so, and its statutes identify those persons entitled to receive welfare benefits, it has created by statute a property-type interest of which the prospective recipient may not be deprived without giving the recipient the opportunity to show that he should not be so deprived.

The Procedural Protections of Procedural Due Process: Notice and Hearing

As guarantors of procedural fairness, the due-process clauses of the Fifth and Fourteenth amendments concentrate on two related requirements: notice and hearing. The notice part means that, before government may deprive a person of life, liberty, or property, government must give the individual adequate and timely information concerning what it proposes to do to him. The hearing part means that the individual must be given an opportunity to tell his side of the story.

The notice requirement is illustrated by the leading case, *Mullane v. Central Hanover Bank & Trust Co.*[16] The Central Hanover Bank and Trust Company administered a common trust fund for the benefit of a large number of small investors. The amount of money invested by any one of these individuals was so small that the services of an institutional investor would have been too expensive. By pooling his investments with those of other small investors, however, each person could obtain the advantages of the bank's trust and investment services. New York law permitted the bank to give its periodic reports to investors by publishing those reports in the newspaper. The likelihood that any given investor would actually "receive" that report by reading it in the newspaper was slight, however. The issue raised by the *Mullane* case was whether this method of "constructive notice" satisfied the notice component of the due-process-of-law requirement. The Court held that the Constitution requires the best notice that is reasonable under the circumstances. The facts of the *Mullane* case illustrate the application of that principle. The bank had on file the names and addresses of some of the common-trust beneficiaries. Concerning others, the bank did not have this information, and it would have been expensive to obtain it; in some cases the cost would have exceeded the value of the beneficiary's investment. Applying the "best notice that is reasonable under the circumstances" test, the Court held that due process required the bank to give actual personal notice to persons in the first category, those whose names and addresses were in the bank's files. As to them the cost of actual notice was small; notice was therefore reasonable and constitutionally required. For members of the second category, however, the analysis was different. The cost of actual notice was substantial and was not warranted by the individual's interest in receiving actual notice.

The due-process hearing requirement is illustrated by *Board of Curators of University of Mo. v. Horowitz.*[17] Barbara Horowitz had been dismissed from her medical-studies program at the University of Missouri while she was doing residency work as part of her fourth year of that program. She brought suit, contending that the Fourteenth Amendment's due-process clause protected her from being dismissed without a hearing, at which she would be informed of the reasons for her proposed dismissal and given the opportunity to present the reasons she should not be dismissed. The Supreme Court ruled against her. She was entitled to a hearing, but due process does not always require a formal hearing, with such trappings as transcribed testimony and both sides represented by counsel. During the period of her clinical work Ms. Horowitz had been informed on numerous occasions that her work was not satisfactory. She knew that dismissal was a distinct possibility if her work did not improve. If she had any favorable evidence that the medical-school authorities should have taken into account, there had been ample opportunity to present it. A more formal hearing was not required.

Irrebuttable Presumptions

There is an analytical overlap between procedural due process and equal protection in the area of what the Supreme Court has termed "irrebuttable presumptions." What is an irrebuttable presumption? Two examples will illustrate. A Connecticut statute provided that students attending the University of Connecticut who were nonresidents at the time they enrolled at the university would not thereafter qualify for resident tuition. The Supreme Court held, in *Vlandis v. Kline*, that this rule was a violation of procedural due process.[18] The rationale was as follows. Some students who are nonresidents at the time they enroll will in fact become Connecticut residents at some later time while they are still in school. Denying them the lower tuition rate is a deprivation of property, because as residents they are entitled to the resident tuition. It is accomplished without procedural due process because they are not given the opportunity to show that in fact they have become residents. Therefore, this "irrebuttable presumption" that nonresident students will always remain nonresidents is a violation of the due-process clause.

The second example is the more famous one; it is the pregnant teachers' case. School boards in some parts of the country, including Cleveland, Ohio, had adopted a rule that any teacher who became pregnant during the course of the school year would be required to take a mandatory maternity leave without pay at a certain point of her pregnancy, typically four or five months. JoCarol LaFleur successfully challenged the Cleveland Board of Education's pregnant teachers' rule on the ground that it was an irrebuttable presumption (*Cleveland Board of Education v. LaFleur*).[19] Her contention, in essence, was this: "It is true that some women are less able to perform their duties as teachers once pregnancy reaches a certain stage. That is not true of all persons, however, and it is not true of me. All I want is a chance to prove that I am one of those whom pregnancy does not incapacitate as a teacher. Forcing me to leave my job by irrebuttably presuming that I am less able to teach because of my pregnancy deprives me of property—my teacher's wages—without a hearing and therefore without due process of law. If the school board provided a hearing, I could show that my abilities as a teacher do not diminish when I am pregnant." The Supreme Court agreed with this argument.

At this point, the astute reader will ask, what about Mr. Murgia, the over-age policeman? Could he not make the same argument made by Ms. LaFleur? The answer is yes. Then why did he lose his case when LaFleur won? The only real factual difference between them is that, whereas Ms. LaFleur would have lost only a few month's pay, Mr. Murgia lost his employment for the rest of his life. The complete identity between Murgia's argument and those of LaFleur (and the Connecticut University student, Vlandis) can be demonstrated by referring once again to the diagrams used in the previous chapter and with modification reproduced on page 173. In all three cases, Vlandis, LaFleur, and Murgia were making exactly the same argument: in a legitimate attempt to solve one of its problems, the state was attempting to identify out of a large group of people (represented by the larger circle) a subgroup (represented by the smaller circle) and to withhold certain benefits from members of that subgroup. In each case, the state acted safely within its constitutional bounds when it treated people within the subgroups less favorably—and none of the plaintiffs in any of the cases contended otherwise. In each of the three cases, the complainant's contention was the same: "The state has a right to target persons falling within the smaller circle for disfavored treatment. The problem is that I have been disfavored because I, who was numbered among the subgroup, should have been considered as an exception."

This circumstance—where the state in effect aims at one class of people, but its program in fact hits not only those people but a few others as well—can be approached either under the equal-protection or the due-process clause. The equal-protection argument is examined in Chapter 14. The due-process argument—which could be made by Murgia just as easily as by Vlandis and LaFleur—is this: "I have been treated as if I were a member of the target class, contained within the smaller circle. In fact, I really don't belong in that circle. I really belong in that part of the larger circle not covered by the smaller circle. The due-

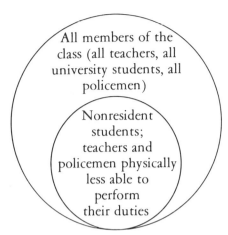

process clause entitles me to a hearing so that I can prove that in fact I do not belong in the smaller circle in which the state has placed me."

Even though the applicable equal-protection and procedural due-process theories are quite different, any case that can be treated as a due-process irrebuttable-presumption problem can also be treated as an equal-protection problem. Yet the results are apt to be diametrically opposed, as comparison of the results in the *Vlandis*, *LaFleur*, and *Murgia* cases demonstrates. The reason is that, if one of these mistargeting cases is treated as an equal-protection case, as in *Murgia*, the reasonable-basis test will apply and government will probably win, unless a suspect classification or fundamental right happens to be involved. (Neither a suspect classification nor a fundamental right was involved in *Murgia*, *Vlandis*, or *LaFleur*.) Treated as a due-process, irrebuttable-presumption case, the pre-merits weighting of the balance scales favors the individual rather than government. The standard, the Supreme Court says, is that irrebuttable presumptions are "not favored," which translates into a weighting against the government.

All of this, of course, makes no sense at all. Any irrebuttable-presumption case can also be analyzed as an equal-protection case. The development of equal-protection doctrine has involved a general rule favoring governmental-policy choices, and two exceptions disfavoring governmental-policy choices where the classification basis is suspect or the individual right is fundamental. The irrebuttable-presumption doctrine superimposes on this equal-protection structure a completely different set of considerations. Its effect is to carve out yet another exception from the reasonable-basis general rule without purporting to do so and without regard for what this does to equal-protection principles. I believe that this circumstance cannot continue to exist and that, in time, the Supreme Court will back away from its flirtation with irrebuttable presumptions. Indeed, I believe that *Murgia* (which was decided after *LaFleur*) may mark the beginning of that development. Notwithstanding the obvious similarities between *Murgia* and *LaFleur*, the Court decided *Murgia* exclusively as a reasonable-basis, equal-protection case, upheld the governmental policy, and never mentioned irrebuttable presumptions.

Indigent Access to Judicial Proceedings

Another area of overlap between the due-process clause and the equal-protection clause involves the problem of poor people, who, because they are poor, do not have the same access to judicial proceedings as rich persons. The problem is illustrated by *Griffin v. Illinois*, probably the leading case in that area.[20] Judson Griffin, who had been convicted of armed robbery in the criminal court of Cook County, Illinois, wanted to appeal his conviction. He could not do so, however, because Illinois law conditioned the right of appeal on the appellant's furnishing a copy of the trial transcript. (The transcript is a record of some of the proceedings before the trial court whose judgment is being appealed. A transcript is helpful to the appellate court in determining whether errors justifying a new trial or reversal of the conviction were committed in the lower court.) Mr. Griffin's problem was that he had no money with which to purchase a transcript. As a consequence he could not appeal his case. For Judson Griffin, therefore, and for other persons convicted of noncapital crimes in Illinois, the right of appeal depended exclusively on how much money the individual had.

The Supreme Court held this Illinois procedure unconstitutional on equal-protection grounds. The opening sentences of Justice Black's majority opinion stated the issue as follows:

> Illinois law provides that "Writs of error in all criminal cases are writs of right and shall be issued of course." The question presented here is whether Illinois may, consistent with the Due Process and Equal Protection Clauses of the Fourteenth Amendment, administer this statute so as to deny adequate appellate review to the poor while granting such review to all others.[21]

The prototype represented by the *Griffin* case—access to judicial proceedings is conditioned upon the payment of money, so that the courts are available for some purposes to rich people but not to poor people—can be treated either as an equal-protection or a due-process issue. The equal-protection argument is a bit easier to understand but more difficult to control. Griffin's equal-protection argument, for example, can be paraphrased as follows: "The Constitution guarantees that government will not treat people unequally. Government makes its courts available for the purpose of assuring that people will not be sent to jail without a fair determination of their guilt. Appellate review is part of this governmentally provided judicial process. In Illinois, it is available to people who have enough money to purchase a transcript. It is not available to me, because I don't have money. That is a clear denial of equal treatment."

The due-process argument, by contrast, does not focus on a comparison of the treatment of different individuals. Rather, it inquires whether imposing burdens on people (such as sending them to jail) and depriving them of benefits without affording certain standards of protection offends the constitutionally guaranteed minimum requirement that persons not be deprived of life, liberty, or property without due process of law. Under the due-process inquiry, the fact that some are treated better than others is irrelevant. The controlling question is whether the particular individual has been afforded the minimum standards required by the Constitution.

Each view has had its advocates. *Griffin v. Illinois* was decided as an equal-protection case, as were other cases involving problems of the indigent criminally accused. Thus, the Supreme Court has held that the equal-protection clause requires the furnishing of a free transcript where a transcript is a prerequisite to appeal.[22] The Court has also held that an indigent has an equal-protection right to the waiving of an appellate filing fee and that, in the first appeal granted by the state as a matter of right, the state must provide counsel.[23]

The difficulty with the equal-protection rationale in this context is that it imposes impossible tasks of linedrawing. In *Griffin*, for example, the Court reasoned that "[T]here can be no equal justice where the kind of trial a man gets depends on the amount of money he has."[24] Notwithstanding the attractiveness of this dictum, the fact is that the quality of legal representation that a person enjoys frequently depends on the amount of money he has. Holding, as the Court did in *Douglas v. California*, that the state is required to provide legal counsel for the first appeal as a matter of right eliminates only a small part of the disparity between the legal representation available to the rich person and the poor person.[25] To the poor person, the state provides a lawyer—an inexperienced recent graduate employed by the legal defender's office. The wealthy person can hire a battery of lawyers, including the most skillful and the most experienced. To the extent that inequality exists, therefore, it exists not because of the governmental action condemned by the Fourteenth Amendment, but for other reasons that have nothing to do with the Constitution or government.

Notwithstanding language like that quoted above, the Supreme Court has in fact drawn some lines that limit the application of the *Griffin v. Illinois* equal-protection holding. The right to counsel on the first, nondiscretionary appeal, declared by *Douglas v. California*, was held not to extend to discretionary appeals in *Ross v. Moffit.*[26]

The problem of the rich person having better access to court proceedings than the poor person is not limited to criminal matters. It is interesting that, while the criminal cases have been decided under the equal-protection clause, in the civil context it has been due process that has carried the day. The leading case involving civil matters is *Boddie v. Connecticut*, which held that Connecticut could not constitutionally require indigent welfare recipients to pay divorce filing fees and costs for service of process—fees that amounted to sixty dollars.[27] The reason that requiring such fees of people who could not pay them violated the due-process clause was as follows. The state of Connecticut had retained for itself the exclusive means of dissolving the marriage relationship. There was no way to get a divorce in Connecticut other than by filing a lawsuit. Conditioning access to the only means by which divorce could be obtained on the payment of a fee that, for an indigent, was impossible to pay constituted a deprivation of due process of law.

Two other civil indigent-access cases have come before the Supreme Court since *Boddie*. Relief was denied in both, and the combined effect appears to be that the unavailability of civil judicial proceedings on account of poverty offends the due-process clause only when, as in the case of divorce, there is absolutely no other relief available. In *United States v. Kras*, the Supreme Court refused to apply the *Boddie* principle to the fifty-dollar filing-fee requirement in voluntary bankruptcy proceedings.[28] One of the reasons was that the "utter exclusiveness" of the divorce action as a means for obtaining a divorce did not apply to bankruptcy. There were other possible means for obtaining relief. Two months later, in *Ortwein v. Schwab*, the Court rejected a challenge to an Oregon statute requiring the payment of a twenty-five-dollar fee as a prerequisite to judicial review of administrative denials of welfare benefits.[29]

While there is an alternate basis for reconciling the holdings in *Boddie*, *Kras*, and *Ortwein* (the Court indicated that the marriage interest in *Boddie* is more fundamental than the interests in the other cases), I believe that the principle evolving from these three cases is that due process of law prevents application of a financial requirement for indigent access to judicial proceedings only where the judicial proceeding provides the exclusive means of securing the indigent's interests. The cases also indicate that the definition of "exclusive" for these purposes is very narrow.

CHAPTER SIXTEEN

The State-Action Limitation

The first three words of the Fourteenth Amendment sentence containing the due-process and equal-protection guarantees are, "No state shall." This means that the equal-protection and due-process provisions are binding only against actions by state governments. An important body of constitutional law has grown up around this "state action" limitation.

The starting point for analysis of the state-action issue is a consideration of the structure of the Fourteenth Amendment. The Fourteenth Amendment consists of five sections. The most important, Section 1, contains two sentences. The purpose of the first sentence was to make the newly freed slaves United States citizens, thereby overturning the Supreme Court's notorious decision in *Dred Scott v. Sandford.*[1] The second sentence, beginning with the words "No state shall," contains the substantive guarantees: privileges or immunities, due process, and equal protection. Sections 2, 3, and 4 are of historical interest and have little importance today. Section 5 provides: "The Congress shall have power to enforce, by appropriate legislation, the provisions of this [amendment]."

One of the earliest Fourteenth Amendment issues was whether the implementing authority that Congress enjoys by virtue of Section 5 gives it the power to pass statutes prohibiting private as well as governmental discrimination. In other words, is Congress's lawmaking authority under Section 5 subject to the limitation in Section 1 that only governmental discrimination is prohibited? If the answer to that question is yes, then Congress's role under Section 5 is a fairly limited one; the Fourteenth Amendment's prohibition against denials of due process and equal protection need no congressional legislation to make them effective, and the congressional role is merely to flesh out the details of the prohibition against state actions. If the answer to the question is no, however, then Section 5 would perhaps be equal in importance to Section 1, because it would provide a constitutional basis for congressional authority to prohibit not just governmental discriminations and due process denials but private ones as well.

This issue was squarely faced in a famous early Supreme Court decision, *The Civil Rights Cases.*[2] *The Civil Rights Cases* were five cases involving discrimination against blacks by privately owned hotels, theatres, and railroads. The discriminatory practices violated a congressional statute, the Civil Rights Act of 1875, enacted pursuant to Section 5 of the Fourteenth Amendment. The holdings of those cases were: (1) the Fourteenth Amendment prohibits only state action and does not prohibit any kind of private, nongovernmental discrimination; and (2) the state-action limitation applies to Section 5 as well as to Section 1. Congress's authority to enact implementing legislation was therefore limited to the enactment of laws prohibiting state discrimination or unfairness.

Analysis of the *Civil Rights Cases* is aided by considering its holdings as the three parts of a syllogism. A syllogism is a tool of logic consisting of a major premise, a minor premise, and a conclusion. As applied to the *Civil Rights Cases,* the three points are:

1. *Major Premise:* The Fourteenth Amendment prohibits only state action.
2. *Minor Premise:* The activity involved in the *Civil Rights Cases* did not involve state action.
3. *Conclusion:* Therefore, the discriminatory practices in the *Civil Rights Cases* did not violate the Fourteenth Amendment.

The *Civil Rights Cases* were decided about one hundred years ago. Since that time, thousands of Fourteenth Amendment cases have been decided. Over that period, the *Civil Rights Cases'* major premise—that the Fourteenth Amendment prohibits only state action—has remained firm. The constitutional law developments pertaining to state action since the *Civil Rights Cases* have involved the minor premise. The problem has been a definitional one: what is meant by "state action" for Fourteenth Amendment purposes? Some of the more important of these developments will now be examined.

Probably the most famous case expanding the category of acts that constitute state action is *Shelley v. Kraemer.*[3] *Shelley v. Kraemer* was a challenge to the constitutionality of a real-estate device known as a restrictive covenant. A restrictive covenant is a written agreement, in a deed or other document, under which the parties agree to restrict the use and occupancy of real property in certain ways. In *Shelley v. Kraemer,* the restrictive covenant restricted the use and occupancy of the property for fifty years to persons of "the Caucasian race." The owners of houses subject to that condition sold to black buyers. Some of the neighboring property owners whose properties were also subject to the restrictive covenants brought suit to enforce the covenants. The state courts agreed with the neighboring property owners and enforced the covenants. On appeal, the United States Supreme Court held that the orders of the state courts violated the Fourteenth Amendment.

The denial of equal protection was clear; the covenant contained a discrimination based on race. But where was the state action? The answer is that it rested in the orders entered by the state courts. A state may act not only through its legislative branch and its executive branch but also through its courts. The restrictive covenants themselves were strictly private conduct; even though discriminatory, they violated no constitutional prohibition. But when the neighboring property owners went to court to enforce the covenants they enlisted an arm of government, the courts; and it was these governmental entities that issued the orders that put teeth into the private discrimination.

Assume that a private person has a backyard neighborhood party to which he invites all of his neighbors except one. The person not invited is Jewish, and the reason for his exclusion is that the host is staunchly anti-Semitic. Assume further that the Jewish neighbor crashes the party and the host sues him for trespassing. Does the *Shelley v. Kraemer* holding mean that the courts may not enforce that kind of private action for trespassing? The answer is that *Shelley v. Kraemer* probably does not reach that kind of judicial enforcement of private discrimination. Then what is the difference? Though a definitive answer cannot be given, my view of the controlling difference between the two cases is that in *Shelley v. Kraemer*, unlike the neighborhood hypothetical, there was no discriminatory practice in the basic transaction between the parties involved. There would never have been any discrimination in *Shelley v. Kraemer* if the state court had not intervened. The Supreme Court's opinion in *Shelley v. Kraemer* repeatedly stresses that there was a willing buyer and a willing seller involved in that case. That is, the black person wanted to buy the property and the owner wanted to sell it to him. In the basic transaction, therefore, there was no discrimination; and there would have been none if the courts—the instruments of government—had stayed out of the picture. That is not true of the neighborhood party. The private discrimination in that hypothetical case existed prior to the judicial involvement.

Much of the state-action controversy has centered on the "governmental function" issue: when private persons or entities do the kinds of things that are traditionally done by government, they may be treated like government for Fourteenth-Amendment purposes. For example, in a series of cases beginning with *Nixon v. Herndon* the Court held that blacks could not constitutionally be excluded from participating in the Texas primary elections.[4] Even though the Democratic party is not an official component of Texas state government, its discriminatory acts constitute state action for Fourteenth-Amendment purposes. The reason is that the Democratic party performs an essential governmental task—the selection of those persons who will be candidates for public office. Many of the candidates will eventually become public officers. Since the function of the Democratic party lies so close to the official governmental activities of the state of Texas, its discriminatory acts will be treated as state action.

Perhaps the leading governmental-function case is *Marsh v. Alabama.*[5] Grace Marsh was a Jehovah's Witness. Like many Jehovah's Witnesses, she devoted time to proselyting for her church. She was convicted under Alabama's criminal-trespass law for distributing religious literature without permission in the town of Chickasaw. Chickasaw, a suburb of Mobile, was a "company town" owned and operated by the Gulf Shipbuilding Corporation. Aside from its private ownership, however, Chickasaw had "all the characteristics of any other American town."[6] The Supreme Court held that under those circumstances Ms. Marsh could not be excluded from proselyting. In spite of being a purely private entity, the Gulf Shipbuilding Corporation had to obey the Fourteenth Amendment as the owner of Chickasaw because, in that capacity, the corporation functioned as a government.

Two cases appear to have diminished somewhat the scope of the governmental-function modification of the state-action doctrine. The first of these is *Jackson v. Metropolitan Edison Co.*[7] The Metropolitan Edison Company is a private electric utility operating in Pennsylvania. It discontinued electrical service to Ms. Jackson, contending that she had failed to pay her bills. She filed suit, arguing that before her electrical service was discontinued she should have been given a hearing and that cutting off her electricity without a hearing deprived her of property without due process of law, in violation of the Fourteenth Amendment. A continued supply of electricity was certainly a property interest for due-process purposes, and she had been given no hearing. The standard Fourteenth Amendment elements of procedural due process were therefore present. But where was the state action? Metropolitan Edison Company was a privately owned corporation.

Ms. Jackson argued that the generation and supply of electricity is the kind of service that government typically either provides itself or authorizes someone else to provide through an exclusive monopoly granted by the state. This was the case with Metropolitan Edison. The only reason that the Metropolitan Edison Company was in a position to sell electricity to anyone was that the state had authorized it to do so. The power company was therefore performing a governmental function and should be governed by the Fourteenth Amendment's guarantee against procedural deprivations of due process.

Compare this argument with that of Irvis in *Moose Lodge No. 107 v. Irvis.*[8] Mr. Irvis was the black guest of a member of a private club that refused to serve liquor to nonwhites. He contended that the club's discrimination amounted to state action for Fourteenth Amendment purposes. He pointed out that the discrimination consisted of refusal to serve him liquor. The authority of the club to serve liquor to him or to anyone else depended exclusively on the club's liquor license. And who had granted the liquor license? The Pennsylvania Liquor Regulatory Commission, a governmental agency of the state of Pennsylvania. Mr. Irvis therefore contended that in its sales of liquor—and its discriminatory practice of refusing to sell to some because of their race—the action of the Moose Lodge was linked to that of the state of Pennsylvania, and the Fourteenth Amendment's equal-protection clause should apply.

In both cases, the Supreme Court rejected these governmental-function arguments. In both cases, the Court's rationale seemed to deemphasize the governmental-function strand of the state-action doctrine and to rely instead on the question of whether the decision to deny due process or equal protection could be attributed to a public entity or was solely a private decision. The Pennsylvania Public Utilities Commission may regulate the Metropolitan Edison Company in many ways, the Court pointed out in *Jackson,* but the decision to cut off Jackson's electricity without a hearing was made by the company alone. No state agency had anything to do with that decision, and it was that decision of which Ms. Jackson complained. Similarly, in the *Moose Lodge* case, the Court reasoned that the state had granted the Lodge's liquor license, but it did not participate in any way in the club's decision to discriminate against Mr. Irvis. The governmental-function aspects of the lodge's activities and the power company's activities, therefore, were not controlling. What was controlling was the fact that in each instance the particular conduct that allegedly violated the Fourteenth Amendment resulted from a purely private decision.

In recent years the Thirteenth Amendment has had an important role in the development of state-action doctrine. The leading case is *Jones v. Alfred Mayer Co.*, which upheld the constitutionality of a section of the Civil Rights Act of 1866 prohibiting private discrimination with respect to transactions in real and personal property.[9] Congress would have lacked authority to enact such legislation pursuant to the Fourteenth Amendment, because it dealt only with private conduct rather than state action. The Court nevertheless sustained Congress's authority to enact this statute, not under the Fourteenth Amendment, but under the Thirteenth. The Thirteenth Amendment consists of two sections. Section 1 outlaws slavery and involuntary servitude (except as a punishment for crime). Section 2 is similar to Section 5 of the

Fourteenth Amendment, giving Congress "power to enforce this [Amendment] by appropriate legislation."

Unlike the Fourteenth Amendment, therefore, the Thirteenth contains no state-action limitations. In *Jones v. Mayer*, the Supreme Court reasoned that Section 2 must have given Congress the authority to do more than abolish slavery and involuntary servitude. That much was accomplished by Section 1, unaided by any congressional legislation. Therefore, the Court reasoned, Section 2 gave Congress the authority to identify and eradicate not only slavery and involuntary servitude but also the "badges," "incidents," and "relics" of slavery. Those issues are largely for congressional determination and lie within the scope of congressional discretion. The Court held that, "when racial discrimination herds men into ghettos and makes their ability to buy property turn on the color of their skin, then it too is a relic of slavery."[10]

The *Jones v. Mayer* holding is a significant one. It gives Congress the authority to prohibit private as well as governmental discrimination. There are, however, two limiting factors: (1) Congress must enact a statute, and (2) the private conduct must be in the area of racial discrimination.

In summary, the major premise of the *Civil Rights Cases*, which has remained the law for over a century, is that the Fourteenth Amendment's guarantees apply only to governmental and not to private action. It is a limitation that applies to the due-process clause as well as equal protection, though most of the litigated state-action cases have been equal-protection, racial-discrimination cases.

Though the *Civil Rights Cases* precedent has remained firm, the equal-protection and due-process guarantees have extended to several areas of conduct that might be considered private. The extension has had two dimensions: enlargement of what constitutes state action under the Fourteenth Amendment, and statutory prohibitions against racial discrimination, enacted under Congress's Thirteenth Amendment powers. The first applies to all Fourteenth Amendment guarantees and the second only to racial discrimination.

CHAPTER SEVENTEEN

The Constitution and the Courts: Policymaking and Adjudication

Chapter 15 discusses some of the meanings of due process of law. Those few words say nothing about free speech or jury trial, yet they guarantee both of these and much more. How has such an apparently expanded interpretation of those words come about? The history of the impairment of the obligation-of-contracts clause is treated in Chapter 9. At one time that clause was considered virtually dormant; today it has new vitality. Since its adoption the contract-clause language has remained unchanged. How, then, did it experience such a change in meaning and impact? The Constitution can be searched in vain for any mention of words such as "irrebuttable presumption" or "right to travel"; yet laws enacted by the people's elected representatives have been stripped of all force and effect because they were found to constitute irrebuttable presumptions or to infringe on the right to travel. Why?

In each instance, the answer is the same: Those results came about because a majority of nine people said that they were required by the United States Constitution. Those nine people are the justices of the United States Supreme Court.

The American Constitution is inseparably bound up with the American people. Our constitutional legacy from Madison is that governmental power derives from the people. In addition, the main function of the Constitution is to secure the rights of the people. Given this intimate relationship between the Constitution and the people, is it a good idea to place the stewardship for securing constitutional rights in the federal judges? Of the three branches of the federal government, the judges have the least requirement to be responsive to the people. The top officials of the legislative and executive branches occupy their positions because the people elected them. There are no elected federal judges; all are appointed. Whether the President and members of Congress can continue in office also depends on the people. Appointments of federal judges are for life. Finally, Article III guarantees that the judges' compensation may not be diminished during their term in office. Probably the most prominent characteristic of the United States judiciary compared to its sister branches, therefore, is the degree of insulation from the people that its occupants enjoy. Chapters 17 and 18 discuss some of the issues raised by the fact that the vindication of a people's Constitution rests primarily with a branch whose officials are deliberately and effectively insulated from direct influence by the people. The starting point is a discussion of judicial review.

Judicial Review

The meaning of the Constitution may be pronounced by lower federal-court judges or by state-court judges; those pronouncements are subject to review and reversal by the United States Supreme Court. Once a majority of the members of that Court have expressed their view of what the Constitution means, there is no review. Their decision is final and binding on all other governmental officials and on everyone in this country. The only way to change their decision is either to persuade the Court to reverse the holding or to obtain a constitutional amendment. The first is a rare occurrence; the judicial doctrine, *stare decisis* (let the decision stand), dictates that, in the interest of stability and predictability, judicial decisions should be reversed only under extraordinary circumstances. The second occurs even more rarely. On only two (or arguably three) occasions has a constitutional amendment overturned a Supreme Court decision.

Each of the three branches of the federal government enjoys a primacy within a particular area of government endeavor. This is one of the bedrock principles of separation of powers. The judiciary's power is the power to interpret the laws. In the landmark decision *Marbury v. Madison* the Supreme Court held that the "laws" with whose interpretation the courts are charged include the Constitution.[1] In the language of the *Marbury* opinion: "It is emphatically the province and duty of the judicial department to say what the law is."[2] This implicitly includes the Constitution as part of "the law."

In a sense the *Marbury* holding is a bootstrap. It declares that the Constitution gives the power of its own interpretation to the courts, and yet *Marbury* itself was an interpretation by a court. Bootstrap or not, *Marbury's* holding that constitutional interpretation is basically a judicial function seems to be supported by constitutional history and by common sense. The most persuasive historical support is found in *The Federalist*, Number 78, in which Hamilton wrote:

> The interpretation of the laws is the proper and peculiar province of the courts. A constitution is in fact, and must be, regarded by the judges as fundamental law. It therefore belongs to them to ascertain its meaning

as well as the meaning of any particular act proceeding from the legislative body.

It is common sense that someone has to determine what the Constitution means. This is particularly important with a constitution that was drafted in terms as broad and vague as those of the United States Constitution. What is meant by free speech and free exercise of religion? Are these guarantees absolutes? Does Congress's exclusive authority to regulate interstate commerce prohibit state regulations if Congress has not acted? The answers to these and many other questions are far from obvious. Yet if our nation is to function as a constitutional republic, answers to constitutional questions must be supplied by someone. The most logical candidates are judges. The traditional province of judges is to deal with issues of law, to say what the law is and what it means. The Constitution is certainly law. The interpretation of the laws has been vested in one branch; it therefore makes sense that that branch would interpret all the laws, including the Constitution.

Moreover, the most important function of the Constitution is the protection of individual rights. In the usual case, this necessarily means minority rights—not just racial or ethnic minorities, but minorities in a much more fundamental sense. Constitutional law protects the rights of the individual against the decisions and acts of government. In the usual case, government acts in the interest of the majority of its citizens. Those who make the laws are elected by the majority. By hypothesis, therefore, the individual rights that come in conflict with government interests will usually be minority rights. That is not only true of Oliver Brown, who sought to integrate the Topeka schools; it was also true of Margaret Kline, JoCarol LaFleur, Robert Murgia, and Leo Nebbia. The most effective protection for the rights of the majority is through the ballot box. If the majority disagrees with what the legislature has done, then, theoretically at least, the majority should be able to effect changes by electing other people. On the other hand, the United States Constitution insulates federal judges from political pressures by providing for their lifetime appointment, rather than election, and by guaranteeing that their compensation shall not be diminished during their time in office. Since their continuance in office does not depend on the will of the majority, federal judges are the most appropriate safeguards of constitutionally guaranteed minority rights.

As a matter of history and as a matter of common sense, therefore, the power of constitutional interpretation belongs in the courts. Alexander Hamilton, in Number 78 of *The Federalist*, expressed the view that "the judiciary from the nature of its functions, will always be the least dangerous to the political rights of the constitution."

Was Hamilton's prediction correct? Has the judiciary in fact proven itself the "least dangerous branch"? A good case can be made for the proposition that it is the most dangerous branch, precisely because of its power to say what the Constitution means. We call that the power of judicial review. The main reason that judicial review is such an important power is that the most significant of the constitutional provisions are cast in such broad, general terms. Consider the language of those provisions:

> The Congress shall have Power . . . To regulate Commerce . . . among the several States (Article I Section 8).

> Congress shall make no law respecting an establishment of religion, or prohibiting the free exercise thereof; or abridging the freedom of speech, or of the press (First Amendment).

> No State shall . . . deprive any person of life, liberty, or property, without due process of law; nor deny to any person within its jurisdiction the equal protection of the laws (Fourteenth Amendment, Section 1).

These provisions do not answer the many specific questions pertaining to interstate commerce, speech and religious activities, fairness, and equality that arise in the course of the American people's activities. They were not intended to provide specific answers. They are the ultimate in breadth, vagueness, and generality. They chart the general course for the ship of state but leave it to the helmsmen to do the steering.

The reason that the Supreme Court is such a powerful institution, therefore, rests on a combination of three factors:

1. The Constitution is the supreme law of the land; any other law that is inconsistent with it is invalid for that reason.
2. The most important provisions of the Constitution are cast in language of extraordinary breadth and vagueness so that the real meaning of this supreme law is vested in the entity that is empowered to say what these broad terms really mean.
3. The interpretive authority and responsibility are vested in the courts—ultimately the United States Supreme Court. They perform the task of pouring content into the vagaries of the Constitution as they decide disputes that come before them on a case-to-case basis.

Judicial Review versus Legislative Policymaking

The discharge of the Supreme Court's responsibility to interpret the Constitution necessarily involves it and the lower courts in a kind of policymaking. (See chapter 4.) Yet policymaking is the primary responsibility of the legislative branch—Congress for the nation as a whole and the state legislatures for their respective states. How then, do the courts go about their job of policymaking—policymaking necessary to their stewardship as interpreters of the Constitution—without infringing on the legislative domain?

That issue is one of the most important and one of the most difficult the courts face. In my opinion, there is no single definitive answer. I believe the most helpful guideline is that courts should always be conscious of the potential infringement of their constitutional interpretive responsibilities on the policymaking authority of the legislature and that, in cases of doubt, they should err on the side of deference to the legislative judgment.

An understanding of the problems of judicial policymaking versus legislative policymaking is assisted more by examples than by abstract discussion. The most egregious examples of judicial abuse of power are provided by the substantive due-process cases.

Today there is almost universal agreement among judges and scholars that the *Lochner* approach to substantive due process was wrong. Why was it wrong? In my view, the *Lochner* approach was wrong because of the extent to which it not only permitted but, indeed, encouraged courts to invade the policymaking domain of the legislature. It has been stated earlier that virtually anything that government does can have some adverse effect on individual interests. That proposition can be expanded: Virtually anything that government does can have some adverse effect on the interests of some individual that can be characterized as liberty or property interests. The *Allgeyer*, *Lochner*, and *Nebbia* cases certainly demonstrate this. As a consequence, judicial authority to invalidate legislative policymaking judgments on substantive due-process grounds gives the courts carte blanche authority to rewrite legislation at will behind the facade of constitutional adjudication.

The point should not be oversimplified. Courts have an obligation to decide constitutional cases that are brought before them. When the constitutional challenge is that there has been a deprivation of life, liberty, or property without due process of law, the courts must decide the question. In the process they must necessarily decide what constitutes the deprivation of life, liberty, or property without due process of law. Should bakery employees be protected from the toll taken on their health by working too many hours in the heat and dust of a bakery? Even more important, who should decide that question, the legislature or the courts? It is basically a public-policy question, the kind of question whose relevant facts are much more susceptible to legislative than to judicial fact finding. Even more important, policymaking under our separation-of-powers system is the primary domain of the legislature. These considerations counsel us, I believe, that courts should upset such legislative policy judgments only under extraordinary circumstances. This is what makes *Nebbia* such a landmark case. It leaves the basic responsibility for policymaking in the legislature and assures that the legislative judgment will be upset only under rare and compelling circumstances.

The New Substantive Due Process

In recent years the *Lochner* approach to substantive due process has shown unmistakable signs of making a comeback. In 1965, in *Griswold v. Connecticut*, the Supreme Court held unconstitutional a Connecticut law that prohibited dissemination of birth-control information; and eight years later, in *Roe v. Wade*, state laws prohibiting abortions were held unconstitutional.[3] In both cases the Court held that the right violated was a right of "privacy" which the Court held to be a "fundamental" right. Reliance was placed on an earlier case, *Skinner v. Oklahoma*, which invalidated an Oklahoma statute requiring sexual sterilization of persons convicted three times of certain felonies.[4]

The Constitution can be searched in vain for any express reference to a right of privacy. Neither in *Griswold* nor in *Roe* did the Court specify where in the Constitution this right is to be found. Justice Douglas, the author of the majority opinion in *Griswold*, found it emanating from a variety of constitutional provisions, including the First, Third, Fourth, Fifth, and Ninth amendments. This is the famous "penumbra" theory. Penumbra means shadow, and the privacy-related shadows cast by each of those amendments—none of which mentions a right of sexual privacy—combined to create the right of sexual privacy that the Court found violated.

In what sense do these cases represent a resurrection of *Lochner*? The Court certainly did not rely on *Lochner* in either opinion, and the words "substantive due process" were never used. Indeed, both the case and the term are anathema to the author of the majority opinion in *Griswold*, Justice Douglas.

I believe that *Griswold* and the abortion cases represent a resurrection of *Lochner* because they vest in the judiciary the license to roam at will through the territory of legislative policymaking. If an unmentioned constitutional right can be pieced together by the judiciary out of bits and scraps that bear some resemblance to a variety of other provisions in the Constitution, then there is little limit to the extent to which judges can substitute their own judgment for that of the legislature. On an even more specific level, I believe that the real basis for *Griswold* and *Roe* is in fact substantive due process. The real basis for the existence of the sexual right of privacy is that sexual privacy is tantamount to "liberty." And where is the only generalized, unspecified constitutional reference to liberty? In the due-process clauses of the Fifth and Fourteenth amendments.

A parenthetical comment is appropriate at this point. In my view *Griswold*, *Roe*, and related decisions represent improper judicial intrusions into fundamental policy decisions that ought to be left to the legislature. It should be noted, however, that these holdings represent at least a potential protection for traditional moral values against possible governmental intrusion. Subsequent cases have begun to characterize those decisions as protecting, for example, "the individual's freedom of choice with respect to certain basic matters of procreation, marriage, and family life."[5] In another case, *Moore v. East Cleveland*, the Supreme Court stated, "Our decisions establish that the Constitution protects the sanctity of the family because the institution of the family is deeply rooted in this Nation's history and tradition."[6]

It would appear that the supporting rationale for *Skinner*, *Griswold*, *Roe*, and the other procreation, sexual-privacy, and abortion cases is the protection of individual choice with respect to family matters. Individual choices in this area rise to the level of fundamental rights. These holdings could provide significant protection, therefore, against any governmental efforts to penalize individual decisions concerning family size or to interfere or impinge in any way on individual decisions related to the family.

CHAPTER EIGHTEEN

The Constitution and the Courts: Internal and External Safeguards

The most disturbing aspect of the substantive due-process cases, both the old and the new, is not simply that judges improperly rejected legislative policy decisions concerning abortion and working hours for bakers. Even more serious is what these cases demonstrate concerning the potential power of the federal courts. Judicial decisions concerning the Constitution are final. The Supreme Court's declaration that states cannot prohibit abortions means that states cannot prohibit abortions unless the Constitution itself is amended. What would prevent the Supreme Court from exercising this power to achieve a truly extreme result, such as abolishing Congress or the Democratic party as unconstitutional?

I have heard law-school professors make the assertion, in all apparent seriousness, that "anyone who thinks that the Constitution has anything to do with constitutional law is being naive. Constitutional law can be found solely in the decisions of the United States Supreme Court." Under this view, the Constitution might as well consist of a single sentence: "There is hereby created a Supreme Court, whose decisions on any issue shall constitute the Supreme Law of the land."

That is not what the Constitution says, and it is clear to me that that is far from a correct characterization of the source and content of constitutional law. The fact that such a view can be seriously asserted by intelligent people, however, demonstrates the rather open-ended nature of judicial authority in entering into policy matters. How open-ended is this authority? Are there any limits?

I believe that there are limits. Some are found in the provisions of the Constitution itself; others are found outside the Constitution. The latter are even more sturdy than the limitations that are constitutionally based. They are rooted in the history and the attitudes of the American people.

Constitutionally Based Limitations on Judicial Power

Hamilton's opinion that the judiciary would be the least dangerous branch was based on some rather specific provisions of the United States Constitution. His reasons were:

> Whoever attentively considers the different departments of power must perceive, that in a government in which they are separated from each other, the judiciary, from the nature of its functions, will always be the least dangerous to the political rights of the constitution; because it will be least in a capacity to annoy or injure them. The executive not only dispenses the honors, but holds the sword of the community. The legislature not only commands the purse, but prescribes the rules by which the duties and rights of every citizen are to be regulated. The judiciary on the contrary has no influence over either the sword or the purse, no direction either of the strength or of the wealth of the society, and can take no active resolution whatever. It may truly be said to have neither Force nor Will, but merely judgment; and must ultimately depend upon the aid of the executive arm even for the efficacy of its judgments.
>
> This simple view of the matter suggests several important consequences. It proves incontestably that the judiciary is beyond comparison the weakest of the three departments of power; that it can never attack with success either of the other two; and that all possible care is requisite to enable it to defend itself against their attacks.[1]

The Constitution also provides for other controls over the judiciary. While a federal judge's salary may not be diminished during his continuance in office, any increases are dependent upon congressional action. Failure to grant increases in the face of inflation amounts to effective decreases. Congress also controls the very existence of every federal court except one. The Supreme Court is the only court created by the Constitution; the existence of others is left to congressional discretion.

Even more important than judges' salaries and the creation of lower federal courts is Congress's control over the federal judiciary's jurisdiction. Jurisdiction is a technical legal term that refers to the power of the courts to act as courts. If a court lacks jurisdiction over a certain category of cases, it is powerless to consider any cases falling within that category. For example, the jurisdiction of many courts is tied to a dollar figure. The federal courts lack jurisdiction over many kinds of cases unless the amount in controversy is over $10,000. Therefore, if an automobile-accident case between citizens of two different states is brought in federal court, but the amount in controversy is $10,000 or less, the federal court has no power to consider it. The case falls outside its jurisdiction.

Who made the decision that in many cases federal courts would have no jurisdiction unless the amount in controversy exceeds $10,000? The answer is Congress. If Congress elected to do so, it could raise that amount to $50,000 or $100,000 or $1,000,000. If it chose to do so, Congress could take away very substantial portions of federal judicial jurisdiction. Indeed, it is arguable that Congress could take away all federal judicial power to act except the power of the Supreme Court to consider cases involving ambassadors, consuls, and other public ministers, and cases in which a state is a party. Those two classes of cases constitute the Supreme Court's original jurisdiction, created by the Constitution itself.

Congress has never exercised its power to cut back the jurisdiction of federal courts in any such radical way. The fact that it holds the power to do so, however, constitutes a very effective control over any extreme use of power by the Courts.

Probably the most important constitutionally specified limitation on the power of the courts is the "case or controversy" requirement found in Article III. Article III limits the power of the federal courts to consideration of cases or controversies. This means that the authority of a federal court to decide any issue—constitutional or otherwise—is limited to those instances in which the question is necessary to the resolution of an actual lawsuit that comes before the court. There are many important constitutional issues that neither the United States Supreme Court nor any other court has ever decided. In many instances the resolution of the issue would be helpful to many people. There could be large savings of time and money for government and its citizens if the constitutional uncertainty were resolved. No matter how intensely all persons affected need and want the constitutional question resolved, however, federal courts are without power to decide it until it becomes necessary to decide it in order to resolve a lawsuit one person brings against another person.

This inability of federal courts to answer constitutional questions, except as they are required to do so in order to decide actual lawsuits pending before them, is what is meant by the provision in Article III limiting federal court jurisdiction to cases or controversies. The courts of some states have the power to issue advisory opinions (opinions rendered for the purpose of general guidance) even though not required to decide a pending case. The federal courts do not have advisory-opinion power. The Constitutional Convention seriously considered a proposal for a Council of Revision, which would have been composed of judges and other government officials and which would have given advance review to enactments of Congress, principally for the purpose of determining their constitutionality.[2] That proposal was rejected. As a consequence, there is no federal governmental authority, judicial or nonjudicial, that can make official declarations concerning the constitutionality of statutes apart from judicial holdings that are required to resolve actual lawsuits.

The reason that Article III's case-or-controversy requirement is such an important limitation on federal judicial power is that it limits the circumstances under which federal courts may decide issues of constitutionality. Control over whether such issues will be presented for decision, and when and where and how they will be presented, lies outside the control of the courts. The decision as to whether to file a lawsuit is made by the person who brings it, not by the judge who hears it. In addition, at any point in the litigation, the parties to the lawsuit may voluntarily settle their difference, at which point the case becomes "moot" so that the court lacks authority to decide the issue, even if it wishes to do so.

The Supreme Court has held that the case-or-controversy requirement includes four elements: standing, ripeness, absence of mootness, and absence of a political question. Any case coming before the courts that fails to satisfy any of these four requirements is not a case or controversy within the meaning of Article III, and the federal courts therefore lack jurisdiction to decide it. Another term frequently used in connection with problems of this type is "justiciability"–that is, if a dispute or other attempt to secure a judicial ruling lacks one of the four case-or-controversy requirements, it is not justiciable.

Each of the four elements of case or controversy, or justiciability, is discussed below.

Standing

This is the best known of the case-or-controversy requirements, the one that is most frequently litigated. The focus of the standing requirement is on the person who brings the lawsuit. That person is called the plaintiff, and in order to satisfy the standing requirement the plaintiff must show that the practice or program he is attacking has a particularized effect on his interests.

The phrase frequently used to describe the standing requirement is "injury in fact." The plaintiff must show that he personally has suffered some kind of injury in fact. Moreover, it must be an injury that has some particularity as to him; he must show that he is injured in some way different from the harm that comes to the general populace because of the practice or program that he is attacking. For example, in *Schlesinger v. Reservists Committee to Stop the War*, a group of present and former members of the military reserves challenged the reserve membership of certain members of Congress.[3] They relied on the provision in Article I Section 6 of the Constitution which states that "no person holding any office in the United States shall be a member of either house during his continuance of office." They contended that holding at the same time a position in Congress and also as a member of the Reserves was in square violation of this constitutional prohibition. On its merits the argument appeared sound. The Court did not decide the merits of that issue, however, because the Reservists' attempt to secure a judicial declaration of that issue was not a case or controversy. It was not justiciable, because the plaintiffs lacked standing. There was no particularized harm to them from the constitutional violation that they asserted. To whatever extent they were harmed by the violation of the "incompatibility clause" in Article I Section 6, it was a harm shared by all American citizens. This is insufficient to satisfy the standing requirement.

Ripeness

Standing deals with the issue of who may bring the suit, and ripeness deals with the issue of when the suit may be brought. More specifically, the ripeness element of justiciability goes to the prevention of litigation that is premature—that is, litigation that the plaintiff attempts to bring prior to the time a real case or controversy has developed.

In 1940 Congress passed the controversial Hatch Act, prohibiting federal employees in the executive branch from taking "any active part in political management or in political campaigns." Following passage of the Hatch Act, but before any of its provisions had been enforced, several federal employees and their union brought suit to prevent the Civil Service Commission from enforcing these prohibitions against political activity, alleging that the prohibitions violated their First Amendment rights. In *United Public Workers v. Mitchell*, the Supreme Court held that the case was not ripe.[4] The federal employees had brought suit because of something they feared might happen in the future: the enforcement of the Hatch Act against them. Their suit assumed the occurrence of future acts that in fact might or might not occur. At the time suit was brought, it was unknown whether the federal employees would engage in political activity, whether that activity would fall within the Hatch Act's prohibitions, and whether prosecutions would be brought against them. The case was therefore not justiciable because of a lack of ripeness.

Any time that a constitutional (or other) challenge is brought in federal court in which the plaintiff's case rests on something that may or may not happen in the future, his case may be dismissed as nonjusticiable because it is not ripe.

Mootness

In a sense, mootness represents the other side of ripeness. Its function is to prevent federal courts from deciding cases that represented genuine cases or controversies at the time they were first brought to federal court but that have since lost their adversary, case-or-controversy quality because of subsequent events. The problem is illustrated by *De-Funis v. Odegaard.*[5] On its merits, *DeFunis* was a reverse-discrimination case, such as the *Bakke* case discussed in Chapter 14. Mr. DeFunis brought suit against the University of Washington, contending that he had not been admitted to that university's law school because of the school's preferential admission program for members of racial minorities. He filed his suit in a Washington state court. The trial court agreed with him and entered an order that he be admitted to the law school. By the time the case reached the Supreme Court, DeFunis was in his final quarter of law school. By the time the Court rendered its decision, DeFunis would have graduated. Therefore, even though the plaintiff had an active case or controversy when the lawsuit was first filed, by the time the Supreme Court rendered its decision that decision would no longer make any difference to Mr. DeFunis, because he would have his law degree. Ruling on the issue under those circumstances was therefore not necessary to decide the particular litigation pending before the Court and would amount to nothing more than an advisory opinion.

Political Question

The first three elements of justiciability—standing, ripeness, and absence of mootness—all have a common feature: all are concerned with whether the case is sufficiently adversary and with whether actual interests of real people have been damaged in a specific and concrete way by the constitutional violation that the plaintiff alleges. The political-question issue is different. The function of the political-question doctrine is to identify those few constitutional issues that, regardless of adversariness, concreteness, imminence, or specificity, simply should not be decided by the courts. The doctrine teaches that there are a few constitutional issues that, as a matter of constitutional law, should be decided by a branch of the government other than the judiciary. In a sense, the political-question doctrine constitutes an exception to *Marbury v. Madison. Marbury* held that it is the province of the courts to say what the law is, including constitutional law. From that basic premise, the political-question doctrine carves out a few substantive areas of constitutional law that are not for judicial decision but are left for ultimate decision by one of the judiciary's sister branches.

At one time the political-question doctrine was of great practical importance, because the courts had held it applicable to the issue of apportionment of state legislatures. Over the almost two centuries of our nation's history up to the 1960s, most state legislatures had become grossly malapportioned. Principally because of population shifts, some legislative districts had many times the number of persons as other legislative districts. The result was that the vote of a person from a larger district counted for only a fraction as much as the vote of someone from a smaller district. On its face, this would appear to present obvious equal-protection problems, but the courts refused to consider the issue because the apportionment of state legislatures was held to be a "political question."[6] If the apportionment of state legislatures raised a constitutional question, it was one of those questions that was not appropriate for judicial decision but that should be left to decision by another branch of government. In the case of legislative apportionment, this meant either the state legislatures themselves or Congress. In *Baker v. Carr*, the Supreme Court reversed its earlier decisions and held that legislative-apportionment issues were not political questions and were therefore subject to judicial determination.[7] General guidelines for identifying political questions were listed in the following famous statement in the *Baker v. Carr* opinion as being

> a textually demonstrable constitutional commitment of the issue to a coordinate political department; or a lack of judicially discoverable and manageable standards for resolving it; or the impossibility of deciding without an initial policy determination of a kind clearly for nonjudicial discretion; or the impossibility of a court's undertaking independent resolution without expressing lack of the respect due coordinate branches of government; or an unusual need for unquestioning adherence to a political decision already made; or the potentiality of embarrassment from multifarious pronouncements by various departments on one question.[8]

After *Baker v. Carr*, what kinds of cases fit within these political-question guidelines? Article IV of the Constitution provides that "The United States shall guarantee to every State in this Union a Republican Form of Government." Whether a state has complied with that obligation is a political question. So, also, it would appear, are some issues (including constitutional issues) concerning how the legislative and executive branches conduct their internal affairs; conduct of foreign relations; and the proposal and ratification of constitutional amendments.

In a sense, it is anomalous to consider these case-or-controversy requirements as "limitations" on the court's jurisdiction, because it is the judges themselves who decide whether the requirements are met in any individual case. For this reason, they are arguably limitations out of which the courts may bootstrap themselves.

In theory, this argument has merit. As a practical matter, however, its impact is limited. It is certainly true that the requirements of standing, ripeness, lack of mootness, and absence of political question are sufficiently broad to permit significant room for judicial manipulation. Indeed, in cases where the case-or-controversy issue is a close one, judicial decisions on those suggest that they may be motivated at least in part by whether the court really wants to reach the merits of the case. But this occurs only in close cases. Considered in the context of the total work of the federal judiciary, it detracts only slightly from the importance of the case-or-controversy limitation on the power of the courts. To take an extreme example, the courts never have decided (and never will decide) an issue of public policy or constitutionality just because a judge reads about it in the newspaper or someone writes him a letter and suggests that it ought to be decided. The core concept–that federal judges decide only those issues that are raised in the context of actual litigation between real parties to a real lawsuit–remains inviolate. If a congressman or state legislator is interested in a particular issue, he is free to deal with it immediately by preparing and introducing a bill. A federal judge does not have that flexibility. His power to deal with an issue is dependent upon the decision of someone totally outside his control to file a lawsuit.

Limitations on Judicial Power Not Contained in the Constitution

The importance of the constitutionally provided limitations on judicial power, discussed above, is fairly obvious. Even more effective, in my opinion, are limitations that are not provided by the Constitution – at least not specifically–but that rest on the nature and structure of American government and the history and attitudes of its people.

The discussion in this chapter began by inquiring whether some extreme hypotheticals could ever come about, such as judicial invalidation of the United States Congress or the Democratic party. Even if all other protective devices failed, the main reason that such an extreme use of judicial power would never occur is that the American people would not stand for it. The only reason the Supreme Court and other federal courts have any power at all is that historically, other branches of government recognize and respect the courts' stewardship over constitutional meaning. In terms of actual physical power to enforce their decisions, the courts have none. They depend on the executive branch to enforce their decisions and on the Congress to appropriate whatever money is needed to enforce them. The real reason those two branches do their part is that the American people–the ultimate repository of all government power–are committed to the rule of law. But since in the final analysis it has no real power other than respect for its authority by its sister branches and by the American people, any radical, gross misuse of power would result in a withdrawal of that respect and an accompanying disintegration of the judicial power.

Is the influence of the American people on their courts limited to the prevention of these extreme, almost doomsdaylike circumstances? In my opinion, it is not so limited. Members of the judiciary, unlike members of the legislative and executive branches, are not subject to election. Are the effects that the American people have on the courts in any way analogous to the election of the President and members of Congress?

I believe that question can best be answered by reference to Richard M. Nixon's 1968 presidential campaign and his subsequent performance as President. People who followed Nixon's campaign knew that he disagreed with the substance of many of the Supreme Court's decisions. While it is impossible to determine why people vote as they do, it must be assumed that at least some people took into account Nixon's views concerning the Supreme Court in making their decision to vote for him. During his subsequent years as President, he had the opportunity to appoint four United States Supreme Court justices. While generalizations are difficult, it is fair to say that in many important areas these appointments have resulted in substantive changes in the Court's decisions. The changes have occurred in the general direction that most people would have inferred that candidate Richard Nixon intended when in 1968 he made his reference to "strict construction" of the Constitution. They are changes that have lasted far beyond the term of the man who made the appointments.

What this history shows, I believe, is that, through their election of the President and his subsequent appointment of Supreme Court justices and federal judges in general, there is a long-range interaction between the people and the federal courts. The Nixon example may be one of the more dramatic, because of Nixon's express campaign references and because of the rather identifiable shifts that the Supreme Court made as a result of the four Nixon appointments. With or without the campaign rhetoric, however, I believe that the long-range interplay between the people and the federal courts, with the President as intermediary, necessarily exists.

In making their choice between presidential candidates, people attempt to select the person whose total views most nearly approximate their own. Similarly, most Presidents recognize that few of their official acts as Chief Executive will have as enduring an effect as their appointment of Supreme Court justices. A President will naturally tend to appoint persons whose judicial philosophy is consistent with the public interest as he perceives it. There will, of course, be some slippage at both stages; Presidents do not always perform exactly as the people who elected them expect them to perform, and the same is true of the appointed federal judges. But over the long run there is a relationship. President Roosevelt was elected in 1932 largely because a majority of the people wanted substantial changes in government. A very important part of those changes came about through the United States Supreme Court—because of President Roosevelt's appointments. The same thing happened with President Nixon. Though the changes are not always as dramatic as in the case of the Roosevelt and Nixon appointments, I believe that with every President there is a long-range transmission of views from the people to the President to the federal courts.

Is it in the interest of sound government that the reaction time between the American people and the judges who serve them should involve a three-step process and that it should be measured in decades? On balance, I believe the answer to that question is yes. The prime function of the federal courts is to decide issues of constitutionality, and with constitutional issues the long run is more important than the short run. Recall that the most important role of the Constitution—and therefore of the judges who interpret it—is the protection of individual rights. Recall also that in the typical case these individual rights are necessarily minority rights. At least over the short run, therefore, popular preferences will not always coincide with those interests for whose protection individual citizens turn to the Constitution.

Whether a substantial number of his constituents agree with the positions taken by the President (or a member of Congress) is quite relevant to the adequacy of his performance. Whether a substantial number of American citizens agree with judicial interpretations of the Constitution is less relevant to the adequacy of the judges' performance. Indeed, in light of the fact that the Constitution usually protects minority rights, additional levels of insulation between the popular will and the stewards of constitutional meaning is not only acceptable but required.

Over the long run, therefore, the reaction chain between the electorate and the courts is just about right: those sentiments that are sufficiently strong to withstand the test of time will have an effect through the election of a President who shares the views of the majority and the appointment of judges who share the President's view. Popular sentiments that are not strong enough to withstand the test of time do not deserve to become part of our constitutional fabric.

Over the long run—probably measured in decades—our constitutional system is theoretically capable of correcting judicial mistakes. I believe that our history shows that this has in fact happened; the substantive due-process cases are probably the best example.

The fact that long-run protections are built into our Constitution should not obscure the magnitude of the potential for mischief over the short run. The problem is accentuated by the fact that the short run—that period of time prior to the correction of judicial error—typically lasts for many years. The old substantive due-process era lasted for forty years. The new substantive due-process era began over a decade ago and is still with us. The modern revival of experimentation with irrebuttable presumptions began in 1973 and has not yet gone away. It would appear, therefore, that, though time is able to heal most of our constitutional wounds, there may be real costs over the short run. In this regard, several considerations need to be taken into account.

First, over the short run, it is not always easy to distinguish constitutional error from constitutional soundness or even brilliance. In my view, the new substantive due-process cases are just as pernicious as the old and maybe more so. In my view, the irrebuttable-presumption doctrine is a mischievous constitutional theory. It represents a complete overlap with equal-protection issues, notwithstanding the fact that it carries a different constitutional standard, and therefore perverts equal-protection doctrine on a willy-nilly basis, dependent on the cases to which the Court decides to apply it. In both of these areas, however, there are many intelligent, responsible, careful students and teachers of constitutional law whose views are just as strongly held and are completely opposite from mine. Obviously, among those who hold the views that I consider erroneous are a majority of the present members of the United States Supreme Court. The assertion that short-run error has occurred in these two instances may therefore be too simple.

Second, assuming over the short run that the courts may make constitutional mistakes, this must be regarded as one of the necessary costs of insulating the judiciary from the immediate pressures of popular sentiment and thereby enabling it more effectively to perform its task as the ultimate protector of individual rights against government intrusion. The assumption that short-run mistakes will occur seems to me unassailable. There is virtually universal agreement that the courts erred in subjecting this nation for almost half a century to judicial policy-making under the aegis of the old substantive due process. The cost of that experiment was high. During those decades, the nation was deprived of many laws that were probably good. Even more important, the nation was deprived of the right to have its elected representatives make the policy judgments that they were elected to make. As high as those costs were, however, they were not as high as the cost of stripping away the judicial insulation from the pressures of current popular view. It would be impossible, even as a theoretical matter, to maintain the judiciary as an independent protector of individual rights in those areas where it made the right decisions without giving it the leeway at the same time to make some mistakes.

The third and final observation is, in a sense, an offshoot of the second. The preceding paragraphs have dealt with the propositions that the long-run benefits of judicial independence are worth its short-run costs and that there are no effective structural devices for cutting down the short-run costs without also eliminating the long-run benefits. The absence of adequate systemic preventives does not mean, however, that the short-run costs are inevitable. There is a preventive. It is the only preventive of short-term judicial errors. It consists of the attitude that the federal judge brings to the performance of his task. Since personal attitude is entirely an individual matter, the extent of the existence or nonexistence of this protective lies wholly in the discretion of the individual judge.

What is the attitude that constitutes this desired protective? The words that most adequately describe it are "judicial restraint." Other people have used other terms. President Nixon's words were "strict constructionist," a phrase that is probably intended to convey the same meaning but in fact conveys no meaning at all. "Strict construction" of a document like the United States Constitution represents nothing less than a strict impossibility. The reason is simply that the United States Constitution is not a strict document. That is, it is not a document whose terms permit only one interpretation, or even a narrow range of interpretations. Strict construction means strict adherence to what the document says. But how does one strictly construe words like freedom of speech, or equal protection of the laws, when the issue is whether a newspaper can be sued for allegedly damaging the reputation of a public official, or whether the state of Massachusetts can require that all of its uniformed policemen retire at age fifty?

For these reasons, I believe that judicial restraint is a more apt term than strict construction. What is meant by judicial restraint? In the great majority of instances where the federal courts have gone wrong in interpreting the Constitution, it is because they have substituted their judgment for the judgment of the legislature in policy matters. There are some exceptions to this generalization—notably the *Dred Scott* decision and the treatment of Japanese-Americans during World War II—but on the whole it is a correct generalization. The power to engage in at least some degree of judgment substitution must be left intact, because any time that a federal court holds a governmental act unconstitutional some level of policymaking is involved. Since the power itself cannot be disturbed, the discretion to exercise retraint in its use must be left in the hands of the judge. The judge's power is an awesome one, and the judge may abuse it. We cannot afford to take it away from him, because that would destroy the more important long-term values of our constitutional system. The extent to which those long-term benefits must be purchased with short-term costs is a function of judicial restraint, the willingness of the judge to be conservative in using the power that he has and that he must have.

What all of this counsels us, I believe, is that weighting the judicial balance scales in favor of government is the best general policy. Judges are not the only governmental servants who take an oath to uphold the Constitution. Congressmen, state legislators, and executive-branch officials at the national and state levels are also duty-bound to uphold the Constitution, including the securing of individual rights. Anyone who has had experience in government knows that most public servants take that obligation seriously and that constitutional concerns play a very prominent role in the legislative process and in governmental decision-making generally. Members of the legislative and executive branches are not and should not be the ultimate interpreters of constitutional issues. Unlike the judges, it is not their sphere of expertise, and they do not enjoy the degree of independence that is conducive to careful and courageous constitutional interpretation. But the point nevertheless stands undiminished that, in the process of making and enforcing the laws and programs whose constitutionality the courts may consider, the other branches of government take constitutional issues into account and in most cases make a conscientious effort to assure that constitutional guarantees are not infringed. In light of that fact, and in light of the further fact that holding a law unconstitutional necessarily imports a substitution of judicial for legislative policymaking, the general approach that courts should bring to their task is one of restraint— of upsetting the legislative judgment only in those instances where the error is quite clear and where the balance scales quite clearly disfavor the policymakers' judgment.

AFTERWORD
What Does the American Constitution Mean to You?

What does the American Constitution mean to you? In large part it means those things that have been discussed in the chapters of this book. It means a government in which no individual holds all power. It means a government whose powers are divided along two planes: among three branches of the national government and between national and state governments. It means the automatic checks against attempts by any governmental official to overstep the bounds of his authority. It means the right to criticize any government official—even the President of the United States—without fear of reprisal. It means the right to have and to practice religious beliefs that are different from those of other religious groups. It means a government that must deal with its people according to minimum standards of equality and fairness. It means a government whose powers derive from the people and in which the ultimate powers are exercised by the people.

Maybe this is all that the Constitution means: the allocation of powers among governmental entities and the protection of individual rights against the exercise of those powers. I believe, however, that, in the case of the American Constitution, the whole is greater than the sum of its parts. In addition to its functions as an allocator of governmental power and protector against abuses of that power, the Constitution, over the two hundred years of our nation's existence, has been an effective symbol of national unity and of our national commitment to law and to human dignity and liberty.

As a symbol, the Constitution has an element of self-fulfillment. Even those who do not really understand why there is a relationship between the Constitution and individual freedoms have a general understanding and acceptance of the fact that there is such a relationship and that it comes about because of a document that is the most unchangeable feature of the entire network of American law. Thus, the Constitution acts as a safeguard of liberties not only directly, because of what it says and does, but also indirectly, because of what people perceive that it says and does. Necessarily, there have been individual dissatisfactions with the results, but as a total matter, the results have been unmatched by the experience of any other country in the world. They have been the kind of results that one would expect from a document created by wise men and upheld for two centuries by a people who know the value of individual liberty.

NOTES

Chapter 1

1. *Quoted in* B. Bailyn, The Great Republic 326–27 (1977).

Chapter 2

1. *Quoted in* C. Bowen, Miracle at Philadelphia 245 (1966).
2. *Id.* at 246.
3. James Madison to Alexander Hamilton, July, 1788, 4 Documentary History of the Constitution 803 (1901).
4. 2 B. Schwartz, The Bill of Rights 983 (1971).

Chapter 3

1. 17 U.S. (4 Wheat.) 316 (1819).

Chapter 4

1. F. Wormuth, The Origins of Modern Constitutionalism 63 (1949).
2. *Id.* at 65.
3. 47 The Federalist 139.
4. Basic Writings of Thomas Jefferson (P. Foner, ed., 1944). Jefferson described the Virginia experience with a constitution which provided for a separation of powers but which omitted checks and balances in the following passage: "The judiciary and the executive members were left dependent on the legislature for subsistence in office, and some of them for their continuance in it. If, therefore, the legislature assumes executive and judiciary powers, no opposition is likely to be made; nor, if made, can be effectual; because in that case they may

put their proceedings into the form of acts of assembly, which will render them obligatory on the other branches. They have accordingly, in many instances decided rights which should have been left to judiciary controversy, and the direction of the executive, during the whole time of their session, is becoming habitual and familiar." *Id.* at 132.

5. 51 THE FEDERALIST 160. J. Reuben Clark, Jr., held to the view that: "It is union of independence and dependence of these branches—legislative, executive and judicial—and of the governmental functions possessed by each of them, that constitutes the marvelous genius of this unravelled document. The Framers had no direct guide in this work, no historical governmental precedent upon which to rely. As I see it, it was here that the divine inspiration came. It was truly a miracle." Church News, Nov. 29, 1952, at 12.

6. Interestingly, although this clause is tucked away in Section 3 between "he shall receive Ambassadors," and "shall commission all Officers," it is interpreted as one of the few most powerful mandates in the entire Constitution.

7. Authority to interpret the laws, particularly constitutionality (judicial review) not clear in the language "judicial Power" in Sections 1 and 2, was made explicit by *Marbury v. Madison,* discussed later.

8. 5 U.S. (1 Cranch) 137 (1803).

9. New York Times Co. v. United States, 403 U.S. 713 (1971).

Chapter 5

1. *See* BOOK OF MORMON, *Mosiah,* 29.

2. United States v. American Tel. & Tel. Co., 551 F.2d 384, 394 (D.C. Cir. 1976).

3. 343 U.S. 579 (1952).

4. 424 U.S. 1 (1976).

5. *See,* for example, the discussion concerning bills of attainder in Chapter 7.

6. A. SCHLESINGER, THE IMPERIAL PRESIDENCY (1973). The President's war power rests on his constitutional role as commander-in-chief of the army and navy and his duty to see that the laws are faithfully executed; Congress, on the other hand, has the exclusive power to declare war.

7. Powell v. McCormack, 395 U.S. 486 (1969).

8. 34 CONG. Q. ALMANAC 11, 14 (1978); TIME, Nov. 20, 1978, at 40; 37 CONG. Q. WEEKLY REP. 65 (1979).

9. 34 CONG. Q. ALMANAC 11, 14 (1978); TIME, Feb. 20, 1978, at 22.

10. *See* Powell v. McCormack, 395 U.S. 486 (1969).

11. 37 CONG. Q. WEEKLY REP. 155 (1979).

12. *Id.*

13. Myers v. United States, 272 U.S. 52 (1926).

14. Humphrey's Executor v. United States, 295 U.S. 602 (1935).

Chapter 6

1. 301 U.S. 1 (1937).

2. 317 U.S. 111 (1942).

3. Steward Machine Co. v. Davis, 301 U.S. 548 (1937); Helvering v. Davis, 301 U.S. 619 (1937).

4. 345 U.S. 22 (1953).

5. 22 U.S. (9 Wheat.) 1 (1824).

6. 325 U.S. 761 (1945).

7. 326 U.S. 572 (1946).

8. 297 U.S. 175 (1936).

9. 377 U.S. 184 (1964).

10. 426 U.S. 833 (1976).

11. *See* Slaughter-House Cases, 83 U.S. (16 Wall.) 36 (1873); Hammer v. Dagenhart, 247 U.S. 251 (1918); National League of Cities v. Usery, 426 U.S. 833 (1976).

Chapter 7

1. 4 C. TORICIA, WHARTON'S CRIMINAL PROCEDURE § 646 (12th ed. 1976).

2. MAGNA CHARTA Sec. 39.

3. Fay v. Noia, 372 U.S. 391, 402 (1963).

4. Baxter v. Palmigiano, 425 U.S. 308 (1976); Bounds v. Smith, 430 U.S. 817 (1977); Johnson v. Avery, 393 U.S. 483 (1969).

5. Fay v. Noia, 372 U.S. 391 (1963); Stone v. Powell, 428 U.S. 465 (1976).

6. United States v. Brown, 381 U.S. 437 (1965); United States v. Lovett, 328 U.S. 303 (1946); Nixon v. Administrator of General Services, 433 U.S. 425 (1977).

7. Duncan v. Louisiana, 391 U.S. 145 (1968) (jury trial required); Baldwin v. New York, 399 U.S. 66 (1970) (jury trial required); Williams v. Florida, 399 U.S. 78, 86–103 (1970) (six-person juries constitutional); Apodaca v. Oregon, 406 U.S. 404 (1972) (non-unanimous verdicts constitutional); Johnson v. Louisiana, 406 U.S. 356 (1972) (non-unanimous verdicts constitutional).

8. *See* Swain v. Alabama, 380 U.S. 202 (1965).

9. Parker v. Gladden, 385 U.S. 363 (1966).

10. WILLIAM PITT, *quoted in* H. BROUGHAM, HISTORICAL SKETCHES OF STATESMEN IN THE TIME OF GEORGE III 22 (1839).

11. Draper v. United States, 358 U.S. 307 (1959), *see especially* at 310–11.

12. 436 U.S. 307 (1978).

13. United States v. Robinson, 414 U.S. 218 (1973).

14. Carroll v. United States, 267 U.S. 132 (1925).

15. Warden v. Hayden, 387 U.S. 294 (1967).

16. *See* Mapp v. Ohio, 367 U.S. 643 (1961).

17. Oaks, *Studying the Exclusionary Rule in Search and Seizure,* 37 U. CHI. L. REV. 665 (1970).

18. *Compare* Illinois v. Vitale, 100 S. Ct. 2260 (1980).

19. Holt v. United States, 218 U.S. 245 (1910); United States v. Wade, 388 U.S. 218 (1967); Gilbert v. California, 388 U.S. 263 (1967).

20. Miranda v. Arizona, 384 U.S. 436 (1966).

21. 1 T. NORTON, THE CONSTITUTION OF THE UNITED STATES 219 (1965).

22. JOHN MILTON, AREOPOGETICA.

Chapter 8

1. *See* Martin v. City of Struthers, 319 U.S. (1943).

2. 348 U.S. 483, 487 (1955).

3. Theoretically, the same issue of the standards by which courts will consider competing interests of government and individuals also applies in the criminal context. The great struggles over constitutional standards, however, have occurred in noncriminal contexts. In the criminal area the presumption of innocence has weighted the scales in favor of the accused individual.

Chapter 9

1. 336 U.S. 525, 533 (1949) (citations omitted).

2. *Id.* at 539.

3. 294 U.S. 511 (1935).

4. 328 U.S. 303 (1946).

5. 17 U.S. (4 Wheat.) 518 (1819).

6. 431 U.S. 1 (1977).

7. 438 U.S. 234 (1978).

8. *Id.* at 245.

9. 260 U.S. 393 (1922).

Chapter 10

1. 418 U.S. 241 (1974).

2. 395 U.S. 367 (1969).

3. *Id.* at 388.

4. 376 U.S. 254 (1964).

5. *Id.* at 279–80.

6. Associated Press v. Walker, 388 U.S. 130, 155 (1967).

7. 418 U.S. 323 (1974).

8. *Id.* at 347.

9. 307 U.S. 496 (1939).

10. *Id.* at 496.

11. *See* Edwards v. South Carolina, 372 U.S. 229 (1963).

12. *See* Cox v. Louisiana, 379 U.S. 559 (1965) (courthouses); Brown v. Louisiana, 383 U.S. 131 (1966) (libraries); Adderley v. Florida, 385 U.S. 39 (1966) (jailhouses); Greer v. Spock, 424 U.S. 828 (1976) (military bases); Secretary of Navy v. Huff, 100 S. Ct. 606 (1980) (military bases).

13. 391 U.S. 367 (1968).

14. *Id.* at 376.

15. *See* Street v. New York, 394 U.S. 576 (1969).

16. 283 U.S. 697 (1931).

17. New York Times Co. v. United States, 403 U.S. 713 (1971).

18. Burstyn Inc. v. Wilson, 343 U.S. 495 (1952); Times Film Corp. v. Chicago, 365 U.S. 43 (1961); Freedman v. Maryland, 380 U.S. 51 (1965); Teitel Film Corp. v. Cusack, 390 U.S. 139 (1968).

19. 283 U.S. 697, 716 (1931).

20. 466 F.2d 1309 (4th Cir. 1972), *cert. denied* 409 U.S. 1063 (1972).

21. 467 F. Supp. 990 (W. D. Wis. 1979). The government dropped the prosecution of this case when defendants appealed because it was discovered that material whose publication the government was trying to prohibit had been published many years before.

22. There can be little question that the material in the *Marchetti* case was sensitive. There may be some doubt about the material in the *Progressive* case, in light of the subsequent dismissal because of earlier publication. It is clear, however, that the district judge who approved the prior restraint considered the subject highly sensitive at the time he entered his order prohibiting the publication.

23. 413 U.S. 15 (1973).

24. *Id.* at 24.

25. *Id.* at 26.

26. 394 U.S. 557, 565 (1969).

27. Paris Adult Theater v. Slaton, 413 U.S. 49 (1973); United States v. Orito, 413 U.S. 139 (1973); United States v. Twelve 200 Foot Reels of Super 8 Millimeter Film, 413 U.S. 123 (1973).

28. 315 U.S. 568 (1942).

29. *Id.* at 571–72.

30. Pittsburgh Press v. Pittsburgh Comm'n. on Human Relations, 413 U.S. 376 (1973).

31. *See* Consolidated Edison Co. of N.Y. v. Public Serv. Comm'n of N.Y., 100 S. Ct. 2326 (1980) and Central Hudson Gas and Elec. Corp. v. Public Serv. Comm'n of N.Y., 100 S. Ct. 2343 (1980), upholding the right of utilities to advertise for mere use of electricity, and to include in monthly bills statements on controversial issues. State bans on these practices were held unconstitutional.

32. *Id.*; Virginia State Bd. of Pharmacy v. Virginia Consumer Council, 425 U.S. 748 (1976); Bigelow v. Virginia, 421 U.S. 809 (1975).

33. Schenck v. United States, 249 U.S. 47, 52 (1919).

Chapter 11

1. 408 U.S. 665 (1972).

2. *Id.* at 690–91.

3. 436 U.S. 547 (1978) (searching newsroom). *Compare* Richmond Newspapers, Inc. v. Virginia, 100 S. Ct. 2814 (1980), which held that in the absence of an overriding interest clearly articulated by judicial findings, criminal trials must be open to the public.

4. 443 U.S. 368 (1979).

5. 441 U.S. 153 (1979).

Chapter 12

1. 340 U.S. 315 (1951); 372 U.S. 229 (1963).

2. *Id.* at 236 (citations omitted).

3. 381 U.S. 479, 484 (1965).

4. 360 U.S. 240 (1959).

5. Barenblatt v. United States, 360 U.S. 109 (1959).

6. Gibson v. Florida Legislative Investigation Comm., 372 U.S. 539 (1963).

Chapter 13

1. 435 U.S. 618 (1978).
2. 370 U.S. 421 (1962).
3. *Id.* at 422.
4. *Id.* at 425.
5. 374 U.S. 203 (1963).
6. Torcaso v. Watkins, 367 U.S. 488 (1961).
7. McCollum v. Board of Educ., 333 U.S. 203 (1948); Zorach v. Clauson, 343 U.S. 306 (1952).
8. *Id.* at 313.
9. L. LEVY, JUDGMENTS: ESSAYS ON AMERICAN CONSTITUTIONAL HISTORY, (1972).
10. 319 U.S. 624 (1943).
11. *Id.* at 642.
12. 406 U.S. 205 (1972).
13. 374 U.S. 398 (1963).
14. 366 U.S. 599 (1961).
15. 435 U.S. 618 (1978).

Chapter 14

1. 60 U.S. (19 How.) 393 (1857).
2. 83 U.S. (16 Wall.) 36, 81 (1873).
3. *Id.* at 68.
4. 427 U.S. 307 (1976).
5. 336 U.S. 106 (1949).
6. 379 U.S. 19 (1964).
7. Brown v. Board of Educ., 347 U.S. 483 (1954); Plessy v. Ferguson, 163 U.S. 537 (1896).
8. Mobile v. Bolden, 100 S. Ct. 1490 (1980); Arlington Heights v. Metropolitan Housing Corp., 429 U.S. 252 (1977); Washington v. Davis, 426 U.S. 229 (1976).
9. Swann v. Charlotte-Mecklenburg Bd. of Educ., 402 U.S. 1 (1971); North Carolina State Bd. of Educ. v. Swann, 402 U.S. 43 (1971).
10. Keyes v. School Dist. No. 1, Denver, Colo., 413 U.S. 189 (1973).
11. Milliken v. Bradley, 418 U.S. 717 (1974).
12. *See* Truax v. Raich, 239 U.S. 33 (1915). *Raich* involved an Arizona law which favored employment of American citizens over aliens. Raich was an Austrian citizen living in Arizona who successfully challenged the law on Fourteenth Amendment grounds.

13. 323 U.S. 214 (1944).

14. *See* Hirabayashi v. United States, 320 U.S. 81 (1943); *Ex parte* Endo, 323 U.S. 283 (1944).

15. Graham v. Richardson, 403 U.S. 365 (1971) (welfare benefits); Sugarman v. Dougall, 413 U.S. 634 (1973) (civil service positions); Nyquist v. Mauclet, 432 U.S. 1 (1977) (financial assistance for education); *In re* Griffiths, 413 U.S. 717 (1973) (membership in bar).

16. 403 U.S. 365 (1971).

17. *See* Hampton v. Mow Sun Wong, 426 U.S. 88 (1976); Mathews v. Diaz, 426 U.S. 67 (1976).

18. 413 U.S. 634, 647 (1973).

19. Foley v. Connelie, 435 U.S. 291 (1978) (policemen); Ambach v. Norwick, 441 U.S. 68 (1979) (schoolteachers).

20. 411 U.S. 677, 686 (1973).

21. Trimble v. Gordon, 430 U.S. 762 (1977).

22. 1980 B.Y.U. L. Rev. 142.

23. 427 U.S. 495 (1976).

24. 411 U.S. 677 (1973).

25. 404 U.S. 71 (1971).

26. 411 U.S. 677 (1973).

27. 429 U.S. 190 (1976).

28. Califano v. Goldfarb, 430 U.S. 199, 207 (1977) (quoting Stanton v. Stanton, 421 U.S. 7, 15 (1975)). *See also* Schlesinger v. Ballard, 419 U.S. 498 (1975); Weinberger v. Wiensenfeld, 420 U.S. 636 (1975); Stanton v. Stanton, 421 U.S. 7 (1975).

29. 316 U.S. 535 (1942).

30. *Id.* at 541.

31. Zablocki v. Redhail, 434 U.S. 374 (1978) (marriage); Skinner v. Oklahoma, 316 U.S. 535 (1942) (procreation); Shapiro v. Thompson, 394 U.S. 618 (1969) (interstate travel); Califano v. Aznavorian, 439 U.S. 170 (1978) (international travel); Griswold v. Connecticut, 381 U.S. 479 (1965) (contraception); Roe v. Wade, 410 U.S. 113 (1973) (abortion).

32. Planned Parenthood of Mo. v. Danforth, 428 U.S. 52, 67–75 (1976).

33. Beal v. Doe, 432 U.S. 438 (1977).

34. Roe v. Wade, 410 U.S. 113, 164 (1973).

35. *Id.* at 163.

36. Harris v. McRae, 100 S. Ct. 2671 (1980); Williams v. Zbaraz, 100 S. Ct. 2694 (1980).

37. 438 U.S. 265 (1978).

38. 443 U.S. 193 (1979).

39. 100 S. Ct. 2758 (1980).

40. Wengler v. Druggists Mutual Ins. Co., 100 S. Ct. 1540, 1545 (1980). *See also* Califano v. Webster, 430 U.S. 313 (1977).

41. 347 U.S. 497 (1954).

Chapter 15

1. 32 U.S. (7 Pet.) 243 (1833).

2. Palko v. Connecticut, 302 U.S. 319 (1937); Duncan v. Louisiana, 391 U.S. 145 (1968).

3. *See generally* Duncan v. Louisiana, 391 U.S. 145 (1968).

4. Michel v. Louisiana, 350 U.S. 91 (1955); Hampton v. Oklahoma, 368 F.2d 9 (10th Cir. 1966); Gasaway v. Page, 303 F. Supp. 391 (N. D. Okla. 1969); Melancon v. McKeithen, 345 F. Supp. 1025 (E. D. La. 1972), *aff'd* 409 U.S. 943 (1972).

5. 83 U.S. (16 Wall.) 36 (1873).

6. *Id.* at 81.

7. 165 U.S. 578 (1897).

8. 262 U.S. 390 (1923) (language classes); 268 U.S. 510 (1925) (public-parochial schools).

9. 198 U.S. 45 (1905).

10. 291 U.S. 502 (1934).

11. *In re* Winship, 397 U.S. 358 (1970); United States v. Agurs, 427 U.S. 97 (1976); United States v. Wade, 388 U.S. 218 (1967).

12. 395 U.S. 337 (1969).

13. 397 U.S. 254 (1970).

14. 408 U.S. 564 (1972).

15. 408 U.S. 593 (1972).

16. 339 U.S. 306 (1950).

17. 435 U.S. 78 (1978).

18. 412 U.S. 441 (1973).

19. 414 U.S. 632 (1974).

20. 351 U.S. 12 (1956).

21. *Id.* at 13 (citation omitted).

22. *See* Long v. District Court, 385 U.S. 192 (1966); Roberts v. LaVallee, 389 U.S. 40 (1967).

23. Burns v. Ohio, 360 U.S. 252 (1959) (waiver of filing fee); Douglas v. California, 372 U.S. 353 (1963) (counsel for appeal).

24. 351 U.S. 12, 19 (1956).
25. 372 U.S. 353 (1963).
26. 417 U.S. 600 (1974).
27. 401 U.S. 371 (1971).
28. 409 U.S. 434 (1973).
29. 410 U.S. 656 (1973).

Chapter 16

1. 60 U.S. (19 How.) 393 (1857).
2. 109 U.S. 3 (1883).
3. 334 U.S. 1 (1948).
4. 273 U.S. 536 (1927).
5. 326 U.S. 501 (1946).
6. *Id.* at 502.
7. 419 U.S. 345 (1974).
8. 407 U.S. 163 (1972).
9. 392 U.S. 409 (1968).
10. *Id.* at 442–43.

Chapter 17

1. 5 U.S. (1 Cranch) 137 (1803).
2. *Id.* at 177.
3. 381 U.S. 479 (1965) (contraception); 410 U.S. 113 (1973) (abortion).
4. 316 U.S. 535 (1942).
5. Kelly v. Johnson, 425 U.S. 238, 244 (1976).
6. 431 U.S. 494, 503 (1977).

Chapter 18

1. 78 THE FEDERALIST.
2. 1 M. FARRAND, THE RECORDS OF THE FEDERAL CONVENTION OF 1787, at 21, 97–98, 108–10, 138–40 (1911); 2 FARRAND, *id.* at 73–80.
3. 418 U.S. 208 (1974).
4. 330 U.S. 75 (1947).
5. 416 U.S. 312 (1974).
6. *See* Colegrove v. Green, 328 U.S. 549 (1946).
7. 369 U.S. 186 (1962).
8. *Id.* at 217.

TABLE OF CASES
(with page references to this volume)

INDEX

Abortion, 44, 132, 153–54, 188–89, 191

Absolutist standard, 89–92, 104, 106, 141, 146

Adams, John, 11, 13

Adams, Samuel, 10, 11, 19

Adversary system, 84–85

Advisory opinions, 193

Affirmative Action. *See* Reverse discrimination

Age, as a classification, 150

Agriculture Department, 51

Agricultural Adjustment Act, 59

Alienage as a classification, 149–51

Amendments of the Constitution. *See* Constitution

Amish School Childrens' case, 135–36

Annapolis Convention, 11

Antifederalists, 19–23

Antitrust. *See* Sherman Antitrust Act

Antitrust Division of the Justice Department, 36–37

Apportionment, 197

Articles of the Constitution. *See* Constitution

Articles of Confederation, 9–14 *passim,* 19, 20, 95

Arbitrariness by government, 42–47 *passim*

Atheism, 132–33

Atheists as public officials, 133

Atomic Energy Act, 114

Bail, 85–86

Balancing test, 61, 90–93, 101–2, 104–5, 125, 136–37, 141, 167

Barbary Pirates, 10

"Best Notice" rule, 170

Bible reading in schools, 130

Bicameral legislature, 27

Bills of attainder, 18, 74, 97–98, 208

Bill of Rights, 2, 7, 17–25 *passim,* 30–31, 72, 104, 140, 159, 161–63; ratification by states, 25; rejected amendment, 25

Black, Hugo, 92

Blackstone, Sir William, 86

Blackmun, Harry A., 156

Breadth and vagueness of Constitution's most important provisions, 186

Brennan, William J., Jr., 150, 156

Building Codes, 98

Bureaucracy, 51–53

Burger, Warren E., 156

Busing, 147

Cabinet, 51

Case or controversy requirement, 193–98

Capital crimes, 78–79

Central Intelligence Agency, 53, 113–14

Checks and balances, 18, 20, 33–39, 205

223

Taxing and spending powers, 28, 59–60

Time, place and manner restrictions, 110

Torture. *See* Cruel and unusual punishment

Treasury Department, 131

Trial transcripts as a requirement for appeals, 174

Trial or trial-type hearing, 161–63, 170–71

Truth prevailing over error, 85

Truman, Harry S., 44

University of California at Davis, 155

University of Washington, 196

"Unquestioned religious exercises," 131

Utilities, 180, 212

Van Buren, Martin, 140

Veto power, 34

Vice-President, 28

Vietnam War, 113

Virginia, experience with reparation of powers, 34, 207–8; ratification of Constitution, 22–23; Virginia Plan, 13–14

Voltaire, 118

War of Independence. *See* Revolutionary War

War powers, 46

War Powers Resolution of 1973, 47

Washington, George, 10, 12, 20, 25

Watergate, 49–50

Webster, Noah, 19

West Coast Program, 147–48, 202

White, Byron R., 156

Wilson, James, 12, 20, 21

World War I, 104, 118

World War II, 147–48

Writ of Habeas Corpus, 18, 72–74

Zoning laws. *See* Eminent domain